A SHORT HISTORY OF THE MIDDLE AGES

A SHORT HISTORY OF THE MIDDLE AGES

THIRD EDITION
BARBARA H. ROSENWEIN

University of Toronto Press

Second edition published by Broadview Press 2004.

LIBRARY AND ARCHIVES CANADA CATALOGUING IN PUBLICATION

Rosenwein, Barbara H.
  A short history of the Middle Ages / Barbara H. Rosenwein.—3rd ed.

Includes bibliographical references and index.
ISBN 978-1-4426-0104-8

  1. Middle Ages. 2. Europe—History—476–1492. I. Title.

D117.R67 2009   940.1   C2009-900441-0

We welcome comments and suggestions regarding any aspect of our publications—please feel free to contact us at news@utphighereducation.com or visit our internet site at www.utphighereducation.com.

North America
5201 Dufferin Street
Toronto, Ontario, Canada, M3H 5T8

2250 Military Road
Tonawanda, New York, USA, 14150

ORDERS PHONE: 1-800-565-9523
ORDERS FAX: 1-800-221-9985
ORDERS EMAIL: utpbooks@utpress.utoronto.ca

UK, Ireland, and continental Europe
NBN International
Estover Road, Plymouth, PL6 7PY, UK
TEL: 44 (0) 1752 202301
FAX ORDER LINE: 44 (0) 1752 202333
enquiries@nbninternational.com

The University of Toronto Press acknowledges the financial support for its publishing activities of the Government of Canada through the Book Publishing Industry Development Program (BPIDP).

Designed by Daiva Villa, Chris Rowat Design.

Printed in Canada

To Jason and Ariana, my dear new children-in-law

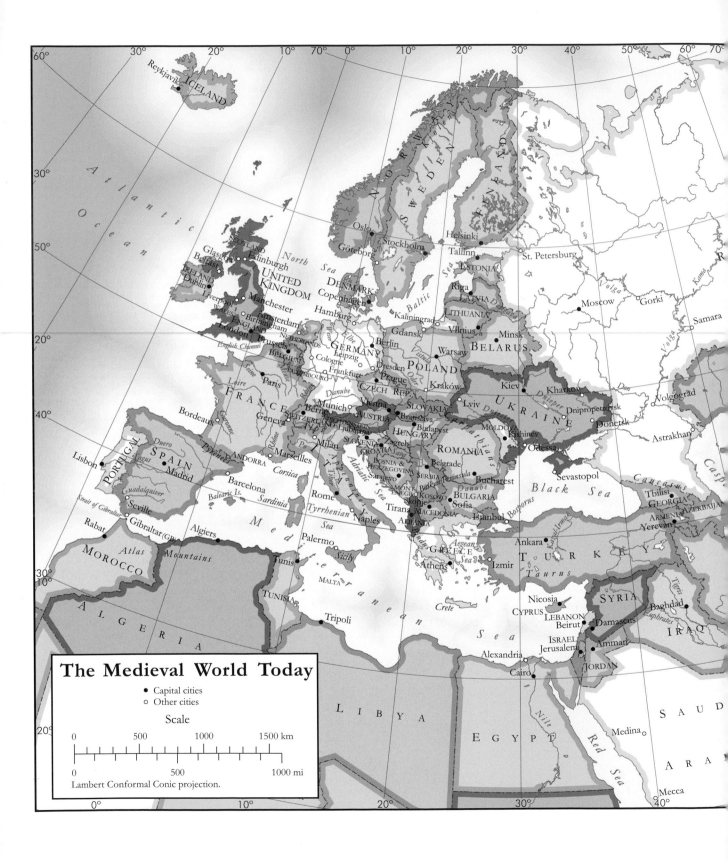

The Medieval World Today

- ● Capital cities
- ○ Other cities

Scale

0 ──── 500 ──── 1000 ──── 1500 km

0 ──── 500 ──── 1000 mi

Lambert Conformal Conic projection.

THE UNION of the Roman empire was dissolved; its genius was humbled in the dust; and armies of unknown barbarians, issuing from the frozen regions of the North, had established their victorious reign over the fairest provinces of Europe and Africa.

Edward Gibbon,
The Decline and Fall of the Roman Empire

IT MAY very well happen that what seems for one group a period of decline may seem to another the birth of a new advance.

Edward Hallett Carr,
What is History?

CONTENTS

MAPS

PLATES

GENEALOGIES

FIGURES

LISTS

ABBREVIATIONS, CONVENTIONS, WEBSITES

ABBREVIATIONS

c. circa. Used in dates to mean that they are approximate.
cent. century
d. date of death
emp. emperor
fl. flourished. This is given when even approximate birth and death dates are unknown.

pl. plural. The plural form of a noun.
  r. rule. Indicates the dates of rule.
sing. singular. The singular form of a noun.

DATE CONVENTIONS

All dates are C.E./A.D. unless otherwise noted (the two systems are interchangeable). The dates of popes are not preceded by *r.* because popes took their papal names upon accession to office, and the dates after those names apply only to their papacies.

WEBSITES

www.rosenweinshorthistory.com = The website for this book, which has practice short answer and essay questions (with sample answers provided), as well as Maps, Genealogies, and Links to other medieval web resources.

http://labyrinth.georgetown.edu = The Labyrinth: Resources for Medieval Studies sponsored by Georgetown University.

http:/www.roman-emperors.org = *De Imperatoribus Romanis*: An Online Encyclopedia of Roman Rulers and Their Families (to 1453).

PREFACE TO THE FIRST EDITION

At the beginning of the first volume of his long and learned trilogy *Suicide in the Middle Ages*, Alexander Murray remarks amiably, "Unconventionally long, the book remains, to the author's certain knowledge, 'a mere introduction.'" Well, if *that* is just an introduction (and it undoubtedly is), then what is *this* book?

It is meant to be an easy pass through a dense thicket. It has been written so that you, the reader, may know enough about the Middle Ages after reading it to move on afterwards with some confidence to meatier fare: to "secondary sources" (so called not because they are "second best" but because they are present-day interpretations of the past) and to "primary sources," the texts, pictures, artefacts, and other bits and pieces of their lives and thought that medieval people left behind.

Because most people read about medieval history in college courses, and because most college courses last at most fifteen weeks, a short textbook may be better than a long one because it can be supplemented without being unduly burdensome. For others—those who may be students no longer but want to pick up a book to learn about the Middle Ages—a short book may well be more pleasant than a long one. But why a survey at all? Because a general orientation is very useful. Without it, primary and secondary sources tend to get unmoored: Abelard becomes a contemporary of Augustine, Murray's suicidal men and women kill themselves everywhere and nowhere.

There are at least two ways to use *A Short History of the Middle Ages* in the classroom. In the first, you read it in one or two weeks—say, at the beginning of the semester—and then refer to it as needed. In the second, you read a chapter or two a week, alongside other readings. This book has lots of maps, genealogies, and plates to help you figure out the context of the other things that you will need or want to study. The index is a handy way to look up names (which are followed by dates where possible), events, and places. Some technical words are explained in a glossary. There are bibliographies after every chapter for further reading. In this way, this book may, if you wish, serve as a permanent reference tool for historical facts.

A Short History of the Middle Ages is meant to be an uncluttered narrative of the whole of the Middle Ages, from about 300 to about 1500 (there are no decisive "start" and "stop" dates, so an author can put them where they seem to make sense). It covers not just Europe (though the focus increasingly moves there) but also the Byzantine and Islamic worlds. I have tried to make "Europe" more than the history of France, England, and Germany, so often the focus of books like this. I have also tried to write not just political history but also social, economic, and cultural history. There is, however, a conscious emphasis on political history, deriving from my twofold conviction that (1) politics tells us a good deal about the uses and distribution of power, always important if we wish to consider general conditions of life; and (2) politics, with its decisive events, provides a nice, clear grid for everything else.

The organization of this book is chronological because everything in a period—culture, social life, political order—is interconnected. It is true that Abelard does not make sense without Augustine before him; theoretically, he could appear in a long chapter on the medieval intellectual tradition. But he makes even less sense outside the context of the rise of cities, a money economy, and new employment opportunities for university men—the world in which he lived, in short—so he comes in a chapter on all those things.

A word on bibliographies: they, like the book, are short. Although they contain only secondary sources, the notes to each chapter contain references to many important primary sources. The notes, then, are meant to serve as a rough and ready bibliography of primary sources.

While preparing this text I have incurred many debts, which I am happy to acknowledge. Anne Wingenter, my research assistant in Spring 2000, ably gathered books for my foray into the realm of the Seljuk Turks. Charles Brauner was kind enough to read and critique my sections on medieval music, Esther Cohen offered useful suggestions for the discussion of the later Middle Ages, and Walter Pohl's advice was invaluable on the "Germans." Via e-mail Monique Bourin advised and aided, while my sister, Naomi Honeth, dispensed sympathy and encouragement. My Loyola colleague Theresa Gross-Diaz shared her thoughts on things medieval (and renaissance) with exemplary generosity. Other colleagues, Blake Dutton and Allen Frantzen, allowed me to draw on their particular expertises in medieval philosophy and Anglo-Saxon respectively. I am grateful to Steven A. Epstein, Paul Freedman, Mayke de Jong, Maureen C. Miller, Julia M.H. Smith, and the anonymous readers solicited by Broadview Press for reading the entire book in manuscript and offering incisive and enormously helpful criticism. Broadview's Betsy Struthers was an able and indefatigable permissions editor, while Paul Heersink showed infinite patience in making the maps. Warm thanks are due as well to production editor Barbara Conolly, assistant production editor Judith Earnshaw, and designer George Kirkpatrick. I owe a different debt to Ian Wood, who once asked me if I might write a book like this; little did he imagine what his words might inspire! Thanks bound up with the very rhythms of daily life go to my family: my parents, Rosaline and Norman Herstein; my husband, Tom; and my children, Frank and Jess. Without them I could not have written even a "short" history. Finally, I am grateful to my students, who tried hard to teach me what needs to be in a book like this—and what does not. I hope they will be pleased with the result.

PREFACE TO THE SECOND EDITION

For the second edition, I have corrected some errors and added some materials, especially on political and economic history. I thank Giles Constable, Adam Kosto, Graham Loud, Michael Morony, Walter Pohl, and Carine van Rhijn for pointing out errors and suggesting changes. Monique Bourin, Riccardo Cristiani, Samuel Leturcq, Rosamond Mack, R.I. Moore, and Anders Winroth generously contributed their expertise to particular sections. Thomas Head shared photographs. Maureen Miller was, as always, a wonderful resource and sounding board. I am indebted to my students in History 310; I wish to thank Jamie McGowan, Eric Nethercott, Susie Newman, and Suzette Vela in particular for their thoughtful suggestions. Paul Heersink prepared new maps with his customary professionalism; George Kirkpatrick worked his magic with the design, and Martin Boyne copyedited with a keen eye. Finally I am grateful to the people at Broadview Press—especially Barbara Conolly, Don LePan, Mical Moser, and Tammy Roberts—for their help and support.

PREFACE TO THE THIRD EDITION

In the third edition I had the opportunity to coordinate the text more closely with my sourcebook, *Reading the Middle Ages: Sources from Europe, Byzantium, and the Islamic World*; to update information; and to choose a few illustrations for extended discussion in a new feature entitled "Seeing the Middle Ages." I have one new piece of advice for student readers: turn first to the Glossary to get the definitions of possibly unfamiliar terms. Then read the book.

I am grateful to Loyola University Chicago and particularly to Dean Isiaah Crawford for financing my trip to Istanbul and Ephesus to see monuments still standing and others under excavation. I thank Paul Cobb, Maureen Miller, Piroska Nagy, Dionysios Stathakopoulos, Bruce Venarde, Anders Winroth, and many anonymous reviewers for their careful reading of the second edition and their thoughtful suggestions for a third. I have benefited enormously from the help, advice, suggestions, and expertise of Maria Aurenhammer, Karl Brunner, Neil Christie, Andrew Donnelly, Ross Brooke Ettle, Elina Gertsman, Zouhair Ghazzal, Mark Humphries, Simon James, Fritz Krinzinger, Sabine Ladstätter, Kristen B. Neuschel, and Christian Sapin. Bert Roest was the ideal fact-checker: immensely erudite, thorough, and zealous. I am grateful as always to the people at Broadview and now University of Toronto Press: Martin Boyne, Laura Cardiff, Judith Earnshaw, Natalie Fingerhut, Melissa Goertzen, Christopher Griffin, Michael Harrison, Tara Lowes, Chris Rowat, and Daiva Villa.

ONE

PRELUDE: THE ROMAN WORLD TRANSFORMED (c.300-c.600)

IN THE THIRD CENTURY, the Roman Empire wrapped around the Mediterranean Sea like a scarf. (See Map 1.1.) Thinner on the North African coast, it bulked large as it enveloped what is today Spain, England, Wales, France, and Belgium, then evened out along the southern coast of the Danube River, following that river eastward, taking in most of what is today called the Balkans (southwestern Europe, including Greece), crossing the Hellespont and engulfing in its sweep the territory of present-day Turkey, much of Syria, and all of modern Lebanon, Israel, and Egypt. All the regions but Italy comprised what the Romans called the "provinces."

This was the Roman Empire whose "decline and fall" was famously proclaimed by the eighteenth-century historian Edward Gibbon. But in fact his verdict was misplaced. The empire was never livelier than at its reputed end. It is true that the old elites of the cities, especially of Rome itself, largely regretted the changes taking place around them c.250-350. They were witnessing the end of their political, military, religious, economic, and cultural leadership, which was passing to the provinces. But for the provincials (the Romans living outside of Italy) this was in many ways a heady period, a long-postponed coming of age. They did not regret the division of the Roman Empire into four parts under the Emperor Diocletian (r.284-305); the partition was tacit recognition of the importance of the provinces. Some did, however, regret losing their place in the sun (as happened c.400-500) to people still farther afield, whom they called "barbarians." In turn, the barbarians were glad to be the heirs of the Roman Empire even as they contributed to its transformation (c.450-600).

North
Sea

Baltic Sea

Britain

FRANKS

Weser

Vistula

BURGUNDIANS

Meuse

VANDALS

Trier

Belgica

Germania

Atlantic
Ocean

Seine

Rhine

Lugdunensis

Noricum

Raetia

Loire

Pannonia

Gaul

Alpes Poen
Alpes Graiae

Roman
until 270

Aquitania

Po

Milan

Sava

Garonne

Rhône

Alpes
Cottiae

Alpes
Maritimes

Dalmatia

Adriatic
Sea

Narbonensis

Italia

Duero

Corsica

Tiber

Dacia
Ripensis

Sard

Hispania

Rome

Macedonia

Lusitania

Pompeii

Tagus

Epirus

Baleares

Sardinia

Tyrrhenian
Sea

Achaia

Baetica

Guadalquiver

M e d i t e r r a n e a n

Sicilia

Dividing line between
Western and Eastern Roman Empire

Mauretania

Carthage

Numidia

Africa proconsularis

Cyr

Legend

VANDALS Peoples

Scale

0

500 km

0

300 mi

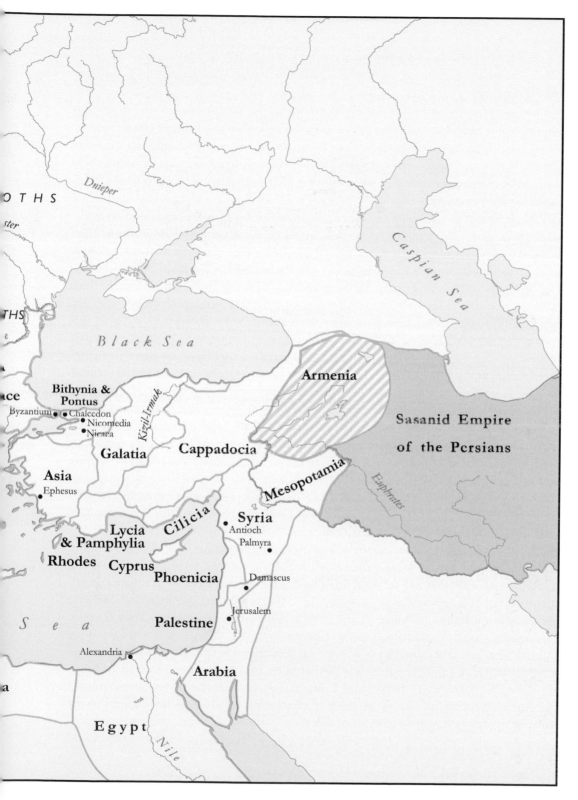

Map 1.1: The Roman Empire in the Third Century

THE PROVINCIALIZATION OF THE EMPIRE (c.250-c.350)

The Roman Empire was too large to be ruled by one man in one place, except in peacetime. This became clear during the "crisis of the third century," when two different groups from two different directions bore down on the borders of the empire. From the north, beyond the Rhine and Danube rivers, came people the Romans called "barbarians"; from the east, the Persians. To contend with these attacks, the Roman government responded with wide-ranging reforms that brought new prominence to the provinces.

Above all, the government expanded the army, setting up new crack mobile forces while reinforcing the standing army. Soldier-workers set up new fortifications, cities hedged themselves with walls, farms gained lookout towers and fences. It was not easy to find enough recruits to man this newly expanded defensive system. Before the crisis, the legions had been largely self-perpetuating. Their soldiers, drawn mainly from local provincial families, had settled permanently along the borders and raised the sons who would make up the next generation of recruits. Now, however, this supply was dwindling: the birthrate was declining, and c.251-266 an epidemic, perhaps of measles or smallpox, ravaged the population further. Recruits would have to come from farther away, from Germania (beyond the northern borders of the empire) and elsewhere. In fact, long before this time, Germanic warriors had been regular members of Roman army units; they had done their stints and gone home. But in the third century the Roman government reorganized the process. They settled Germanic and other barbarian groups within the empire, giving them land in return for military service.

The term "crisis of the third century" refers not only to the wars that the empire had to fight on its borders, but also to a political succession crisis that saw more than twenty men claim, then lose (with their lives), the title of emperor between the years 235 and 284. (See list on p. 355: Late Roman Emperors; but note that this list names only the most important emperors!) Most of these men were the creatures of the army, chosen to rule by their troops. Often competing emperors wielded authority in different regions at the same time. They had little interest in the city of Rome, which, in any case, was too far from any of the fields of war to serve as military headquarters. For this reason Emperor Valerian (r.253-259) shifted the imperial residence and mint from Rome to Milan. Soon other favored imperial places—Trier, Sardica, Nicomedia, and, eventually, Constantinople—joined Milan in overshadowing Rome. The new army and the new imperial seats belonged to the provinces.

The primacy of the provinces was further enhanced by the need to feed and supply the army. To meet its demand for ready money, the Roman government debased the currency, increasing the proportion of base metals to silver. While helpful in the short term, this policy produced severe inflation. Strapped for cash, the state increased taxes and used its power to requisition goods and services. To clothe the troops it confiscated uniforms; to arm them it set up weapons factories staffed by artisans who were bound to produce a regular quota for the state. Food for the army had to be produced and delivered; here too the state depended on the labor of growers, bakers, and haulers. New taxes assessed on both land and individual "heads" were collected. The wealth and labor of the empire moved inexorably toward the provinces, to the hot spots where armies were clashing.

The whole empire, organized for war, became militarized. In about the middle of the third century, Emperor Gallienus (r.253–268) forbade the senatorial aristocracy — the old Roman elite — to lead the army; tougher men from the ranks were promoted to command positions instead. It was no wonder that those men also became the emperors. They brought new provincial tastes and sensibilities to the very heart of the empire, as we shall see.

Diocletian, a provincial from Dalmatia (today Croatia), brought the crisis under control, and Constantine (r.306–337), from Moesia (today Serbia and Bulgaria), brought it to an end. For administrative purposes, Diocletian divided the empire into four parts, later reduced to two. Although the emperors who ruled these divisions were supposed to confer on all matters, the reform was a harbinger of things to come, when the eastern and western halves of the empire would go their separate ways. Meanwhile, the wars over imperial succession ceased with the establishment of Constantine's dynasty, and political stability put an end to the border wars.

A New Religion

The empire of Constantine was meant to be the Roman Empire restored. Yet nothing could have been more different from the old Roman Empire. Constantine's rule marks the beginning of what historians call "Late Antiquity," a period transformed by the culture and religion of the provinces.

The province of Palestine — to the Romans of Italy a most dismal backwater — had been in fact a hotbed of creative religious and social ideas around the beginning of what we now call the first millennium. Chafing under Roman domination, experimenting with new notions of morality and new ethical lifestyles, the Jews of Palestine gave birth to religious groups of breathtaking originality. One coalesced around Jesus. After his death, under the impetus of the Jew-turned-Christian Paul (d.c.65), a new and radical brand of monotheism under Jesus' name was actively preached to Gentiles (non-Jews), not only in Palestine, but beyond. Its core belief was that men and women were saved — redeemed and accorded eternal life in heaven — by their faith in Jesus Christ.

At first Christianity was of nearly perfect indifference to elite Romans, who were devoted to the gods who had served them so well over years of conquest and prosperity. Nor did it attract many of the lower classes, who were still firmly rooted in old local religious traditions. The Romans had never insisted that the provincials whom they conquered give up their beliefs; they simply added official Roman gods into local pantheons. For most people, both rich and poor, the rich texture of religious life at the local level was both comfortable and satisfying. In dreams they encountered their personal gods, who served them as guardians and friends. At home they found their household gods, evoking family ancestors. Outside, on the street, they visited temples and monuments to local gods, reminders of home-town pride. Here and there could be seen monuments to the "divine emperor," put up by rich town benefactors. Everyone engaged in the festivals of the public cults, whose ceremonies gave rhythm to the year. Paganism was thus at one and the same time personal, familial, local, and imperial.

But Christianity had its attractions too. Romans and other city-dwellers of the middle class could never hope to become part of the educated upper crust, but

Map 1.2:
Christian Churches Founded before the Great Persecution of Diocletian (304)

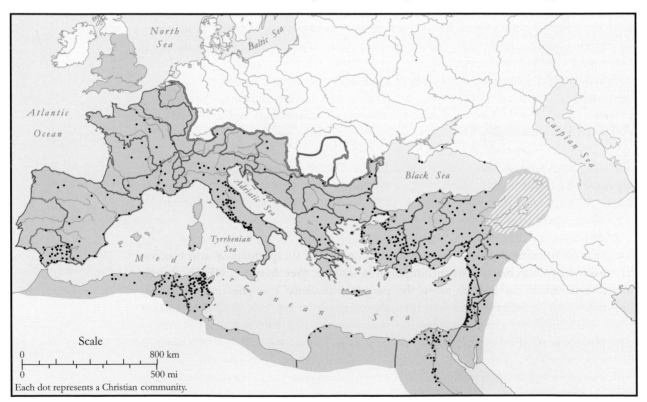

Scale
0 ———————— 800 km
0 ———————— 500 mi
Each dot represents a Christian community.

Christianity gave them dignity by substituting "the elect" for the elite. Education, long and expensive, was the ticket into Roman high society. Christians had their own solid, less expensive knowledge. It was the key to an even "higher" society. Saint Perpetua (*d*.203), imprisoned and awaiting martyrdom, debated her pagan father with the assurance of a Socrates:

> "Father, do you see this vase here...?" "Yes, I do," said he. And I told him:
> "Could it be called by any other name than what it is?" And he said: "No."
> "Well, so too I cannot be called anything other than what I am, a Christian."[1]

Christianity attracted as well those provincials who had never been given the chance to feel truly Roman. (Citizenship was not granted to all provincials until 212.) The new religion was confident, hopeful, and universal. As the empire settled into an era of peaceful complacency in the second century, its hinterlands opened up to the influence of the center, and vice versa. Men and women whose horizons in earlier times would have stretched no farther than their village now took to the roads as traders—or confronted a new cosmopolitanism right at their doorsteps. Uprooted from old traditions, they found comfort in small assemblies—churches—where they were welcomed as equals and where God was the same, no matter what region the members of the church hailed from.

The Romans persecuted Christians—after besting her father in debate, Perpetua went off joyfully to her martyrdom—but at first only locally, sporadically, and above all in times of crisis. At such moments the Romans feared that the gods were venting their wrath on the empire because Christians would not carry out the proper sacrifices. True, the Jews also refused to honor the Roman gods, but the Romans could usually tolerate—just barely—Jewish practices as part of their particular cultural identity. Christians, however, among whom numbered even Romans, claimed God not only for themselves but for all. Major official government persecutions of Christians began in the 250s, with the third-century crisis.

Meanwhile the Christian community organized itself. By 304, on the eve of the last great persecution, when perhaps only 10 per cent of the population was Christian, numerous churches dotted the imperial landscape. (See Map 1.2.) Each church was two-tiered: at the bottom were the people (the "laity"), at the top the clergy (from *kleros*, or "Lord's portion"). In turn, the clergy were supervised by their bishop (in Greek *episkopos*, "overseer"), assisted by his "presbyters" (the priests who served with the bishops), deacons, and lesser servitors. Some bishops—those of Alexandria, Antioch, Carthage, Jerusalem, and Rome (whose bishop was later called the "pope")—were more important than others. No religion was better prepared for official recognition.

This it received in 313, in the so-called *Edict of Milan*. Emperors Licinius and Constantine declared toleration for all the religions in the empire "so that whatever divinity is enthroned in heaven may be gracious and favorable to us."[2] In fact, the *Edict* helped Christians above all: they had been the ones persecuted and now, in addition to enjoying the toleration declared in the *Edict*, they regained their property. Constantine was the chief force behind the *Edict*: it was issued just after his triumphant battle at the Milvian Bridge against his rival emperor Maxentius in 312, a victory that he attributed to the God of the Christians. Constantine seems to have converted to Christianity; he certainly favored it, building and endowing church buildings, making sure that property was restored to churches that had been stripped during the persecutions, and giving priests special privileges. Under him, the ancient Greek city of Byzantium became a new Christian city, residence of emperors, and named for the emperor himself: Constantinople. The bishop of Constantinople became a patriarch, a "superbishop," equal to the bishops of Antioch and Alexandria, although not as important as the bishop of Rome. In one of the crowning measures of his career, Constantine called and then presided over the first ecumenical (universal) church council, the Council of Nicaea, in 325. There the assembled bishops hammered out some of the canon law and doctrines of the Christian church.

With Constantine's conversion and his privileging of Christianity, it was simply a matter of time before most people considered it both good and expedient to convert. Though after Constantine's time several emperors espoused "heretical" — unacceptable — forms of Christianity, and one (Julian, the "Apostate") professed paganism, the die had been cast. Anti-pagan legislation culminated in two edicts issued in 391 and 392, when Emperor Theodosius I (r.379-395) outlawed all the old public and private cults. Christianity was now the official religion of the Roman Empire. In some places, Christian mobs took to smashing local pagan temples. At Carthage in 401, Saint Augustine (354-430), bishop of Hippo and the most influential of the Church Fathers in the West, told his congregation that "all superstition of pagans and heathens should be annihilated."[3] In this way — via law, coercion, and conviction — a fragile religion hailing from one of the most backward of the provinces triumphed everywhere in the Roman world.

But even before its victory, Christianity had been torn by rival factions. North African Donatists — who considered themselves purer than other Christians because they had not backpedaled during the period of persecutions — fought bitterly with Catholics all through the fourth century, willingly killing and dying for their cause. As paganism gave way, Christian disagreements came to the fore: what was the nature of God? where were God and the sacred to be found? how did God relate to humanity? In the fourth and fifth centuries, Christians fought with each other ever more vehemently over doctrine and over the location of the holy.

The men we call the "Church Fathers" were the victors in the battles over doctrine. Already in Constantine's day, Saint Athanasius (c.295-373)—then secretary to the bishop of Alexandria, later bishop there himself—led the challenge against the beliefs of the Christians next door. He called them "Arians," rather than Christians, after the priest Arius (250-336), another Alexandrian and a competing focus of local loyalties. Athanasius promoted his views at the Council of Nicaea (325) and won. It is because of this that he is the orthodox catholic "Father" and Arius the "heretic." For both Athanasius and Arius, God was triune, that is, three persons in one: the Father, the Son, and the Holy Spirit. Their debate was about the nature of these persons. For the Arians, the Father was pure Godhead while the Son was created ("begotten"), flesh but not quite flesh, and thus neither purely human nor purely divine. To Athanasius and the assembled bishops at Nicaea, this was heresy—the wrong "choice" (the root meaning of the Greek term *hairesis*)—and a damnable faith. The Council of Nicaea wrote the party line: the Father and Son were co-eternal and equal in divinity. Arius was condemned and banished. His doctrine, however, persisted. It was the brand of Christianity that Wulfilas (c.311-383), a Gothic bishop with Roman connections, preached to the Goths along the Danube, at the same time translating the Bible into the Gothic language.

Arianism was only the tip of the iceberg. Indeed, the period 350-450 might be called the "era of competing doctrines." As church councils met—especially Ephesus (431) and Chalcedon (451)—to shave ever more closely the contours of right doctrine, dissent multiplied. Monophysites (a later, convenient term for those who opposed the rulings of Chalcedon) held that the "flesh" that God had assumed as Christ was nevertheless divine. Eventually this view, which tended to assimilate human flesh to Christ's and thus divinize humankind, became the doctrine of the Armenian, Coptic (Egyptian), and Ethiopian Christian churches. On the other hand, Pelagius (from Britain, *d.* after 418) was interested less in the nature of Christ than in that of humanity: for him conversion bleached out sins, and thereafter people could follow God by their own will. Entirely opposite to Pelagius was Saint Augustine, for whom human beings were capable of nothing good without God's grace working through them: "Come, Lord, act upon us and rouse us up and call us back! Fire us, clutch us, let your sweet fragrance grow upon us!"[4]

These debates were carried on everywhere, and with passion. Gregory of Nyssa reported that at Constantinople,

> if one asks anyone for change, he will discuss with you whether the Son is
> begotten or unbegotten. If you ask about the quality of bread you will

receive the answer, "the Father is greater, the Son is less." If you suggest a bath is desirable, you will be told "there was nothing before the Son was created."[5]

Like arguments over sports teams today, these debates were more than small talk: they identified people's loyalties. They also brought God down to earth. God had debased himself to take on human flesh. It was critical to know how he had done so and what that meant for the rest of humanity.

For these huge questions, Saint Augustine wrote most of the definitive answers for the West, though they were certainly modified and reworked over the centuries. In the *City of God*, a huge and sprawling work, he defined two cities: the earthly one in which our feet are planted, in which we are born, learn to read, marry, get old, and die; and the heavenly one, on which our hearts and minds are fixed. The first, the "City of Man," is impermanent, subject to fire, war, famine, and sickness; the second, the "City of God," is the opposite. Only there is true, eternal happiness. Yet the first, however imperfect, is where the institutions of society—local churches, schools, governments—make possible the attainment of the second. Thus "if anyone accepts the present life in such a spirit that he uses it with the end in view of [the City of God], ... such a man may without absurdity be called happy, even now."[6] In Augustine's hands, the old traditions of the ancient world were reused and reoriented for a new Christian society.

THE SOURCES OF GOD'S GRACE

The City of Man was fortunate. There God had instituted his church. Christ had said to Peter, the foremost of his apostles (his "messengers"):

> Thou art Peter [*Petros*, or "rock" in Greek]; and upon this rock I will build my church, and the gates of hell shall not prevail against it. And I will give to thee the keys of the kingdom of heaven. And whatsoever thou shalt bind upon earth, it shall be bound also in heaven; and whatsoever thou shalt loose on earth, it shall be loosed also in heaven. (Matt. 16:18-19)

Although variously interpreted (above all by the popes at Rome, who took it to mean that they were the successors of Saint Peter, the first bishop of Rome), no one doubted that this declaration confirmed that the all-important powers of binding (imposing penance on) and loosing (forgiving) sinners were in the hands of Christ's earthly heirs, the priests and bishops. In the Mass, the central liturgy of the earthly church, the bread and wine on the altar became the body and blood of Christ, the

"Eucharist." Through the Mass the faithful were joined to one another; to the souls of the dead, who were remembered in the liturgy; and to Christ himself.

The Eucharist was one potent source of God's grace. There were others. Above all, there were certain people so beloved by God, so infused with his grace, that they were both models of virtue and powerful wonder-workers. These were the saints. In the early church, the saints had largely been the martyrs, but martyrdom ended with Constantine. The new saints of the fourth and fifth centuries were "athletes" of God: like Saint Symeon Stylites (396–459), they climbed tall pillars and stood there for decades; or, like Saint Antony (250–356), they entered tombs to fight, heroically and successfully, with the demons (whose reality was as little questioned as the existence of germs is today). These were neither flights of fancy nor the deeds of madmen. They were considered socially responsible acts by the surrounding community. Purged of sin by their ascetic rigors — giving up their possessions, fasting, praying, not sleeping, not engaging in sex — and fearless in the face of the demons, holy men and women were intercessors with God on behalf of their neighbors and those who sought them out from afar. Saint Athanasius told the story of Saint Antony: after years of solitude and asceticism the saint emerged

> as if from some shrine, initiated into the mysteries and filled with God.... When he saw the crowd, he was not disturbed, nor did he rejoice to be greeted by so many people. Rather, he was wholly balanced, as if he were being navigated by the Word [of God] and existing in his natural state. Therefore, through Antony the Lord healed many of the suffering bodies of those present, and others he cleansed of demons. He gave Antony grace in speaking, and thus he comforted many who were grieved and reconciled into friendship others who were quarreling.[7]

Healer of illnesses and of disputes, Antony brought spiritual, physical, and civic peace. This was power indeed.

But who would control it? Bishop Athanasius of Alexandria laid claim to Antony's legacy by writing about it. Yet writing was only one way to appropriate and harness the power of the saints (and also of making sure that demons were not craftily standing in for them). When holy men and women died, their power lived on in their relics (whatever they left behind: their bones, hair, clothes, sometimes even the dust from their tombs). In the fourth century, pious people knew this very well. They wanted access to these "special dead." Rich and influential Romans got their own holy monopolies by simply moving saintly bones home with them:

> [Pompeiana] obtained the body [of the martyr Maximilianus] from the

magistrate and, after placing it in her own chamber, later brought it to Carthage. There she buried it at the foot of a hill near the governor's palace next to the body of [Saint] Cyprian [bishop of Carthage]. Thirteen days later [Pompeiana] herself passed away and was buried in the same spot.[8]

With enough wealthy ladies like Pompeiana, the saints were likely to be appropriated by laypeople, buried on private estates, and made the focal point of noble family burials. What place would the churches, the clergy, and the wider community have in this privatized system? Churchmen like Saint Ambrose (339–397), bishop of Milan, did not need to think twice. He had the newly discovered relics of Saints Gervasius and Protasius moved from their original resting place into his newly built cathedral and buried under the altar, the focus of communal worship. He allied himself, his successors, and the whole Christian community of Milan with the power of those saints. No single rich patron could thereafter control them. Ambrose set the pattern: henceforth bishops would oversee the disposition of relics.

Art from the Provinces to the Center

Just as Christianity came from the periphery to transform the center, so too did provincial artistic traditions. Classical Roman art, nicely exemplified by the wall paintings of Pompeii (Plate 1.1 and Plate 1.2), was characterized by light and shadow, a sense of atmosphere—of earth, sky, air, light—and a feeling of movement, even in the midst of calm. Figures—sometimes lithe, sometimes stocky, always "plastic," suggesting volume and real weight on the ground—interacted, touching one another or talking, and caring little or nothing about the viewer. In Plate 1.1 the craggy mountains are the focus. A shepherd, painted with sketchy lines, pushes a goat toward a shrine, perhaps to sacrifice the animal. On the left, another goat frolics. Shadowy shepherds and goats appear in the distance. The scene is tranquil yet suggests both the grandeur of nature and the solemnity of the occasion. Plate 1.2 pictures a moment well known to Romans from their myths. A nude man—thus clearly an athlete—stands in quiet triumph while people kiss his hands and feet. Any Roman would know, from the "iconography"—the symbolic meaning of the elements—that the man is Theseus and that he has just slain the Minotaur (dying in the doorway on the left), who had demanded a tribute of Athenian youths each year in return for peace. The artist has chosen to depict the very instant that Theseus emerges from the Minotaur's lair, the intended victims crowding around him to express their gratitude. Even though the story is illustrated for the viewers' pleasure, the figures act as if no one is looking at them. They are self-absorbed, glimpsed as if through a window onto their private world.

Plate 1.1: Landscape, Pompeii (*c*.79). The Roman artist of this painting created the illusion of space, air, and light directly on the flat surface of a wall (probably of a house).

Plate 1.2: Theseus the Minotaur Slayer, Pompeii (*c.*79). Theseus, hero of a Greek myth and here portrayed as both triumphant and beloved, adorned the wall of a private house at Pompeii.

The relief on a Roman sarcophagus (stone coffin) carved in the second century (Plate 1.3) depicts the funeral procession of the mythical hero Meleager. It shows that even in the medium of sculpture, classical artists were concerned with atmosphere and movement, figures turning and interacting with one another, and space created by "perspective," where some elements seem to recede while others come to the fore.

But even in the classical period there were other artistic conventions and traditions in the Roman Empire. For many years these provincial artistic traditions had been tamped down by the juggernaut of Roman political and cultural hegemony. But in the third century, with the new importance of the provinces, these regional traditions re-emerged. As provincial military men became the new heroes and emperors, artistic tastes changed as well. The center—Rome, Italy, Constantinople—now borrowed its artistic styles from the periphery.

To understand some of the old regional traditions, consider the sculpted head of a woman from Palmyra, Syria (Plate 1.4); a large stone coffer for holding the bones of the dead from Jerusalem (Plate 1.5); and a tombstone from the region of Carthage—Tunis, Tunisia today—(Plate 1.6). All of these were made in either the first or second century C.E., under the shadow of Roman imperial rule. Yet they are little like Roman works of art. Above all, the artists who made these pieces valued decorative elements. The Jerusalem coffer plays with formal, solemn patterns of light and shadow. The tombstone flattens its figures, varying them by cutting lines for folds, hands, and eyes. Any sense of movement here comes from the incised patterns, certainly not from the rigidly frontal figures. Although the head from Palmyra is more classical, it

Plate 1.3: Meleager on a Roman Sarcophagus (2nd cent.). This relief depicts part of the story of the hero Meleager, who awarded the hide of a ferocious boar to Atalanta, a huntress who had aided him in pursuing it. Meleager's uncles were furious that the prize had been awarded to a woman, and in the ensuing dispute Meleager killed them. The loss of her brothers so pained Meleager's mother that she impulsively brought about her son's death. Here, on the left, Meleager slays one of his uncles; on the right, mourners carry home the hero's dead body.

Plate 1.4: Head from Palmyra (1st half of 1st cent.). Compare this fragment of a woman's head with the head of Theseus in Plate 1.2 to see the very different notions of the human body and of beauty that co-existed in the Roman Empire.

too is created by an artist in love with decoration. The lady's hair is a series of rings and lines; her pupils are spirals.

There may be something to the idea that such works of art were "inferior" to Roman products—but not much. The artists who made them had their own values and were not particularly interested in classical notions of beauty. The Palmyra head is clearly the work of a sculptor who wanted to show the opposite of human interaction. His lady takes part in no familiar mythological story for viewers to enjoy. She has been "abstracted" from any natural context. Her very hair, eyebrows, and eyes are simple shapes: coils, crescent moons, concentric circles. All of this emphasizes her otherworldliness. Here is a woman who is deeply contemplative. Her eyes, the most prominent feature of her face, gaze outward beyond the viewer, transcending the here and now.

The same emphasis on transcendence explains the horizontal zones of the limestone tombstone (Plate 1.6). It may seem absurd to compare this piece with the Pompeian painting of mountains and shepherd (Plate 1.1). Yet it is crucial to realize that the subjects are largely the same: people and animals participating in a religious sacrifice. It is the approach that is different. On the provincial tombstone, the stress is on hierarchical order. In the center of the top zone is a god. In the middle zones are people busying themselves with proper religious ceremonies. At the bottom, the lowest rung, are three people praying. The proper order of the cosmos, not the natural

Plate 1.5: Decorated Coffer from Jerusalem (1st cent.?). The human figure was of no interest to the carver of this stone chest, whose formal floral and architectural motives seemed more appropriate for its sober contents: the bones of the dead.

order, is the focus. This tombstone is no window onto a private world; rather it teaches and preaches to those who look at it.

The extraordinary development of the fourth century was the center's appropriation of these provincial artistic styles. The trend is graphically illustrated by a marble base made at Constantinople *c.*390 to support a gigantic ancient obelisk, transported at great cost from Egypt and set up with considerable difficulty at the Hippodrome, the great sports arena. (For the location of the Hippodrome, see Map 4.1 on p. 140.) The four-sided base depicts the games and races that took place in the stadium. The side shown in Plate 1.7 is decisively divided into two tiers: at the top is the imperial family and other dignitaries, formal, frontal, staring straight ahead. Directly in the center is the imperial group, higher than all others. Beneath, in the lower tier, are bearded, hairy-coated barbarians, bringing humble offerings to those on high. The two levels are divided by a decorative frame, a rough indication of the "sky boxes" inhabited by the emperor and his retinue. The folds of the drapery are graceful but stylized. The hairstyles are caps. The ensemble is meant to preach eternal truths: the

Plate 1.6 (facing page): Tombstone, near Carthage (2nd cent.?). The stiff, frontal figures on this relief show a delight in order, hierarchy, and decoration.

Plate 1.7: Base of the Hippodrome Obelisk (*c.*390). Nothing illustrates changing imperial artistic tastes so well as this carving, placed right in the middle of the most imperial part of Constantinople. It was inspired more by the style of Plate 1.6 than by the traditional classical style of Plate 1.3.

Plate 1.8: Saint Cyprian Fresco (2nd half of 4th cent.). Painted in a small room within a *titulus*, or community church, in a posh neighborhood of Rome, the figure of Cyprian commands the lower wall. Above and to the sides (not pictured here) are depictions of his trial and martyrdom. The painting marks a very early example of the translation (transfer) of relics from outside of Rome to a place within the city. Arranged at the initiative of a private patron, the translation reflects the sort of lay practices that Ambrose was determined to stop.

highness of imperial power and its transcendence of time and place.

This style of art was not Christian in origin, but it was quickly adopted by Christians at the time. It was suited to a religion that saw only fleeting value in the City of Man, that sought to transcend the world, and that had a message to preach. A good example is the flat image of Saint Cyprian (in this case, the martyred bishop of Antioch) in Plate 1.8, the central figure of a fresco painted on the wall of a Roman *confessio*—an oratory, or place of prayer—in the second half of the fourth century. Here Cyprian serves as a "publicity agent" for his tomb, originally visible just behind him through the grill-covered opening. The fresco, like the tombstone in Plate 1.6, emphasizes hierarchy—Cyprian is on top; humble people grovel at his feet; and he is at the center of all other activity. Like the figures on the bottom of the tombstone, he prays, his hands raised in the ancient "orant" position. Like those figures, too, he has no weight, exists in no landscape, interacts with no one. We shall continue to see the influence of this transcendent style throughout the Middle Ages.

Nevertheless, beginning around the very same time as this image of Saint Cyprian was produced, more classical artistic styles were making a brief comeback even in a Christian context. Sometimes called the "renaissance of the late fourth and early fifth centuries," this was the first of many recurring infusions of the classical spirit in medieval art. Consider the sarcophagus of Junius Bassus, carved in 359 (Plate 1.9). The bottom central panel depicts a man on a horse-like donkey. Two young men greet him, one peeking out from behind an oak tree, the other laying down a cloak. The rider's garment drapes convincingly around his body, which has weight, volume, and plasticity. There is a sense of depth and lively human interaction, just as there was in the Meleager sarcophagus. But this is a Christian coffin, and the rider is Christ, entering Jerusalem.

THE BARBARIANS

The classicizing style exemplified by Junius Bassus' coffin did not long survive the sack of Rome by the Visigoths in 410. The sack was a stunning blow. Like a married cou-

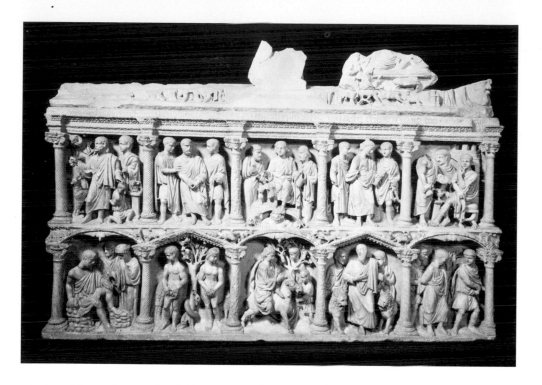

ple in a bitter divorce, both Romans and Goths had once wooed one another; they then became mutually and comfortably dependent; eventually they fell into betrayal and strife. Nor was the Visigothic experience unique. The Franks, too, had been recruited into the Roman army, some of their members settling peacefully within the imperial borders. The Burgundian experience was similar.

The Romans called all these peoples "barbarians." They called some of them "Germani" — Germans — because they materialized from beyond the Rhine, in Germania. Historians today tend to differentiate these peoples linguistically: "Germanic peoples" are those who spoke Germanic languages. Whatever name we give them (they certainly had no collective name for themselves), these peoples were long used to a settled existence. Archaeologists have found in northern Europe evidence of small hamlets built and continuously inhabited for centuries by Germanic groups before they entered the empire. At Wijster, one of their settlements near the North Sea (today in the Netherlands), for example, about fifty or sixty families lived in a well-planned community, with hedged streets and carefully aligned houses. Elsewhere, smaller hamlets were the rule. Whether due to their contacts with the Romans or because of indigenous practices, Germanic society was not egalitarian: we can see the evidence of social inequalities in the different sorts of houses that archaeologists have uncovered: long wooden houses for the well-off, sunken cottages for lesser folk. Supporting themselves by herding and farming, Germanic traders bartered with Roman provincials along the empire's border.

Plate 1.9: Sarcophagus of Junius Bassus (359). Like the Meleager relief (Plate 1.3), the figures on this sarcophagus, carved nearly in the round, gesture and interact. But their subject is now entirely Christian. Reading the scenes from left to right, they portray: (top) Abraham and Isaac; Peter's arrest; Christ enthroned between Saints Peter and Paul, his feet resting on the scarf of Heaven; Christ's arrest; the judgment of Pilate; (bottom) Job sitting on the dunghill, comforted by friends; Adam and Eve; Christ's triumphal entry into Jerusalem; Daniel (clothed by a later, prudish carver, but originally naked) in the lion's den; the arrest of Saint Paul.

There was no biological distinction between "Germanic" traders and "Roman" ones, nor was there any biological distinction between different Germanic tribespeople. However, there were ethnic differences — differences created by preferences and customs surrounding food, language, clothing, hairstyle, behaviors, and all the other elements that go into a sense of identity. But these ethnicities were in constant flux as tribes came together and broke apart.

The "ethnogenesis" of the Goths, for example — the ethnicities that came into being and changed over time — made them not one people but many. If it is true that a people called the "Goths" (Gutones) can be found in the first century C.E. in what is today northwestern Poland, that does not mean that they much resembled those "Goths" who, in the third century, organized and dominated a confederation of steppe peoples and forest dwellers of mixed origins north of the Black Sea (today Ukraine). The second set of Goths was a splinter of the first; by the time they got to the Black Sea, they had joined with many other groups. In short, the Goths were multiethnic.

Taking advantage — and soon becoming a part — of the crisis of the third century, the Black Sea Goths invaded and plundered the nearby provinces of the Roman Empire. The Romans responded at first with annual payments to buy peace, but soon they stopped, preferring confrontation. Around 250, Gothic and other raiders and pirates plundered parts of the Balkans and Anatolia (today Turkey). It took many years of bitter fighting for Roman armies, reinforced by Gothic and other mercenaries, to stop these raids. Afterwards, once again transformed, the Goths emerged as two different groups: eastern (later, Ostrogoths), again north of the Black Sea, and western (later, Visigoths), in what is today Romania. By the mid-330s the Visigoths were allies of the empire and fighting in their armies. Some rose to the position of army leaders. By the end of the fourth century, many Roman army units were made up of whole tribes — Goths or Franks, for example — fighting as "federates" for the Roman government under their own chiefs.

This was the marriage. It fell apart under the pressure of the Huns, a nomadic people from the semi-arid, grass-covered plains (the "steppeland") of west-central Asia, who invaded the Black Sea region in 376, attacking and destroying its settlements like lightning and moving into Romania. The Visigoths, joined by other refugees driven from their settlements by the Huns, petitioned Emperor Valens (r.364-378) to be allowed into the Empire. He agreed; we have seen that barbarians had long been settled within the borders as army recruits. But in this case the numbers were unprecedented: tens of thousands, perhaps even up to 200,000. The Romans were overwhelmed, unprepared, and resentful. About two centuries later a humanitarian crisis was recalled by the Gothic historian Jordanes:

[The Goths] crossed the Danube and settled Dacia Ripensis, Moesia and Thrace by permission of the Emperor. Soon famine and want came upon them, as often happens to a people not yet well settled in a country. Their princes ... began to lament the plight of their army and begged Lupicinus and Maximus, the Roman commanders, to open a market. But to what will not the "cursed lust for gold" compel men to assent? The generals, swayed by avarice, sold them at a high price not only the flesh of sheep and oxen, but even the carcasses of dogs and unclean animals, so that a slave would be bartered for a loaf of bread or ten pounds of meat. When their goods and chattels failed, the greedy trader demanded their sons in return for the necessities of life. And the parents consented even to this.[9]

The parents did not consent for long. In 378 the Visigoths rebelled against the Romans, killing Emperor Valens at the battle of Adrianople. Thereafter, again bound as federates to serve the Romans, the Visigoths under Alaric began in about 397 to seek a place for permanent settlement. Moving first to Greece, then to Italy, taking Rome for a few days in 410, the Visigoths settled in Gaul, south of the Loire, in 418. By 484 they had taken most of Spain as well.

Meanwhile, beginning late in 406, perhaps also impelled by the Huns, other barbarian groups — Alans, Vandals, and Sueves — entered the Empire by crossing the Rhine River. They first moved into Gaul, then into Spain. The Vandals crossed into North Africa; the Sueves remained in Spain, but most of their kingdom was conquered by the Visigoths in the course of the sixth century. When, after the death in 453 of Attila, a powerful leader of the Huns, the empire that he had created along the Danubian frontier collapsed, still other groups moved into the Roman empire Ostrogoths, Rugi, Gepids — each with a "deal" from the Roman government, each with the hope of working for Rome and reaping its rewards. In 476 the last Roman emperor in the West, Romulus Augustulus, was deposed by Odoacer, a barbarian (from one of the lesser tribes, the Sciri) leading Roman troops. Odoacer promptly had himself declared King of Italy and, in a bid to "unite" the empire, sent Augustulus' imperial insignia to Emperor Zeno (r.474-491). But Zeno in his turn authorized Theodoric, king of the Ostrogoths, to attack Odoacer in about 490. Theodoric's conquest of Italy succeeded. Not much later the Franks, long used to fighting for the Romans, conquered Gaul under Clovis (r.481-511), a Roman official and king of the Franks, by defeating a provincial governor of Gaul and several barbarian rivals. Meanwhile other barbarian groups set up kingdoms of their own.

Around the year 500 the former Roman Empire was no longer a scarf flung around the Mediterranean; it was a mosaic. (See Map 1.3.) Northwest Africa was now the Vandal Kingdom, Spain the Visigothic kingdom, Gaul the Kingdom of the Franks, and Italy the Kingdom of the Ostrogoths. The Anglo-Saxons occupied southeastern Britain; the Burgundians formed a kingdom centered in what is today Switzerland. Only the eastern half of the Empire—the long end of the scarf—remained intact.

THE NEW ORDER

Map 1.3: The Former Western Empire, *c.*500

What was new about the "new order" of the sixth century was less the rise of barbarian kingdoms than it was, in the West, the decay of the cities and corresponding liveliness of the countryside, the increased dominance of the rich, and the quiet domestication of Christianity. In the East, the Roman Empire continued, made an ill-fated bid to expand, and finally retrenched as an autonomous entity: the Byzantine Empire.

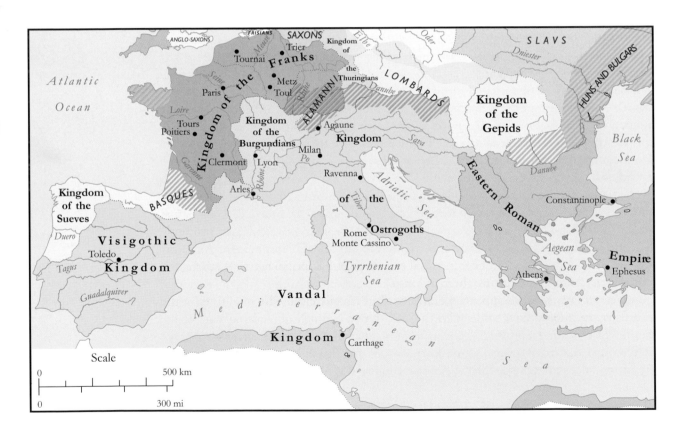

The Ruralization of the West

Where the barbarians settled, they did so with only tiny ripples of discontent from articulate Roman elites. It used to be thought that the Roman Empire granted the invaders vast estates confiscated from Roman landowners. It now seems that the new tribal rulers were often content to live in cities or border forts, collecting land taxes rather than land.

For Romans, the chief objection to the new barbarian overlords was their Arian Christian beliefs. (Recall that Wulfilas had preached that brand of Christianity to the Goths.) Clovis, king of the Franks, may have been the first Germanic king to overcome this problem. (If so, Sigismund, king of the Burgundians, was a close second.) Clovis flirted with Arianism early on, but he soon converted to the Catholic Christianity of his Gallic neighbors. Bishop Avitus of Vienne wrote him a congratulatory letter: "Now the bright glory of [the Eastern Roman Empire] adorns *your* part of the world also."[10]

In other respects as well, the new rulers took over Roman institutions; they issued laws, for example. The *Visigothic Code*—drawing on Roman imperial precedents like the *Theodosian Code* (see p. 54), on the regulations for rural life found in Roman provincial law codes such as *The Farmer's Law*, and possibly on tribal customary law as well—was drawn up during the course of the fifth through seventh centuries. Sigismund, king of the Burgundians, issued a code of Burgundian laws in 517. A Frankish law code was compiled under King Clovis, fusing provincial Roman and Germanic procedures into a single whole.

Written in Latin, these laws revealed their Roman inspiration even in their language. Barbarian kings, some well educated themselves, often depended on Roman advisors to write up their letters and laws. In Italy, in particular, an outstanding group of Roman administrators, judges, and officers served Ostrogothic King Theodoric the Great (r.493–526). They included the encyclopedic Cassiodorus (490–583), author of the *Institutes of Christian Culture*, and the learned Boethius (480–524), who wrote the tranquil *Consolation of Philosophy* as he awaited execution for treason. Since the fourth century, Romans had become used to barbarian leaders; in the sixth, there was nothing very strange in having them as kings.

Far stranger was the disappearance of the urban middle class. The new taxes of the fourth century had much to do with this. The town councillors—the *curiales*, traditional leaders and spokesmen for the cities—had been used to collecting the taxes for their communities, making up any shortfalls, and reaping the rewards of prestige for doing so. In the fourth century, new land and head taxes impoverished the *curiales*, while very rich landowners—out in the countryside, surrounded by their bodyguards and slaves—simply did not bother to pay. Now the tax burdens fell on poorer

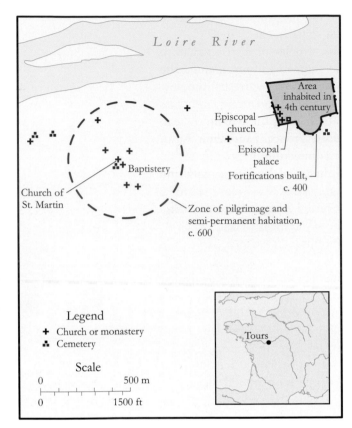

Map 1.4: Tours, *c.*600

people. Families pressed to pay taxes they could not afford escaped to the great estates of the rich, giving up their free status in return for land and protection. By the seventh century, the rich had won; the barbarian kings no longer bothered to collect general taxes.

The cities, most of them walled since the time of the crisis of the third century, were no longer thriving or populous, though they remained political and religious centers. For example, the episcopal complex at Tours (in Gaul) was within the walls of a fortification thrown up *c.*400. (See Map 1.4.) Although it still functioned as an institution of religion and government, almost no one lived in the city any longer. But outside of Tours, in a cemetery that the Romans had carefully sited away from ordinary habitation, a new church rose over the relics of the local saint, Martin. This served as a magnet for the people of the surrounding countryside and even further away. A baptistery was constructed nearby, to baptize the infants of pilgrims and others who came to the tomb of Saint Martin hoping for a miracle. Sometimes people stayed for years. Gregory, bishop of Tours (*r.*573-594), our chief source for the history of Gaul in the sixth century, described Chainemund, a blind woman:

> She was a very pious woman, and full of faith she went to the venerable church of the blessed bishop Martin. She was ... also covered with abrasions on her entire body. For a sickness had attacked all her limbs with sores, and her appearance was so horrible and so repulsive to look at that she was considered by the people as a leper. Every day she felt her way and went to the church of the glorious champion. After almost three years, while she was standing in front of his tomb, her eyes were opened and she saw everything clearly. All the weakness in her limbs disappeared ... and a healthy skin grew back.[11]

With people like Chainemund flocking to the tomb, it is no wonder that archaeologists have found evidence of semi-permanent habitations right at the cemetery.

War and plague no doubt reduced the overall population, but it is impossible to gauge the precise toll. More calculable were changes in styles of life. The shift from urban to rural settlements brought with it a new localism. The active long-distance trade of the Mediterranean slowed down, though it did not stop. But now this trade penetrated very little beyond the coast. This is nicely illustrated by the story of pottery, a cheap necessity of the ancient world. In the sixth century, fine mass-produced African red pottery adorned even the most humble tables along the Mediterranean Sea coast. Inland, however, most people had to make do with local handmade wares, as regional networks of exchange eroded long-distance connections.

For some—the rich—the new disconnection of the rural landscape with the wider world had its charms. When they were inclined, they could still take advantage of luxury goods. In some regions they could even enjoy a life of splendid isolation:

> On the summit of the high rock a magnificent palace is built.... Marble columns hold up the imposing structure; from the top you can see boats gliding by on the surface of the river in summertime.... Water is channeled off along ducts following the contours of the mountain.... On these slopes, formerly sterile, Nicetius has planted juicy vines, and green vineshoots clothe the high rock that used to bear nothing but scrub. Orchards with fruit-trees growing here and there fill the air with the perfume of their flowers.[12]

The owner of this haven was Nicetius, bishop of Trier. He retreated to it when his pastoral cares gave him the chance. Bishops like Nicetius were among the rich; most rose to their episcopal status in their twilight years, after they had married and had sired children to inherit their estates. (Their wives continued to live with them but— or so it was expected—not to sleep with them.) Great lay landlords, kings, queens, warriors, and courtiers controlled and monopolized most of the rest of the wealth of the West, now based largely on land.

Monasteries, too, were beginning to become important corporate landowners. In the sixth century many monks lived in communities just far enough away from the centers of power to be holy, yet near enough to be important. Monks were not quite laity (since they devoted their entire life to religion), yet not quite clergy (since they were only rarely ordained), but something in between and increasingly admired. It is often said that Saint Antony was the "first monk," and though this may not be strictly true, it is not far off the mark. Like Antony, monks lived a life of daily martyrdom, giving up their wealth, family ties, and worldly offices. Like Antony, who toward the end of his life came out of the tombs he had once retreated to in order to be with others, monks lived in communities. Some communities were of men only, some of women, some of both (in separate quarters). Whatever the sort, monks lived in obedience to a "rule" that gave them a stable and orderly way of life.

The rule might be unwritten, as it was at Saint-Maurice d'Agaune, a monastic community set up in 515 by Sigismund on the eve of his accession to the Burgundian throne. The monks at Agaune, divided into groups that went to the church in relay, carried out a grueling regime of non-stop prayer every day. Built outside the Burgundian capital of Geneva, high on a cliff that was held to be the site of the heroic martyrdom of a Christian Roman legion, this monastery tapped into a holy landscape and linked it to Sigismund and his episcopal advisors.

Other rules were written. Caesarius, bishop of Arles (r.502-542) wrote one for his sister, the "abbess" (head) of a monastery of women. He wrote another for his nephew, the "abbot" of a male monastery. In Italy, Saint Benedict (d.c.547) wrote the most famous of the monastic rules some time around 540. With its adoption, much later, by the Carolingian kings of the ninth century, it became the monastic norm in the West. Unlike the rule of Agaune, where prayer was paramount, the *Benedictine Rule* divided the day into discrete periods of prayer, reading, and labor. Nevertheless, the core of its program, as at Agaune, was the "liturgy"—not just the Mass, but an elaborate round of formal worship that took place seven times a day and once at night. At these specific times, the monks chanted—that is sang—the "Offices," much of which consisted of the psalms, a group of 150 poems in the Old Testament:

> During the winter season, Vigils [the Night Office] begin with the verse
> "Lord, open my lips and my mouth shall proclaim your praise." [Ps. 51:17]
> After this has been said three times, the following order is observed: Psalm
> 3 with "Glory be to the Father"; Psalm 94 with a refrain, or at least chanted [sung]; an Ambrosian hymn [i.e., a hymn written by St. Ambrose]; then
> six psalms with refrain.[13]

By the end of each week the monks were to have completed all 150 psalms.

Benedict's monastery, Monte Cassino, was in the shadow of Rome, far enough to be an "escape" from society but near enough to link it to the papacy. Pope Gregory the Great (590-604), arguably the man most responsible for making the papacy the greatest power in Italy, took the time to write a biography of Benedict and praise his Rule. Monasteries, by their ostentatious rejection of wealth and power, became partners of the powerful. The monks were seen as models of virtue, and their prayers were thought to reach God's ear. It was crucial to ally with them.

Little by little the Christian religion was domesticated to the needs of the new order, even as it shaped that order to fit its demands. Chainemund was not afraid to go to the cemetery outside of Tours. There were no demons there; they had been driven far away by the power of Saint Martin. The fame of Saint Benedict, Gregory reported, drew "pious noblemen from Rome," who "left their sons with him to be schooled in the service of God."[14] Benedict's monasteries had become the perfectly acceptable alternatives to the old avenues to prestige: armies and schools. Saint Radegund, founder of a convent at Poitiers (not far from Tours), obtained a fragment of the Holy Cross and other precious relics for her nuns. As one of her hagiographers, Baudonivia, wrote, "She got what she had prayed for: that she might glory in having the blessed wood of the Lord's cross enshrined in gold and gems and many of the relics of the saints that had been kept in the [Eastern half of the Roman Empire] living in that one place [her monastery]."[15] The reliquaries that "enshrined" the relics were themselves precious objects, like the so-called reliquary of Theuderic (Plate 1.10), a small box made of cloisonné enamel (bits of enamel framed by metal), garnets, glass gems, and a cameo. Holy tombs and relics brought the sacred into the countryside, into city convents, into the texture of everyday life.

Plate 1.10: Reliquary of Theuderic (late 7th cent.) Shaped like a miniature sarcophagus, this reliquary is inscribed on the back, "Theuderic the priest had this made in honor of Saint Maurice." Paying for the creation of a reliquary — suitable housing for the remains of the saints — was itself an act of piety. Theuderic must have given this to the monastery of Saint-Maurice d'Agaune in the late seventh century.

SCOTS

PICTS

ANGLES

SAXONS

BRITONS

North Sea

NORSE

SWEDES

DANES

Baltic Sea

FINNS

LITHUANIANS

PRUSSIANS

EASTERN SLAVS

Atlantic Ocean

FRISIANS

SAXONS

Elbe

THURINGIANS

WESTERN SLAVS

Oder

Vistula

Brittany
(Frankish Dependency)

Austrasia

Tertry
Soissons

Reims

Cologne
Mainz

Neustria

Seine

Metz

Frankish

Loire

Kingdoms

Tours

Poitiers

Burgundy

Aquitaine

Garonne

Rhône

Bavarians
(Frankish Dependency)

SLAVS

Dnieper

Avar Khaganate

BULGARS

**Suevian
Kingdom**
(Conquered by
Visigoths, 584)

BASQUES

Ebro

Milan

Lombard

Rhône

Adriatic Sea

SOUTHERN

SLAVS

Danube

Visigothic   Kingdom

Toledo

Córdoba

Kingdom

Rome

Black

Constantinople

Chalcedon
Nicaea

M e d i t

E a s t e r n   R o m a n   E m p i r e

BERBERS

Carthage

Ephesus

Antio

Dama

Sea

Jerusalem

Alexandria

GARAMANTES

BERBERS

Scale

0

800 km

0

500 mi

Lambert Conformal Conic projection.

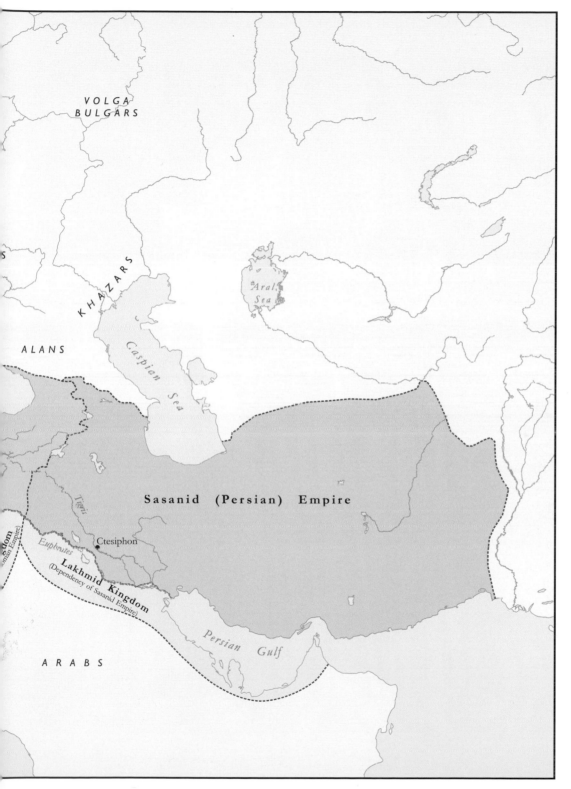

Map 1.5: Europe and the Eastern Roman Empire, *c.*600

VOLGA
BULGARS

KHAZARS

ALANS

*Aral
Sea*

*Caspian
Sea*

Sasanid (Persian) Empire

Tigris

Euphrates

● Ctesiphon

Lakhmid Kingdom
(Dependency of Sasanid Empire)

Persian Gulf

ARABS

MAXIMIANVS

Plate 1.11: Mosaic from San Vitale, Ravenna (c.540–548). Flanked on one side by churchmen (holding a cross and a Bible) and on the other by military men (holding spears and a shield inscribed with the sign of Christ), Emperor Justinian is here depicted in an offertory procession, during which the items for the Mass are brought to the altar. He himself carries the paten, which contains the Eucharistic bread. By both his position in the composition and his role in the Mass, he is thus made the link between heavenly and earthly orders.

The Retrenchment of the East

After 476 there was a "new order" in the East as well, but it was much less obvious. For one thing, there was still an emperor with considerable authority. The towns continued to thrive, and their middle classes even experienced renewed prosperity and influence. The best of the small-town educated elite went off to Constantinople, where they found good jobs as administrators, civil servants, and financial advisors. While barbarian kings in the West were giving in to the rich and eliminating general taxes altogether, the eastern emperors were collecting state revenues more efficiently than ever. When Hagia Sophia ("Holy Wisdom"), the great church of Constantinople, burned to the ground, Emperor Justinian (r.527–565) dipped into the treasury to hire 10,000 workers to rebuild it. They covered its domed ceiling with gold and used 40,000 pounds of silver for its decoration.

Nevertheless, the eastern Roman Empire was not the old Roman Empire writ small. It was becoming a "Middle Eastern state," more akin to Persia than to Gaul. When the Visigoths sacked Rome, the eastern Emperor Theodosius II (r.408–450) did not send an army; he built walls around Constantinople instead. When the roads fell into disrepair, Justinian let many of them decay. When the Slavs pressed on the Roman frontier in the Balkans, Justinian let them enter. Borrowing the ceremony and pomp of the Persian "king of kings" for himself, Justinian was pleased to be represented in the mosaics of San Vitale at Ravenna (Plate 1.11) in a crown and jewels, his head surrounded by a gleaming halo, his ministers—both secular and ecclesiastic—flanking him on both sides. At San Vitale, he is almost an icon, a simplified, radically "abstracted" image of a person suffused with divinity. The Saint Cyprian of Plate 1.8 is another example of this genre.

Icons, perhaps originally the creation of the Coptic Christians of Egypt, were another Middle Eastern product crucial above all to the culture of the eastern Romans. Without denigrating relics, eastern Christians found that icons—whether painted, woven, or carved—gave them more important access to the sacred. In the sixth-century Egyptian tapestry shown in Plate 1.12, the Virgin, dressed in the purple robes of an empress, sits on a gem-encrusted throne with the Christ Child in her lap. Like the Eucharist, icons concentrated and transmuted spiritual into material substance.

The fifth and sixth centuries brought retrenchment. For the first time emperors issued compendia of Roman laws. The *Theodosian Code*, which gathered together imperial "constitutions" (general laws) alongside "rescripts" (rulings on individual cases), was published in 438. The barbarian law codes of the sixth century attempted to match this achievement, but they were overshadowed by the great legal initiatives of Justinian, which included the *Codex Justinianus* (529), an imperial law code; the *Digest* (533), an orderly compilation of Roman juridical thought; and the *Institutes* (534), a

textbook for lawyers. From then on the laws of the eastern Roman Empire were largely (though not wholly) fixed, though Justinian's books were soon eclipsed by short summaries in Greek, while in the West they had little impact until the twelfth century.

Under Justinian, this redefined Roman Empire sought to recapture its past glory. It quickly took North Africa from the Vandals in 534. It added a strip of southeastern Spain in 552. Meanwhile Justinian's armies pressed on to wrench—but with great difficulty—Italy from the Ostrogoths. The first two enterprises were fairly successful; eastern Roman rule lasted in North Africa for another century. The last venture, however, was a disaster. The long war in Italy, which began in 535 and ended only in 552, devastated the country. Soon the Lombards, Germanic warriors employed by Justinian to help take Italy, returned to Italy on their own behalf. By 572 they were masters of part of northern Italy and, further south, of Spoleto and Benevento. (See Map 1.5.)

For the eastern Roman Empire, the western undertaking was a sideshow. The empire's real focus was on the Sasanid Empire of the Persians. The two "super–powers" confronted one another with wary forays throughout the sixth century. They thought that to the winner would come the spoils. Little did they imagine that the real winner in the Middle East would be a new and unheard of group: the Muslims.

★   ★   ★   ★

The crisis of the third century demoted the old Roman elites, bringing new groups to the fore. Among these were the Christians, who insisted on one God and one way to understand and worship him. Made the official religion of the empire in 391-92, Christianity redefined the location of the holy: no longer was it in private households or city temples but in the precious relics of the saints, icons, and the Eucharist; in those who ministered on behalf of the church on earth (the bishops); and in those who led lives of ascetic heroism (the monks).

Politically the empire, once a vast conglomeration of conquered provinces, was in turn largely conquered by its periphery. In spite of themselves, the Romans had tacitly to acknowledge and exploit the interdependence between the center and the hinterlands. They invited the barbarians in, and then declined to recognize the needs of their guests. The repudiation came too late. The barbarians were part of the empire, and in the western half they took it over. In the next century they would show how much they had learned from their former hosts.

212 Roman citizenship granted to all free inhabitants of the provinces

235–284 Crisis of the Third Century

284–305 Reign of Diocletian

306–337 Reign of Constantine

313 *Edict of Milan*

325 Council of Nicaea

378 Emperor Valens killed by Visigoths

391–92 Emperor Theodosius outlaws all pagan cults; Christianity becomes the official religion of the Roman Empire

410 Visigoths sack Rome

476 Deposition of Romulus Augustulus

*c.*540 *The Benedictine Rule* written

527–565 Emperor Justinian

590–604 Pope Gregory the Great

NOTES

1. *The Passion of SS. Perpetua and Felicitas*, in *Medieval Saints: A Reader*, ed. Mary-Ann Stouck, Readings in Medieval Civilizations and Cultures 4 (Peterborough, ON, 1999), p.22.

2. *The Edict of Milan*, in *Reading the Middle Ages: Sources from Europe, Byzantium, and the Islamic World*, ed. Barbara H. Rosenwein (Peterborough, ON, 2006), p.3.

3. Quoted in Ramsay MacMullen, *Christianizing the Roman Empire (A.D. 100–400)* (New Haven, 1984), p.95.

4. *The Confessions of Saint Augustine* 8.4, trans. Rex Warner (New York, 1963), p.166.

5. Quoted in W.H.C. Frend, *The Rise of the Monophysite Movement: Chapters in the History of the Church in the Fifth and Sixth Centuries* (Cambridge, 1972), p.xii.

6. Augustine, *City of God*, in *Reading the Middle Ages*, p.26.

7. Athanasius, *Life of St. Antony of Egypt*, in *Reading the Middle Ages*, p.42.

8. *Acta Maximiliani* 3,4, ed. and trans. H. Musurillo, *The Acts of the Christian Martyrs* (Oxford, 1972), p.248, quoted in Peter Brown, *The Cult of the Saints: Its Rise and Function in Latin Christianity* (Chicago, 1981), p.33.

9. Charles Christopher Mierow, trans., *The Gothic History of Jordanes* (Princeton, 1915), pp.88–89.

10. Avitus of Vienne, *Letter to Clovis*, in *Reading the Middle Ages*, p.59.

11. Gregory of Tours, *The Miracles of the Bishop Saint Martin*, trans. Raymond Van Dam in his *Saints and Their Miracles in Late Antique Gaul* (Princeton, 1993), p.210.

12. Venantius Fortunatus, quoted in Georges Duby, *The Early Growth of the European Economy: Warriors and Peasants from the Seventh to the Twelfth Century* (Ithaca, 1974), p.58, spelling and punctuation slightly modified.

13. *The Benedictine Rule*, in *Reading the Middle Ages*, p.31.

14. Gregory the Great, "The Life and Miracles of Saint Benedict," in *Medieval Saints: A Reader*, p.177.

15. Baudonivia, *The Life of St. Radegund*, in *Reading the Middle Ages*, p.56.

FURTHER READING

Brown, Peter. *The Cult of the Saints*. Chicago, 1981.

—. *The World of Late Antiquity, 150-750*. London, 1971.

Gaddis, Michael. *There Is No Crime for Those Who Have Christ: Religious Violence in the Christian Roman Empire*. Berkeley, 2005.

Geary, Patrick J. *The Myth of Nations: The Medieval Origins of Europe*. Princeton, 2002.

Heinzelmann, Martin. *Gregory of Tours: History and Society in the Sixth Century*. Trans. Christopher Carroll. Cambridge, 2001.

Kitzinger, Ernst. *Early Medieval Art*. Rev. ed. Bloomington, 1983.

Macmullen, Ramsay. *Voting about God in Early Church Councils*. New Haven, 2006.

Moorhead, John. *Justinian*. London, 1994.

Pohl, Walter, with Helmut Reimitz, eds. *Strategies of Distinction: The Construction of Ethnic Communities, 300-800*. Leiden, 1998.

Rapp, Claudia. *Holy Bishops in Late Antiquity: The Nature of Christian Leadership in an Age of Transition*. Berkeley, 2005.

Wolfram, Herwig. *The Roman Empire and Its Germanic Peoples*. Trans. Thomas J. Dunlap. Berkeley, 1997.

To test your knowledge of this chapter, please go to www.rosenweinshorthistory.com and click "Study Questions."

PART I
THREE
CULTURES
FROM ONE

TWO

THE EMERGENCE OF SIBLING CULTURES (c.600-c.750)

THE RISE of Islam in the Arabic world and its triumph over territories that had for centuries been dominated by either Rome or Persia is the first astonishing fact of the seventh and eighth centuries. The second is the persistence of the Roman Empire both politically, in what historians call the "Byzantine Empire," and culturally, in the Islamic world and Europe. By 750 three distinct and nearly separate civilizations—Byzantine, European, and Islamic—crystallized in and around the territory of the old Roman Empire. They professed different values, struggled with different problems, adapted to different standards of living. Yet all three bore the marks of common parentage—or, at least, of common adoption. They were sibling heirs of Rome.

SAVING BYZANTIUM

In the seventh century, the eastern Roman Empire was so transformed that historians by convention call it something new, the "Byzantine Empire," from the old Greek name for Constantinople: Byzantium. (Often the word "Byzantium" alone is used to refer to this empire as well.) War, first with the Sasanid Persians, then with the Arabs, was the major transforming agent. Gone was the ambitious imperial reach of Justinian; by 700, Byzantium had lost all its rich territories in North Africa and its tiny Spanish outpost as well. (See Map 2.1.) True, it held on tenuously to bits and pieces of Italy and Greece. But in the main it had become a medium-sized state, in the same location but about two-thirds the size of Turkey today. Yet, if small, it was also tough.

Sources of Resiliency

Byzantium survived the onslaughts of outsiders by preserving its capital city, which was well protected by high, thick, and far-flung walls that embraced farmland and pasture as well as the city proper (see Map 4.1 on p. 140). Within, the emperor (still calling himself the Roman emperor) and his officials serenely continued to collect the traditional Roman land taxes from the provinces left to them. This allowed the state to pay regular salaries to its soldiers, sailors, and court officials. The navy, well supplied with ships, patrolled the Mediterranean Sea. It was proud of its prestigious weapon, Greek Fire — a mixture of crude oil and resin, heated and projected via a tube over the water, where it burned and engulfed enemy ships. The armies of the empire, formerly posted as frontier guards, were now pulled back and set up as regional units within the empire itself. These armies and their regions, both called "themes," were led by *strategoi* (sing. *strategos*), generals who were gradually given responsibility for both military and regional civil matters. They countered enemy raids while remaining close to sources of supplies and new recruits. Each soldier was given land in his

Map 2.1: The Byzantine Empire, *c.*700

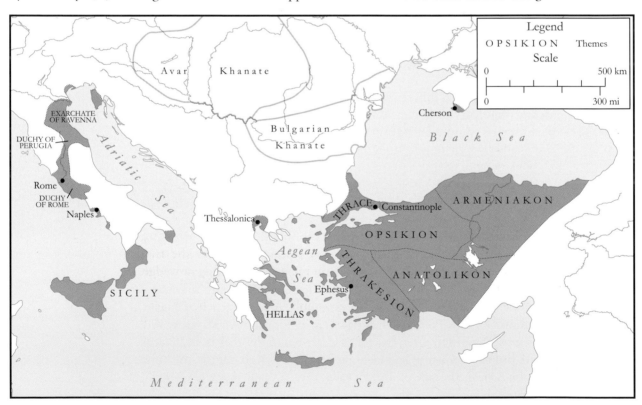

theme to help him purchase his uniform and arms. In this way, the themes maintained the traditions of the imperial Roman army: well trained and equipped, Byzantium's troops served as reliable defenders of their newly compact state.

The Invaders and Their Consequences

The Sasanid Empire of Persia, its capital at Ctesiphon, its ruler styled "king of kings," was as venerable as the Roman Empire—and as ambitious. (See Map 1.5 on pp. 50-51.) King Chosroes II (r.591-628), not unlike Justinian a half-century before him, dreamed of recreating past glories. In his case the inspiration was the ancient empire of Xerxes and Darius, which had sprawled from a lick of land just west of Libya to a great swath of territory ending near the Indus River. Taking advantage of a dispute between two claimants to the imperial throne during the first decade of the seventh century, Chosroes marched into Byzantine territory in 607. By 613 he had taken Damascus, by 614 Jerusalem. The whole of Egypt fell to the Persians in 619. But Emperor Heraclius (r.610-641) rallied his troops and turned triumph into defeat; all territories taken by the Persians were back in Byzantine hands by 630. (For Heraclius and his successors, see list on p. 357: Byzantine Emperors and Empresses.) On a map it would seem that nothing much had happened; in fact, the cities fought over were depopulated and ruined, and both Sasanid and Byzantine troops and revenues were exhausted.

Meanwhile, the Byzantines had to contend with Slavs and other groups north of the Danube. Again Map 1.5 makes the situation clear. Slavs—farmers and stockbreeders in the main—were pushing into the Balkans, sometimes accompanied by Avars, multi-ethnic horseback warriors and pastoralists. In 626, just before Heraclius wheeled around and bested the Persians on his frontiers, he was confronted with Avars and their Sasanid allies besieging—unsuccessfully, as it turned out the very walls of Constantinople. It took another half-century for the Bulgars, a Turkic-speaking nomadic group, to become a threat, but in the 670s they began moving into what is today Bulgaria, defeating the Byzantine army in 681. By 700 very little of the Balkan Peninsula was Byzantine. (See Map 2.1.) The place where once the two halves of the Roman Empire had met (see Map 1.1 on pp. 22-23) was now a wedge that separated East from West.

An even more dramatic obliteration of the old geography took place when attacks by Arab Muslims in the century after 630 ended in the conquest of Sasanid Persia and the further shrinking of Byzantium. We shall soon see how and why the Arabs poured out of Arabia. But first we need to know what the shrunken Byzantium was like.

Decline of Urban Centers

The city-based Greco-Roman culture on which the Byzantine Empire was originally constructed had long been gradually giving way. Invasions and raids hastened this development. Many urban centers, once bustling nodes of trade and administration, disappeared or reinvented themselves. Some became fortresses; others were abandoned; still others remained as skeletal administrative centers. The public activities of marketplaces, theaters, and town squares yielded to the pious pursuits of churchgoers or the private ones of the family.

Figure 2.1 (facing page): Late Antique Ephesus

The story of Ephesus is unique only in its details. Ephesus had once been an opulent commercial and industrial center. Turned to rubble by an earthquake near the end of the third century, it rebuilt itself on a grand scale during the course of the fourth and especially the fifth centuries. Imagine it in about 500. (See Fig. 2.1, concentrating on the labels in red.) It had two main centers, both fitting comfortably within the old walls that had been constructed in the Hellenistic period. The most important center was the Embolos, a grand avenue paved with marble. Extending the length of more than two football fields, the Embolos began at its west end on a Market Square and the Library of Celsus, while it opened out on its east end onto the so-called State Agora, only bits of which were restored after the earthquake. All along the Embolos' length were statues, monumental fountains, and arcades. Along its north side were the Baths of Varius and other public buildings. Flanking its south were poor living quarters built over the rubble of once-elegant "terrace houses." There was no question about the religious affiliation of this sector of the city: the Embolos was well Christianized by numerous crosses etched onto the marble slabs of its fountains and paving stones. Small churches were scattered about the vicinity.

The second center of Ephesus around 500 was to the northwest, nearer the harbor. Here numerous old temples and cultural centers were now being reused for homes, baths, and churches. Richly furnished houses were erected in the Harbor Baths, while a chapel was built in the Byzantine palace and a church was constructed in the Stadium. Above all, there was the new Church of St. Mary, the seat of the bishopric, which had been built into the southern flank of an old temple (the Olympieion) next to the bishop's palace and the baptistery.

In short, Ephesus around 500 suggests the comfortable integration of Christian and old Roman institutions. Baths expressed the value of cleanliness; temples were turned into churches; a chapel nestled in the shadow of the old Stadium. Grand fountains and heroic statues continued to be built along the Embolos by proud city benefactors.

But the events of the sixth and seventh centuries transformed the city. The Persian wars disrupted Ephesus' trade and threatened its prosperity. Repeated visitations of bubonic plague began in 541, the time of Justinian, and recurred in virulent attacks

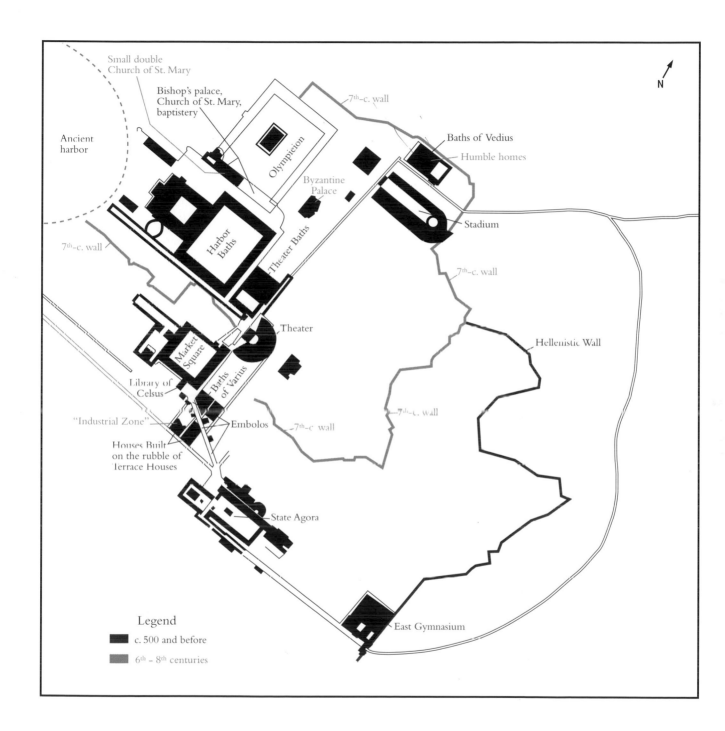

Small double
Church of St. Mary

Bishop's palace,
Church of St. Mary,
baptistery

Ancient
harbor

Olympieion

7th-c. wall

Baths of Vedius

Humble homes

Byzantine
Palace

7th-c. wall

Harbor
Baths

Theater Baths

Stadium

7th-c. wall

Theater

Hellenistic Wall

Market
Square

Baths of Varius

Library of
Celsus

"Industrial Zone"

Embolos

7th-c. wall

7th-c. wall

Houses Built
on the rubble of
Terrace Houses

State Agora

N

Legend

■ c. 500 and before

■ 6th – 8th centuries

East Gymnasium

until about 750. This Plague of Justinian was the first pandemic (widespread epidemic) in the historical record, taking in most of the old Roman Empire and extending to Persia in one direction and to Ireland in the other. Ephesus could not have been spared its grim demographic toll. The residences along the length of the Embolos were destroyed in 614, perhaps as the result of an earthquake or of Persian invasions. Arab attacks on Ephesus began in 654-655.

In the face of these disasters, the face of Ephesus changed. (Consider Fig. 2.1 again, now focusing on the elements in green.) As if tightening its belt, the city put up new walls to enclose the harbor area. The Embolos lost its centrality. Its southern flank became an "industrial zone": mills, stone-cutting and ceramic factories, and other workshops were built on the edge of where the terrace houses had once stood. No doubt this location protected the harbor from both noise and pollution. A road south of the Embolos became the workaday thoroughfare, while the "Byzantine palace," closely protected by the seventh-century walls, became the new center of administration.

Yet the new walls did not stave off disaster and decay. The Baths of Vedius were destroyed—though some families made their homes in the rubble until the roof collapsed, probably at the end of the sixth century. The Church of St. Mary itself was partially destroyed—perhaps in the early seventh century—and rebuilt as two separate smaller churches within the original space. Finally, in the wake of the Arab attacks, the bishop abandoned his palace by the harbor and moved to a church about a mile and a half outside of the city.

The fate of Ephesus—much reduced in size but nevertheless still a center of production and habitation—was echoed in many cities circling the eastern Mediterranean in Syria, Palestine, and Egypt. Elsewhere, the urban centers of the Byzantine Empire became little more than fortresses in the course of the seventh and eighth centuries. Constantinople itself was spared this fate only in part. As with other cities, its population shrank, and formerly inhabited areas right within the walls were abandoned or turned into farms. As the capital of both church and state, however, Constantinople boasted an extraordinarily thriving imperial and ecclesiastical upper class. It also retained some trade and industry. Even in the darkest days of the seventh-century wars, it had taverns, brothels, merchants, and a money economy. Its factories continued to manufacture fine silk textiles. Although Byzantium's economic life became increasingly rural in the seventh and eighth centuries, institutions vital to urban growth remained at Constantinople, ensuring a revival of commercial activity once the wars ended.

RURALIZATION

With the decline of cities came the rise of the countryside. Agriculture had all along been the backbone of the Byzantine economy. Apart from large landowners—the state, the church, and a few wealthy individuals—most Byzantines were free or semi-free peasant farmers. In the interior of Anatolia, on the great plateau that extends from the Mediterranean to the Black Sea, peasants must often have had to abandon their farms when Arab raiders came. Some may have joined the other pastoralists of the region, ready to drive their flocks to safety. Elsewhere (and, in times of peace, on the Anatolian plains as well), peasants worked small plots (sometimes rented, sometimes owned outright), herding animals, cultivating grains, and tending orchards.

The so-called *Farmer's Law*, which seems to reflect rural conditions in parts of the empire during the eighth century, paints a picture of insular village communities composed of small households, where land transactions needed only a few witnesses to be valid:"If two farmers agree one with the other before two or three witnesses to exchange lands and they agreed for all time, let ... their exchange remain firm and secure and unassailable."[1]

But if insular socially, these villages were nevertheless subject as never before to imperial rule. With the disappearance of the traditional town councillors—the *curiales*—cities and their rural hinterlands were now controlled directly by the reigning imperial governor and the local "notables"—a new elite consisting of the bishop and big land owners favored by the emperor. Freed from the old buffers between itself and commoners, the state adopted a thoroughgoing agenda of "family values," narrowing the grounds for divorce, setting new punishments for marital infidelity, and prohibiting abortions. Legislation gave mothers greater power over their offspring and made widows the legal guardians of their minor children. Education was still important—the young Saint Theodore of Sykeon, for example, joined the other boys at his village school, where presumably he learned some classical Greek literature—but now for many pious Christians the classical heritage took second place to the Psalter, the book of 150 psalms in the Old Testament thought to have been written by King David. Thus, at the age of twelve, Saint Theodore

> wanted to imitate David in his holy hymn-writing and accordingly began to learn the Psalter. With difficulty and much labor he learnt as far as the sixteenth psalm, but he could not manage to get the seventeenth psalm by heart. He was studying it in the chapel of the holy martyr Christopher (which was near the village) and as he could not learn it, he threw himself on his face and besought God to make him quick of learning in his study of the psalms. And the merciful God, Who said, "Ask and it shall be given you," [Matt. 7:7] granted him his request.[2]

Such piety was partly a response to crisis. What had provoked God's anger, unleashing war, plague, earthquakes? What would appease Him? The armies thought they knew: they attributed Arab victories to the biblical injunction against graven images. Around the year 723, the Caliph Yazid II (r.720-724) prohibited depictions of all things that breathed; Byzantine soldiers—though not at all Muslim—listened. They feared that Christian icons revived pagan idolatry. As iconoclastic (anti-icon or, literally, icon-breaking) feeling grew, some churchmen became outspoken in their opposition to icons, while others, especially monks, defended them.

Byzantine emperors, who were religious as well as political figures, sided with their troops. They had other good reasons to oppose icons. As mediators between human beings and God, icons undermined the emperor's exclusive place in the divine and temporal order. In 726, in the wake of a terrifying volcanic eruption in the middle of the Aegean Sea, Emperor Leo III the Isaurian (r.717-741) had his officers tear down the great golden icon of Christ at the Chalke, the gateway to the imperial palace, and replace it with a cross. A crowd of women protested in fury. Thus was launched the long iconoclastic period. Leo ordered all icons destroyed, and the ban lasted until 787. It was revived, in modified form, between 815 and 843.

During the iconoclastic period many works of art were destroyed, and few new ones were produced. Yet artistic activity did not end entirely. Painters blotted out the figures of saints, substituting birds or animals; minters replaced the images of Christ on imperial coins with crosses. Weavers still made textiles enlivened by abstract designs or figures of hunters to decorate the tunics of the wealthy. In Plate 2.1, which illustrates fragments of a silk band woven during the iconoclastic period, two mirror-image archers wearing elegant bands on their own tunics aim their bows at two rampant tigers.

Behind the iconoclastic movement lay a great revulsion not so much against artistic representation as against sullying the divine. At the Synod of 754, a meeting of over 300 bishops and Emperor Constantine V (r.741-775), the assembly argued eloquently that Christ himself had declared he should be represented through the bread and wine—and in no other way. As for the saints, they

> live on eternally with God, although they have died. If anyone thinks to call them back again to life by a dead art, discovered by the heathen, he makes himself guilty of blasphemy.... It is not permitted to Christians ... to insult the saints, who shine in so great glory, by common dead matter.[3]

Iconoclasm had a thousand intimate consequences. Anyone with a portable icon at home had to destroy it or adore it in secret. The effects on the monasteries were

Plate 2.1: Silk Band (8th or 9th cent.). Although this particular weaving probably comes from Egypt, which was under Islamic rule at the time, it echoes the patterns and motifs of textiles produced even at Constantinople during the iconoclastic period.

dramatic: their treasuries were raided and properties confiscated. Most extreme was one zealous *strategos*, Michael Lachanodracon, who forced all the monks in his theme to marry or suffer blinding and exile. In this way, iconoclasm destroyed communities that might otherwise have served as centers of resistance to imperial power. That was perhaps incidental. The most important point was that it made the Byzantines, in the eyes of the movement's defenders, the "people of God."

THE RISE OF THE "BEST COMMUNITY": ISLAM

The Muslims also considered themselves God's people. In the Qur'an, the "recitation" of God's words, Muslims are "the best community ever raised up for mankind ... having faith in God" (3:110). The community's common purpose is "submission to God," the literal meaning of "Islam." The Muslim (a word that derives from "Islam") is "one who submits." Under the leadership of Muhammad (*c.*570-632) in Arabia, Islam created a new world power in less than a century.

The Shaping of Islam

"One community" was a revolutionary notion for the disparate peoples of Arabia (today Saudi Arabia), who converted to Islam in the course of the early seventh century. Pre-Islamic Arabia lay between the two great empires of the day — Persia and Byzantium — and felt the cross-currents as well as the magnetic pull of their economies and cultures. Its land supported Bedouins: nomads (the word "arab" is derived from the most prestigious of these, the camel-herders) and semi-nomads. But by far the majority of the population was neither; it was sedentary. To the southwest, where rain was adequate, farmers worked the soil. Elsewhere people settled at oases, where they raised date palms (a highly prized food); some of these communities were prosperous enough to support merchants and artisans. Both the nomads and the settled population were organized as tribes — communities whose members considered themselves related through a common ancestor.

Herding goats, sheep or camels, the nomads and semi-nomads lived in small groups, largely making do with the products (leather, milk, meat) of their animals, and raiding one another for booty — including women. "Manliness" was the chief Bedouin virtue; it meant not sexual prowess (though polygyny — having more than one wife at a time — was practiced) but bravery, generosity, and a keen sense of honor. Lacking written literature, the nomads were proud of their oral culture of storytelling and poetry.

Islam began as a religion of the sedentary, but it soon found support and military strength among the nomads. The movement began at Mecca, a commercial center and the launching pad of caravans organized to sell Bedouin products—mainly leather goods and raisins—to the more urbanized areas at the Syrian border. (See Map 2.2.) Mecca was also a holy place. Its shrine, the Ka'ba, was rimmed with hundreds of idols. Within its sacred precincts, where war and violence were prohibited, pilgrims bartered and traded.

Muhammad, the prophet of Islam, was born in this commercial and religious center around 570. Orphaned as a child, he came under the guardianship of his uncle, a leader of the Quraysh tribe, which dominated Mecca and controlled access to the Ka'ba. Muhammad became a trader, married, had children, and seemed comfortable and happy. But he sought something more: he would sometimes leave home, escaping to a nearby mountain to pray.

Map 2.2: The Islamic World to 750

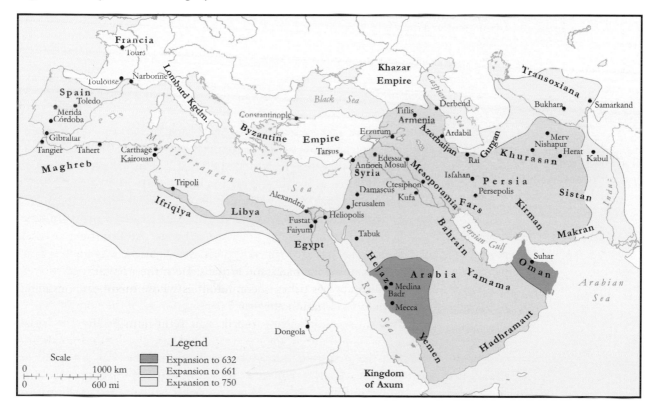

In about 610, on one such retreat, Muhammad heard a voice calling on him to worship God (the Arabic word for God is Allah). After he solemnly assented, the voice gave him further messages—they continued, intermittently, for the rest of his life. Later, when they had been written down and arranged—a process that was completed in the seventh century, but after Muhammad's death—these messages became the Qur'an, the holy book of Islam. The Qur'an is understood to be God's revelation as told to Muhammad by the angel Gabriel, then recited in turn by Muhammad to others. Its first chapter—or sura—is the *fatihah*, or Opening:

> In the name of God
>   the Compassionate the Caring
> Praise be to God
>   lord sustainer of the world
> the Compassionate the Caring
> master of the day of reckoning
> To you we turn to worship
>   and to you we turn in time of need
> Guide us along the road straight
> the road of those to whom you are giving
>   not those with anger upon them
>   not those who have lost the way.[4]

The Qur'an continues with a far longer sura, followed by others (114 in all) of gradually decreasing length. For Muslims the Qur'an covers the gamut of human experience—the sum total of history, prophecy, and the legal and moral code by which men and women should live—as well as the life to come.

Banning infanticide, Islam gave girls and women new dignity. It allowed for polygyny, but this was limited to four wives at one time, all to be treated equally. It mandated dowries and offered some female inheritance rights. At first women even prayed with men, though that practice ended in the eighth century. The nuclear family (newly emphasized, as was happening around the same time at Byzantium as well; see p. 67) became more important than the tribe. In Islam there are three essential social facts: the individual, God, and the *ummah*, the community of the faithful. There are no intermediaries between the divine and human realms, no priests, Eucharist, relics, or icons.

Not all welcomed the new religion. Muhammad's insistence that paganism be abandoned threatened Quraysh tribal interests, so bound up with the Ka'ba. Its leaders tried to thwart his missionary efforts. When some of Muhammad's followers at Medina, an oasis about 200 miles to the northeast of Mecca, invited him to join them, he agreed. In 622 he made the *Hijra*, or flight from Mecca to Medina, where he was greeted not only as a religious but also as a secular leader. This joining of the political and religious spheres set the pattern for Islamic government thereafter. After Muhammad's death, the year of the *Hijra*, 622, became the year 1 of the Islamic calendar, marking the establishment of the Islamic era.

Muhammad consolidated his position as a religious and secular leader by asserting hegemony over three important groups: the Jews, the Meccans, and the nomads. At Medina itself he took control by ousting and sometimes killing his main competitors, the Jewish clans of the city. Against the Meccans he fought a series of battles; the battle of Badr (624), waged against a Meccan caravan, marked the first Islamic military victory. After several other campaigns, Muhammad triumphed and took over Mecca in 630, offering leniency to most of its inhabitants, who in turn converted to Islam. Meanwhile, Muhammad allied himself with numerous nomadic groups, adding their contingents to his army. Warfare was thus integrated into the new religion as a part of the duty of Muslims to strive in the ways of God; *jihad*, often translated as "holy war," in fact means "striving." Through a combination of military might, conversion, and negotiation, Muhammad united many, though by no means all, Arabic tribes under his leadership by the time of his death in 632.

Gradually, new, defining practices for Muslims were instituted. There was the *zakat*, a tax to be used for charity; Ramadan, a month of fasting to mark the battle of Badr, the *hajj*, an annual pilgrimage to Mecca to be made at least once in a believer's lifetime, and the *salat*, formal worship at least three times a day (later increased to five), including the *shahadah*, or profession of faith: "There is no god but God, and Muhammad is His prophet." The place of worship was known as a "mosque." Breaking with Jewish practices, Muhammad had the Muslims turn their prayers away from Jerusalem, the center of Jewish worship, and toward Mecca instead. Detailed regulations for these practices, sometimes called the "five pillars of Islam," were worked out in the eighth and early ninth centuries.

Out of Arabia

"Strive, O Prophet," says the Qur'an, "against the unbelievers and the hypocrites, and deal with them firmly. Their final abode is Hell; And what a wretched destination" (9:73). Cutting across tribal allegiances, the Islamic *ummah* was itself a formidable "supertribe" dedicated to victory over the enemies of God. After Muhammad's death, armies of Muslims led by caliphs—a title which at first seems to have derived from *khalifat Allah*, "deputy of God," but which later came to mean the deputy of the Apostle of God, Muhammad—moved into Sasanid and Byzantine territory, toppling or crippling the once great ancient empires. (See Map 2.2.) Islamic armies captured the Persian capital, Ctesiphon, in 637 and continued eastward to take Persepolis in 648, Nishapur in 651, and then, beyond Persia, Kabul in 664 and Samarkand in 710. To the west, they picked off, one by one, the great Mediterranean cities of the Byzantine Empire: Antioch and Damascus in 635, Alexandria in 642, Carthage in 697. By the beginning of the eighth century, Islamic warriors held sway from Spain to India.

It was an astonishing triumph, but one not hard to understand with the benefit of hindsight. The Arabs were formidable fighters, and their enemies were relatively weak. The Persian and Byzantine Empires had exhausted one another after years of fighting. Nor were their populations particularly loyal; some — Jews and Christians in Persia, Monophysite Christians in Syria — even welcomed the invaders. In large measure they were proved right: the Muslims made no attempt to convert them, imposing a tax on them instead.

Although Arabic culture was not strikingly city-based, Muhammad himself was attached to Mecca and Medina, and the Muslims almost immediately fostered urban life in the regions that they conquered. In Syria and Palestine, most of the soldiers settled within existing coastal cities; their leaders, however, built palaces, hunting lodges, and caravanserai to house travelers in the countryside. Everywhere else the invaders created large permanent camps of their own, remaining separate from the indigenous populations. Some of these camps were eventually abandoned, but others — such as those at Baghdad and Cairo — became centers of new and thriving urban agglomerations.

Men and women living along the Mediterranean — in Syria, Palestine, North Africa, and Spain — went back to work and play much as they had done before the invasions. Safe in Muslim-controlled Damascus, where he served as a minister to the caliph, Saint John of Damascus (*d*.749) thundered against iconoclasm: "I do not worship matter [i.e., the paint and wood of an icon]; I worship the God of matter, who became matter for my sake."[5] He would never have been able to write such words within the Byzantine Empire. Maps of the Islamic conquest divide the world into Muslims and Christians. But the "Islamic world" was only slightly Islamic; Muslims constituted a minority of the population. Then, even as their religion came to predominate, they were themselves absorbed, at least to some degree, into the cultures that they had conquered.

The Culture of the Umayyads

Dissension, triumph, and disappointment accompanied the naming of Muhammad's successors. The caliphs were not chosen from the old tribal elites but rather from a new inner circle of men close to Muhammad. The first two caliphs, Abu-Bakr and Umar, ruled without serious opposition. They were the fathers of two of Muhammad's wives. But the third caliph, Uthman, husband of two of Muhammad's daughters and great-grandson of the Quraysh leader Umayyah, aroused resentment. (See Genealogy 2.1: Muhammad's Relatives and Successors to 750.) His family had come late to Islam, and some of its members had once even persecuted Muhammad. The opponents of the Umayyads supported Ali, the husband of Muhammad's daughter Fatimah. After a group of discontented soldiers murdered Uthman, civil war broke out between the Umayyads and Ali's faction. It ended when Ali was killed in 661 by one of his own erstwhile supporters. The caliphate remained thereafter in Umayyad hands until 750.

Yet the *Shi'ah*, the faction of Ali, did not forget their leader. They became the "Shi'ites," faithful to Ali's dynasty, mourning his martyrdom, shunning the "mainstream" caliphs of the other Muslims ("Sunni" Muslims, as they were later called), awaiting the arrival of the true leader—the *imam*—who would spring from the house of Ali.

Meanwhile, the Umayyads made Damascus, previously a minor Byzantine city, into their capital. Here they adopted many of the institutions of the culture that they had conquered, issuing coins like those of the Byzantines (in the east they used coins based on Persian models), and employing former Byzantine officials as administrators (John of Damascus came from such a family). Under Caliph 'Abd al-Malik (r.685-705, but who was fully recognized only in 692), Jerusalem—already sacred to Jews and Christians—became an Islamic Holy City. Building the mosque known as the Dome of the Rock, 'Abd al-Malik laid claim to the religious and artistic inheritances of the past for Islam itself. (See Plate 2.2.) Arabic, the language of the Qur'an, became the official tongue of the Islamic world. As translators rendered important Greek and other texts into this newly imperial language, it proved to be both flexible and capacious. Around this time, Muslim scholars determined the definitive form of the Qur'an and began to compile pious narratives about the Prophet's sayings, or *hadith*. A new literate class—composed mainly of the old Persian and Syrian elite, now converted to Islam and schooled in Arabic—created new forms of prose and poetry. A commercial revolution in China helped to vivify commerce in the Islamic world. At hand was a cultural flowering in a land of prosperity.

THE MAKING OF WESTERN EUROPE

No reasonable person in the year 750 would have predicted that, of the three heirs of the Roman Empire, Western Europe would be the one eventually to dominate the

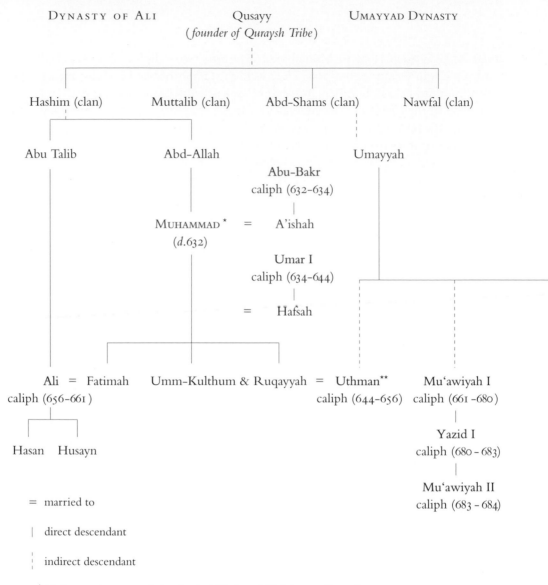

DYNASTY OF ALI   Qusayy   UMAYYAD DYNASTY
(*founder of Quraysh Tribe*)

Hashim (clan)   Muttalib (clan)   Abd-Shams (clan)   Nawfal (clan)

Abu Talib   Abd-Allah   Umayyah

Abu-Bakr
caliph (632-634)

MUHAMMAD*   =   A'ishah
(*d.*632)

Umar I
caliph (634-644)

=   Hafsah

Ali   =   Fatimah   Umm-Kulthum & Ruqayyah   =   Uthman**   Mu'awiyah I
caliph (656-661)   caliph (644-656)   caliph (661-680)

Hasan   Husayn   Yazid I
caliph (680 - 683)

Mu'awiyah II
caliph (683 - 684)

=   married to

| direct descendant

⋮   indirect descendant

* Muhammad was married to both A'ishah and Hafsah as well as others
** Uthman was married to two of Muhammad's daughters, Umm-Kulthum and Ruqayyah

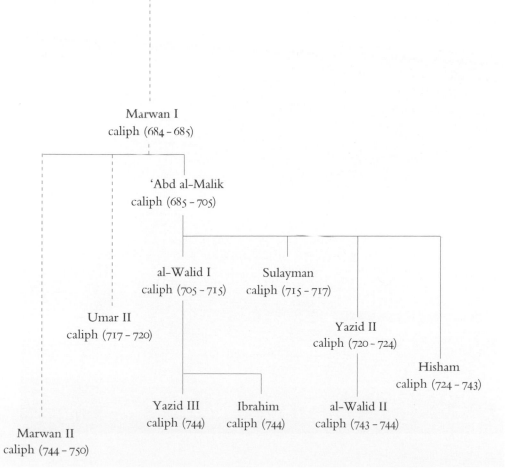

Genealogy 2.1:
Muhammad's Relatives
and Successors to 750

Marwan I
caliph (684 – 685)

'Abd al-Malik
caliph (685 – 705)

al-Walid I
caliph (705 – 715)

Sulayman
caliph (715 – 717)

Umar II
caliph (717 – 720)

Yazid II
caliph (720 – 724)

Hisham
caliph (724 – 743)

Yazid III
caliph (744)

Ibrahim
caliph (744)

al-Walid II
caliph (743 – 744)

Marwan II
caliph (744 – 750)

Plate 2.2: Dome of the Rock (691). Rivaling great Christian churches like Hagia Sophia (see p. 54) in its size and opulence, the Dome of the Rock was covered with mosaics both inside and out. The use of a dome, of arches on piers and marble columns (looted from older buildings), and the construction technique of stone and brick masonry were all borrowed from the Byzantines. But, while admittedly absorbing many non-Arab traditions, the conquerors also asserted, in the same building, their separate and triumphant identity. In this plate, the motifs of Byzantine and Persian crowns and jewels are engulfed by plant forms that function like trophies of victory on the wall. Above the crowns you can just make out a band of Arabic writing. Such bands run along most of the building, and many of the inscriptions concern the place of Christ in God's scheme. "Say only the truth about Jesus over whom you dispute: he is the son of Mary! It is not fitting that God should beget or father a child," reads one, thus challenging the very notion of Christ's divine paternity. In this way, the building recognizes the importance of Christ in his very own city, but at the same time it reinterprets his meaning in accordance with Islamic tradition.

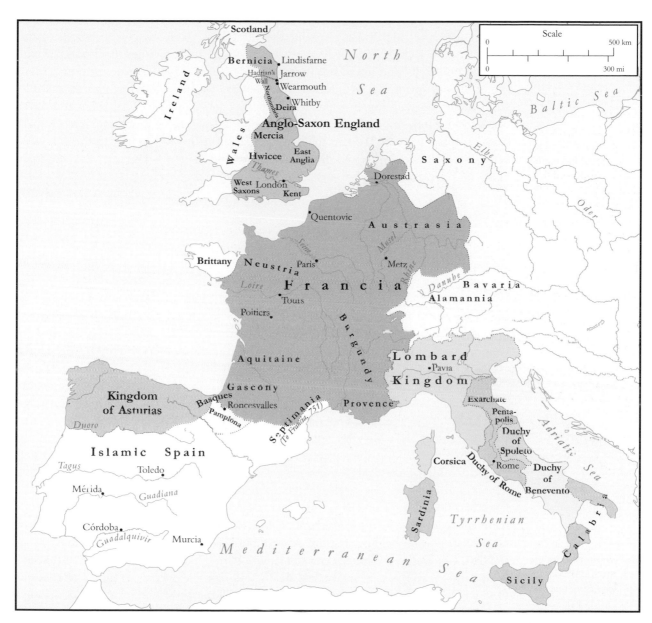

Map 2.3: Western Europe, *c*.750

world. While Byzantium cut back, reorganized, and forged ahead, while Islam spread its language and rule over a territory that stretched nearly twice the length of the United States today, Western Europe remained an impoverished backwater. Fragmented politically and linguistically, its cities (left over from Roman antiquity) mere shells, its tools primitive, its infrastructure—what was left of Roman roads, schools, and bridges—collapsing, Europe lacked identity and cohesion. That these and other strengths did indeed eventually develop over a long period of time is a tribute in part to the survival of some Roman traditions and institutions and in part to the inventive ways in which people adapted those institutions and made up new ones to meet their needs and desires.

Impoverishment and Its Variations

Taking in the whole of Western Europe around this time means dwelling long on its variety. Dominating the scene was Francia. To its south were Spain (ruled first by the Visigoths, and then, after c.715, by the Muslims) and Italy (divided between the pope, the Byzantines, and the Lombards). To the north, joined to rather than separated from the Continent by the lick of water called the English Channel, the British Isles were home to a plethora of tiny kingdoms, about three quarters of which were native ("Celtic") and the last quarter Germanic ("Anglo-Saxons").

There were clear differences between the Romanized south—Spain, Italy, southern Francia—and the north. (See Map 2.3.) Travelers going from Anglo-Saxon England to Rome would have noticed them. There were many such travelers: some, like the churchman Benedict Biscop, were voluntary pilgrims; others were slaves on forced march. Making their way across England, voyagers such as these would pass fenced wooden farmsteads, each with a rectangular "hall" for eating and sleeping, a few outbuildings serving as sheds, and perhaps a sunken house, its floor below the level of the soil, its damp atmosphere suitable for weaving. (Even royal complexes were made of wood and looked much like humble villages: see Figure 2.2.) Most farmsteads—each held by a family—were built in clusters of four to five, making up tiny hamlets. Peasants planted their fields with barley (used to make a thick and nourishing ale) as well as oats, wheat, rye, beans, and flax. Two kinds of plows were used. One was heavy: it had a coulter and moldboard, often tipped with iron, to cut through and turn over heavy soils. The other was a light "scratch plow," suitable for making narrow furrows in light soils. Because the first plow was hard to turn, the fields it produced tended to be long and rectangular in shape. The lighter plow was more agile: it was used to cut the soil in one direction and then at right angles to that, producing a square field. There were many animals on these farms: cattle, sheep, horses, pigs, and dogs. In some cases, the peasants who worked the land and tended the animals were relatively independent, owing little to anyone outside their village. In other instances, regional lords—often kings—commanded a share of the peasants' produce and, occasionally, labor services. But all was not pastoral or agricultural in England: here and there, and especially toward the south, were commercial settlements—real emporia.

Crossing the Channel, travelers would enter northern Francia, also dotted with emporia (such as Quentovic and Dorestad) but additionally boasting old Roman cities, now mainly religious centers. Paris, for example, was to a large extent an agglomeration of churches: Montmartre, Saint-Laurent, Saint-Martin-des-Champs— perhaps 35 churches were jammed into an otherwise nearly abandoned city. In the countryside around Paris the lands and vineyards, largely held by aristocrats, were tended by tenants, each family with its own plot. Moving eastward, our voyagers would pass through thick forests and land more often used as pasture for animals than for cereal cultivation. Along the Mosel River they would find villages with fields, meadows, woods, and water courses, a few supplied with mills and churches. Some of the peasants in these villages would be tenants or slaves of a lord; others would be independent farmers who owned all or part of the land that they cultivated.

Southern Francia and much of Italy, by contrast, still had an urban feel. Here the great hulks of Roman cities, with their stone amphitheaters, baths, and walls, dominated the landscape even though, as at Byzantium, their populations were much diminished. The countryside had once been organized into great estates farmed by slave gangs. These had long ago disappeared, and many of the farms abandoned. The remaining peasants settled in small hamlets scattered sparsely across the countryside. They cultivated their own plots, but, as elsewhere, few were landowners. Most were tenant farmers, owing a proportion of their produce to an aristocratic lord. The soil of this region was lighter than in the north, easily worked with scratch plows to produce the barley and rye (in northern Italy) and wheat (elsewhere) that were the staples—along with meat and fish—of the peasant diet.

By 700, there was little left of the old long-distance Mediterranean commerce of the ancient Roman world. But, although this was an impoverished society, it was not without wealth or lively patterns of exchange. In the first place, money was still minted, but increasingly in silver rather than gold. The change of metal was due in part to a shortage of gold in Europe. But it was also a nod to the importance of small-scale commercial transactions—sales of surplus wine from a vineyard, say, for which small coins were the most practical. In the second place, North Sea merchant-sailors—carrying, for example, ceramic plates and glass vessels—had begun to link northern Francia, the east coast of England, Scandinavia, and the Baltic Sea. Brisk trade gave rise to new emporia and revivified older Roman cities along the coasts. In the third

SEEING THE MIDDLE AGES

Figure 2.2 (facing page): Yeavering, Northumberland

In *The Ecclesiastical History of the English People*, the monk-historian Bede (see p. 88) wrote of the proselytizing work of Paulinus in the north of England in the 620s: "So great is said to have been the fervor of the faith of the Northumbrians and their longing for the washing of salvation [i.e., baptism] that once when Paulinus came to the king and queen in their royal palace at *Ad Gefrin*, he spent thirty-six days there occupied in the task of catechizing and baptizing."[1] Where was *Ad Gefrin* and what was this "royal palace" like? Bede mentioned that it was near the river Glen. Aerial photographs of the region taken in the late 1940s and early 1950s revealed its probable location in Bernicia, not far from Lindisfarne (see Map 2.3) at Yeavering, a crest of land strategically situated on a lowland route between the eastern coast of England and the inland. Farmland now, Yeavering's cropmarks showed the outlines of buildings under the topsoil. (Cropmarks are variant crop growths caused by different levels of moisture beneath. Pits or troughs under the topsoil hold more water than the rest of the terrain, and plants that find this moisture grow taller than their neighbors.)

Archaeological excavations undertaken by Brian Hope-Taylor on the site from 1953 to 1962 revealed that the outlines were not structures but rather the post-holes and foundations of large wooden buildings.

In Figure 2.2, the major buildings of the royal settlement at Yeavering were "reconstructed" by Simon James, an archaeologist and archaeological illustrator, for an exhibition on Anglo-Saxon art and culture held at the British Museum in 1984. James's vision, reproduced here with the addition of identifying letters in red, relied not only on Hope-Taylor's reports but also on what was known from other sources about Anglo-Saxon building materials, heights, and shapes.

It is an imaginative vision: a line of people and animals snakes along a path. One of the people carries a cross: is he Paulinus, processing from the triangular assembly place, E, where he addressed the great throng, to the great hall, B? In the distance are older buildings aligned north and south.

The one here labeled G was, according to Hope-Taylor, a simple dwelling (since pottery and a loom weight were found there). The larger building, F, was probably a temple, since graves were clustered around its southern end and ox skulls—evidence of feasting—were piled up at its eastern door.

The reconstruction "freezes" a changing community, showing it at its most advanced development. The building complex B-C-D was the newest phase of a series of buildings on the spot. For example, a hall had once stood where we here see a fenced-in courtyard (C).

The illustrator had to make some hard choices. Consider the double fence-like structure that ends in a circular "fort" (A). This fence continued, curving around outside and to the east of the settlement, ending with another circular structure nearly touching the first. No one lived within this "great enclosure," as Hope-Taylor calls it; it probably had little defensive significance. But it may have functioned as a sign of power as well as the site of public gatherings, a market, or a communal cattle corral. It posed a dilemma for the illustrator: had he shown all of it, the central structures of the royal complex—the assembly place and great hall—would have had to recede toward the back, belying their real importance in the social and political life of the royal complex.

Further Reading

Hamerow, Helena. *Early Medieval Settlements: The Archaeology of Rural Communities in North-West Europe 400-900*. Oxford, 2002.

Hope-Taylor, Brian. *Yeavering: An Anglo-British Centre of Early Northumbria*. London, 1977.

The Making of England: Anglo-Saxon England: Anglo-Saxon Art and Culture, AD 600-900. Edited by Leslie Webster and Janet Backhouse. London, 1991.

Welch, Martin. *Discovering Anglo-Saxon England*. University Park, PA, 1992.

Note

1. Bede, *The Ecclesiastical History of the English People*, ed. Judith McClure and Roger Collins (Oxford, 1994), p.97.

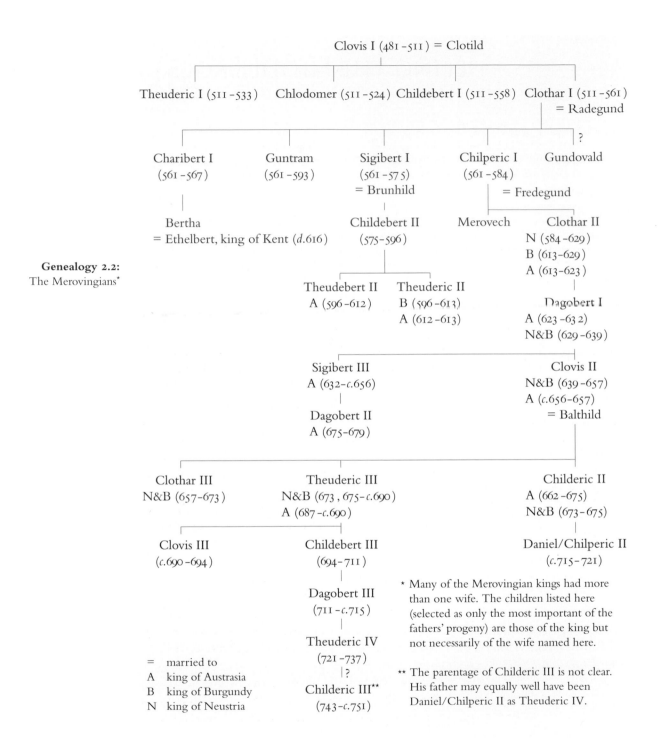

Genealogy 2.2:
The Merovingians*

Clovis I (481–511) = Clotild

Theuderic I (511–533)   Chlodomer (511–524)   Childebert I (511–558)   Clothar I (511–561)
= Radegund

?

Charibert I   Guntram   Sigibert I   Chilperic I   Gundovald
(561–567)   (561–593)   (561–575)   (561–584)
                                     = Brunhild   = Fredegund

Bertha   Childebert II   Merovech   Clothar II
= Ethelbert, king of Kent (d.616)   (575–596)   N (584–629)
                                                                            B (613–629)
                                                                            A (613–623)

                          Theudebert II   Theuderic II   Dagobert I
                          A (596–612)   B (596–613)   A (623–632)
                                           A (612–613)   N&B (629–639)

                                Sigibert III   Clovis II
                                A (632–c.656)   N&B (639–657)
                                                                            A (c.656–657)
                                Dagobert II   = Balthild
                                A (675–679)

Clothar III   Theuderic III   Childeric II
N&B (657–673)   N&B (673, 675–c.690)   A (662–675)
                        A (687–c.690)   N&B (673–675)

Clovis III   Childebert III   Daniel/Chilperic II
(c.690–694)   (694–711)   (c.715–721)

                        Dagobert III   * Many of the Merovingian kings had more
                        (711–c.715)   than one wife. The children listed here
                                                (selected as only the most important of the
                        Theuderic IV   fathers' progeny) are those of the king but
                        (721–737)   not necessarily of the wife named here.

=   married to |?
A   king of Austrasia   ** The parentage of Childeric III is not clear.
B   king of Burgundy   Childeric III**   His father may equally well have been
N   king of Neustria   (743–c.751)   Daniel/Chilperic II as Theuderic IV.

place, a gift economy—that is, an economy of give and take—was flourishing. Booty was seized, tribute demanded, harvests hoarded, and coins struck, all to be redistributed to friends, followers, dependents, and the church. Kings and other rich and powerful men and women amassed gold, silver, ornaments, and jewelry in their treasuries and grain in their storehouses to give out in ceremonies that marked their power and added to their prestige. Even the rents that peasants paid to their lords, mainly in kind, were often couched as "gifts."

Politics and Culture

If variations were plentiful in even so basic a matter as material and farming conditions, the differences were magnified by political and cultural conditions. We need now to take Europe kingdom by kingdom.

Francia

Francia comes first because it was the major player, a real political entity that dominated what is today France, Belgium, the Netherlands, Luxembourg, and much of Germany. In the seventh century, it was divided into three related kingdoms—Neustria, Austrasia, Burgundy—each of which included parts of a fourth, southern region, Aquitaine. By 700, however, the political distinctions between them were melting, and Francia was becoming one kingdom.

The line of Clovis—the Merovingians—ruled these kingdoms. (See Genealogy 2.2: The Merovingians.) The dynasty owed its longevity to biological good fortune and excellent political sense: it allied itself with the major lay aristocrats and ecclesiastical authorities of Gaul—men and women of high status, enormous wealth, and marked local power. To that alliance, the kings brought their own sources of power: a skeletal Roman administrative apparatus, family properties, appropriated lands once belonging to the Roman state, and the profits and prestige of leadership in war.

The royal court—which moved with the kings as they traveled from one palace to another, as they had no capital city—was the focus of political life. Here gathered talented young men, clerics-on-the-rise, aristocratic scions. The most important courtiers had official positions: there was, for example, the referendary and the cup-bearer. Highest of all was the "mayor of the palace," who controlled access to the king and brokered deals with aristocratic factions.

Queens were an important part of the court as well. One of them, Balthild (d.680), had once been among the unwilling travelers from England. Purchased there as a slave by the mayor of the palace of Neustria, she parlayed her beauty into marriage with the king himself. (Merovingian kings often married slaves or women captured in war. By avoiding wives with powerful kindred, they staved off challenges to their royal authority.) Balthild's biographer described how kindly she cared for the young men at court: "to the princes she showed herself a mother, to the priests as a daughter, and to the young and the adolescents as the best possible nurse." When her husband, King Clovis II, died, Balthild served as regent for her minor sons, acting, in effect, as king during this time. She arranged, "through the advice of the great magnates," (as her biographer put it) that one of her sons become king of Austrasia, and she maintained the prestige of the royal line through her extraordinary generosity: "Who, then, is able to say how many and how great were the sources of income, the entire farms and the large forests she gave up by donating them to the establishments of religious men ...?"[6] By the end of her life, Balthild was counted a saint.

Important as the court was as a focus of power, aristocrats usually stayed at "home," though in fact they might (like kings) have many homes, scattered in many regions. Tending to their estates, honing their skills in the hunt, aristocratic men regularly led armed retinues to war. They proved their worth in the regular taking of booty and rewarded their faithful followers afterwards at generous banquets.

And they bedded down. The bed—or rather the production of children—was the focus of marriage, the key to the survival of aristocratic families and the transmission of their property and power. Though churchmen had many ideas about the value of marriage, they had nothing to do with the ceremony; no one married in a church. Rather, marriage was a family affair, and a very expensive one. There was more than one form of marriage: in the most formal, the husband-to-be gave to his future bride a handsome dowry of clothes, bedding, livestock, and land. Then, after the marriage was consummated, he gave his wife a morning gift of furniture and perhaps the keys to the house. Very rich men often had, in addition to their wife, one or more "concubines" at the same time. These enjoyed a less formal type of marriage, receiving a morning gift but no dowry.

The wife's role was above all to maintain the family. We have already seen how important the metaphor of motherhood was for Balthild, even in connection with unrelated men at court. A woman passed from one family (that of her birth) to the next (that of her marriage) by parental fiat. When they married, women left the legal protection of their father for that of their husband. Did women have any freedom of action? Yes. For one thing, they had considerable control over their dowries. Some participated in family land transactions: sales, donations, exchanges. Upon the death of their husbands, widows received a portion of the household property. Although inheritances generally went from fathers to sons, many fathers left bequests to their daughters, who could then dispose of their property more or less as they liked. In 632, for example, the nun Burgundofara, who had never married, drew up a will giving to her monastery the land, slaves, vineyards, pastures, and forests that she had received from her two brothers and her father. In the same will, she gave other property near Paris to her brothers and sister.

Burgundofara's generous piety was extraordinary only in degree. The world of kings, queens, and aristocrats intersected with that of the church. The arrival (c.590) on the Continent of the fierce Irish monastic reformer Saint Columbanus (543–615) marked a new level of association between the two. Columbanus's brand of monasticism, which stressed exile, devotion, and discipline, made a powerful impact on Merovingian aristocrats. They flocked to the monasteries that he established in both Francia and Italy, and they founded new ones themselves on their own lands in the countryside. In Francia alone there was an explosion of monasteries: between the years 600 and 700, an astonishing 320 new houses were established, most of them outside of the cities. Some of the new monks and nuns were grown men and women, others were young children, given to a monastery by their parents. This latter practice, called oblation, was not only accepted but even considered essential for the spiritual well-being of both children and their families.

Irish monasticism introduced aristocrats on the Continent to a deepened religious devotion. Those who did not actively join or patronize a monastery still read, or listened to others read, books preaching penance, and they chanted the psalms. The Merovingian laity developed a culture of domestic piety at about the same time as the Byzantines did.

Deepened piety did not, in this case, lead to the persecution of others—something that (as we shall see) happened in later centuries. In particular, where Jews were settled in Western Europe—along the Mediterranean coast and inland, in Burgundy, for example—they remained integrated into every aspect of secular life. They used Hebrew in worship, but otherwise they spoke the same languages as Christians and used Latin in their legal documents. Their children were often given the same names as Christians (and Christians often took biblical names, such as Solomon); they dressed as everyone else dressed; and they engaged in the same occupations. Many Jews planted and tended vineyards, in part because of the importance of wine in synagogue services, in part because the surplus could easily be sold. Some were rich landowners, with slaves and dependent peasants working for them; others were independent peasants of modest means. While some Jews lived in cities—the few that remained—most, like their Christian neighbors, lived on the land.

THE BRITISH ISLES

Roman Britain had been as habituated to barbarian defenders—in this case Saxons—as the rest of the empire. When the last of the Roman garrisons left England in 410 for service elsewhere, the Saxons gradually took over in the southeast, helped by massive invasions of their brethren from the Continent. The old and new tribes together are called "Anglo-Saxons"; where they conquered—in the southeastern lowlands of the British Isles — most Christians were absorbed as slaves into the pagan culture of the invaders. Elsewhere — in what is today the north and west of England, Scotland, and Ireland — Celtic kingdoms survived. Wales was already Christian when, in the course of the fifth century, Ireland and Scotland were converted by missionaries. (Saint Patrick, apostle to the Irish, is only the most famous of these.) These Celtic kingdoms supported relatively non-hierarchical church organizations. Rural monasteries often served as the seats of bishoprics as well as centers of population and settlement. Abbots and abbesses, often members of powerful families, enjoyed considerable power and prestige.

The Anglo-Saxon quadrant of the British Isles was reintroduced to Christianity from two different directions: the Celtic north and the Roman south. The Anglo-Saxon king of Northumbria Oswald (*r*.633-641), a convert to Christianity during his period of exile in Ireland, called for missionaries to come to his kingdom to preach. Monks and a bishop arrived from Ireland, setting up a monastery at Lindisfarne, just off the coast of Northumbria, and, as the English historian and monk Bede (673?-735) put it about a century later,

from that time, as the days went by, many came from the country of the Irish into Britain and to those English kingdoms over which Oswald reigned, preaching the word of faith with great devotion.... Churches were built in various places and the people flocked together with joy to hear the Word [of God].[7]

In the south, Christianity arrived from the Continent, most spectacularly in 597 when missionaries sent from Rome by Pope Gregory the Great came to the court of King Ethelbert of Kent (*d*.616). Under their leader, Augustine (not the fifth-century bishop of Hippo!), the missionaries converted the king. He was primed for the change, having long before married a Christian Merovingian princess, who arrived in Kent with a bishop in her entourage.

Augustine had in mind more than the conversion of a king: he wanted to set up an English church on the Roman model, with ties to the pope and a clear hierarchy. He divided England into territorial units (dioceses) headed by an archbishop and bishops. Augustine himself became archbishop of Canterbury. There he set up the model English ecclesiastical complex: a cathedral, a monastery, and a school to train young clerics.

There was nothing easy or quick about the conversion of England. Everywhere paganism maintained its attractive hold. Once converted, the Christians of the north and south differed in their interpretation of the religious life and in the organization of the church. Above all, they clashed in their calculations of the date of Easter. Everyone agreed that they could not be saved unless they observed the day of Christ's

Plate 2.3 (facing page): Belt Buckle from Sutton Hoo (early 7th cent.). Beginning in 1939 and continuing through the 1980s, archaeologists excavated seventeen curious mounds at Sutton Hoo, a barren stretch of land in southeast England. Their finds included numerous Anglo-Saxon cremations and burials, the bones of horses, spears, shields, helmets, large open boats, jewelry, silver bowls, and many other objects, including this heavy buckle made of gold.

Resurrection properly and on the right date. But what was the right date? Each side was wedded to its own view. A turning point came at the Synod of Whitby, organized in 664 by the Northumbrian King Oswy to decide between the Roman and Irish dates. When Oswy became convinced that Rome spoke with the very voice of Saint Peter, the heavenly doorkeeper, he opted for the Roman calculation of the date and embraced the Roman church as a whole.

The pull of Rome—the symbol, in English clerics' view, of the Christian religion itself—was almost physical. Benedict Biscop (c.630-690), a Northumbrian aristocrat-turned-abbot and founder of two important English monasteries, Wearmouth and Jarrow, made numerous arduous trips to Rome. He brought back books, saints' relics, liturgical vestments, and even a cantor to teach his monks the proper melodies in a time before written musical notation existed. A century later, the Anglo-Saxon monk Winfrith changed his name to the more Roman-sounding Boniface (c.672-754) after he went to Rome to get a commission from Pope Gregory II (r.715-731) to preach the Word to people living east of the Rhine. Though they were already Christian, their brand of Christianity was not Roman enough for Saint Boniface.

As Roman culture confronted Anglo-Saxon, the results were particularly eclectic. This is best seen in the visual arts. The Anglo-Saxons, like other barbarian (and, indeed, Celtic) tribes, had artistic traditions particularly well suited to adorning flat surfaces. Belt buckles, helmet nose-pieces, brooches, and other sorts of jewelry of the rich were embellished with semi-precious stones and enlivened with decorative patterns, often made up of intertwining snake-like animals. A particularly fine example is a buckle from Sutton Hoo (see Plate 2.3), perhaps the greatest archaeological find for the Anglo-Saxon period.

The conversion of England meant that the books associated with Christianity would became essential parts of its learned culture, and English artists soon combined their native decorative traditions with classical pictorial style to produce illuminations perfectly suited to flat pages. Consider the Lindisfarne Gospels, which were probably made at the monastery of Lindisfarne in the first third of the eighth century. (The Gospels are the four canonical accounts of Christ's life and death in the New Testament.) The artist of this sumptuous book was clearly uniting Anglo-Saxon, Irish, and Roman artistic traditions when he introduced each Gospel with three full-page illustrations: first, a portrait of the "author" (the evangelist); then an entirely ornamental "carpet" page; finally, the beginning words of the Gospel text. Plates 2.4 to 2.6 illustrate the sequence for the Gospel of Luke. The figure of Luke (see Plate 2.4), though clearly human, floats in space. His "throne" is a square of ribbons, his drapery a series of loopy lines. The artist captures the essence of an otherworldly saint without the distraction of three-dimensionality. The carpet page (see Plate 2.5), with its interlace panels, has some of the features of the Sutton Hoo brooch as well as Irish interlace patterns. It is more than decorative, however: the design clearly evokes a cross. The next page (see Plate 2.6) begins with a great letter, Q (for the first word, "quoniam"), as richly decorated as the cross of the carpet page; gradually, in the course of the next few words, the ornamentation diminishes. In this way, after the fanfare of author and carpet pages, the reader is ushered into the Gospel text itself.

The amalgamation of traditions in England is perhaps most clearly illustrated by the so-called Franks Casket, probably made in Northumbria around the same time as — or a bit later than — the Lindisfarne Gospels. Carved out of whale bone, this box is decorated with scenes from Roman, Jewish, Christian, and Germanic tales. The front panel (Plate 2.7), for example, melds a Christian story with one from the Anglo-Saxon tradition. On the left, the princess Beadohild is tricked by Weyland the Smith into bearing his son, the hero Widia. Weyland, an otherworldly figure of incredible skill at the forge, was celebrated in the Anglo-Saxon poems *Beowulf* and *Deor*. On the right side of the same panel, the Magi bring gifts to Christ, seated on Mary's lap. That, of course, was a story from the Gospels. Yet both scenes play on the same theme: a mother who bears the son of an otherworldly father.

Just as the Anglo-Saxons held on to their artistic styles and their legends after they were Christianized, so they retained their language. In England, the vernacular — the language of the people, as opposed to Latin — was quickly turned into a written language and used in every aspect of English life, from government to entertainment. But the same was true in Ireland; the uniqueness of Anglo-Saxon culture should not be exaggerated. The model for the Franks Casket probably came from a similar one carved earlier in Francia or Italy, and certainly comparable cultural creativity and the fusion of diverse elements were equally characteristic of early medieval Ireland and Scotland.

THE SOUTH: SPAIN AND ITALY

It is just possible that the exemplar for the Franks Casket came from Spain, which boasted an equally lively mix of cultures. Here, especially in the south and east, some Roman cities had continued to flourish after the Visigothic invasions. Merchants from Byzantium regularly visited Mérida, for example, and the sixth-century bishops

✝ Lucas tïtulus ⁊

on ginneð   goð spell

Incipit euangelium   secun dum lucam ∴

QUO
NIAM

QUIDE

MULTI

TISUNTORDINA

RENARRATIONEM

Plate 2.7: Franks Casket (1st half of 8th cent.). Made up of panels of carved whalebone, the Franks Casket combines not only various literary traditions but also some artistic ones. The whole idea of having figural scenes on a casket was classical, but the style here is Anglo-Saxon. Compare the style of cloaks and figures on the left (the Weyland scene) with Luke in Plate 2.4.

there constructed lavish churches and set up a system of regular food distribution. Under King Leovigild (r. 569–586), all of Spain came under Visigothic control. Under his son Reccared (r. 586–601), the monarchy converted from Arian to Catholic Christianity. This event (587) cemented the ties between the king and the Hispano-Roman population, which included the great landowners and leading bishops. Two years later, at the Third Council of Toledo, most of the Arian bishops followed their king by announcing their conversion to Catholicism, and the assembled churchmen enacted decrees for a united church in Spain.

Thereafter, the bishops and kings of Spain cooperated to a degree unprecedented in other regions. While the king gave the churchmen free rein to set up their own hierarchy (with the bishop of Toledo at the top) and to meet regularly at synods to regulate and reform the church, the bishops in turn supported the king. They even anointed him, daubing him with holy oil in a ritual that paralleled the ordination of priests and echoed the anointment of kings in the Old Testament. While the bishops in this way made the king's cause their own, their lay counterparts, the great landowners, helped supply the king with troops.

Unlike the Merovingians, however, the Visigothic kings were not able to establish a stable dynasty. The minority of a king's son almost always sparked revolts by rival families, and the child's deposition was often accompanied by wholesale slaughter of his father's followers and confiscation of their lands. This may help to explain why Visigothic courtiers painted a particularly lustrous picture of their kings, resplendent and dazzling, their throne "radiant with shining gold," and why royal laws punished treason by death or blinding.[8]

It was precisely the centralization of the Visigothic kingdom that proved its undoing. In 711, a small Islamic raiding party killed the Visigothic king and thereby dealt the whole state a decisive blow. Between 712 and 715, armies led by Arabs took over the peninsula through a combination of war and diplomacy. The Treaty of Tudmir, drawn up in 713, shows how one local lord, Theodemir (Arabized as Tudmir), worked out an arrangement with the invaders that allowed the Christians in Murcia (in southeast Spain) to continue their lives as before. In exchange, they promised not to aid the enemies of the Muslims and to pay their new overlords a yearly tax.

The conquest of Spain was less Arabic or Islamic than Berber. The generals who led the invasion of Spain were Arabs, to be sure; but the rank-and-file fighters were Berbers from North Africa. While the Berbers were converts to Islam, they did not speak Arabic, and the Arabs considered them crude mountainfolk, only imperfectly Muslim. Perhaps a million people settled in Spain in the wake of the invasions, the Arabs taking the better lands in the south, the Berbers getting less rich properties in the center and north. Most of the conquered population consisted of Christians, along with a sprinkling of Jews. A thin ribbon of Christian states—Asturias, Pamplona, and so on survived in the north. There was thus a great variety of religions on the Iberian Peninsula. (See Map 2.3.) The history of Spain would for many centuries thereafter be one of both acculturation and war.

Unlike Visigothic Spain, Lombard Italy presented no united front. In the center of the peninsula was the papacy, always hostile to the Lombard king in the north. (See Map 2.3.) To Rome's east and south were the dukes of Benevento and Spoleto. Although theoretically the Lombard king's officers, in fact they were virtually independent rulers. Although many Lombards were Catholics, others, including important kings and dukes, were Arian. The "official" religion varied with the ruler in power. Rather than signal a major political event, then, the conversion of the Lombards to Catholic Christianity occurred gradually, ending only in the late seventh century. Partly as a result of this slow development, the Lombard kings, unlike the Visigoths, Franks, or even Anglo-Saxons, never enlisted the wholehearted support of any particular group of churchmen.

Yet the Lombard kings did not lack advantages. They controlled extensive estates, and they made use of the Roman institutions that survived in Italy. The Lombard kings made the cities their administrative bases, assigning dukes to rule from them and setting up one, Pavia, as their capital. Recalling emperors like Constantine and Justinian, the kings built churches and monasteries at Pavia, maintained city walls, and minted coins. Revenues from tolls, sales taxes, port duties, and court fines filled their coffers.

Emboldened by their attainments in the north, the Lombard kings tried to make some headway against the independent dukes of southern Italy. But that threatened to surround Rome with a unified Lombard kingdom. The pope, fearing for his own position, called on the Franks for help.

THE POPE: MAN IN THE MIDDLE

By the end of the sixth century, the pope's position was ambiguous. Bishop of Rome, he wielded real secular power within the city as well as a measure of spiritual leadership farther afield. Yet in other ways he was just a subordinate of Byzantium. Pope Gregory the Great (590-604), whom we have already met a number of times, laid the foundations for the papacy's later spiritual and temporal ascendancy. (See Popes and Antipopes to 1500 on pp. 359-62.) During Gregory's tenure, the pope became the greatest landowner in Italy; he organized Rome's defense and paid for its army; he heard court cases, made treaties, and provided welfare services. The missionary expedition he sent to England was only a small part of his involvement in the rest of Europe. A prolific author of spiritual works, Gregory digested and simplified the ideas of Church Fathers such as Saint Augustine, making them accessible to a wider audience. In his *Moralia in Job*, he set forth a model of biblical exegesis that was widely imitated for centuries. His handbook for clerics, *Pastoral Care*, went hand-in-hand with his practical church reforms in Italy, where he tried to impose regular episcopal elections and enforce clerical celibacy.

On the other hand, even Gregory was only one of many bishops in the former Roman Empire, now ruled from Constantinople. For a long time the emperor's views on dogma, discipline, and church administration prevailed at Rome. However, this authority began to unravel in the seventh century. In 692, Emperor Justinian II convened a council that determined 102 rules for the church. When he sent the rules to Rome for papal endorsement, Pope Sergius I (687-701) found most of them acceptable, but he was unwilling to agree to the whole because it permitted priestly marriages (which the Roman church did not want to allow), and it prohibited fasting on Saturdays in Lent (which the Roman church required). Outraged by Sergius's refusal, Justinian tried to arrest the pope, but Italian armies (theoretically under the emperor's command) came to the pontiff's aid instead. Justinian's arresting officer was reduced to cowering under the pope's bed. Clearly Constantinople's influence and authority over Rome had become tenuous. Sheer distance as well as diminishing imperial power in Italy meant that the popes had in effect become the leaders of non-Lombard Italy.

The gap between Byzantium and the papacy widened in the early eighth century, when Emperor Leo III tried to increase the taxes on papal property to pay for his wars against the Arabs. Gregory II, the pope who later commissioned Saint Boniface's evangelical work (see above, p. 89), responded by leading a general tax revolt. Meanwhile, Leo's fierce policy of iconoclasm collided with the pope's tolerance of images. For Gregory, as for Saint John of Damascus, holy images could and should be venerated, though not worshiped.

Increasing friction with Byzantium meant that when the pope felt threatened by the Lombard kings, as he did in the mid-eighth century, he looked elsewhere for support. Pope Stephen II (752-757)

> besought the pestilential king of the Lombards for the flocks God had entrusted to him and for the lost sheep —[in short,] for the entire exarchate of Ravenna and for the people of the whole of this province of Italy, whom that impious king had deceived with devilish trickery and was now occupying. He was getting nowhere with him; and in particular he saw that no help would come his way from the imperial power [at Byzantium].... He sent word incessantly to the king of the Franks [Pippin III]: the king must dispatch his envoys here to Rome; he must have them summon [the pope] to come to [the king].[9]

Pippin listened to the pope's entreaties and marched into Italy with an army to fight the Lombards. The new Frankish/papal alliance would change the map of Europe in the coming decades.

★ ★ ★ ★

The "fall" of the Roman Empire meant the rise of its children. In the East the Muslims swept out of Arabia—and promptly set up a Roman-style government where they conquered. The bit in the east that they did not take—the part ruled from Constantinople—still considered itself the Roman Empire. In the West, impoverished kingdoms looked to the city of Rome for religion, culture, and inspiration. However much East and West, Christian and Muslim, would come to deviate from and hate one another, they could not change the fact of shared parentage.

CHAPTER TWO KEY EVENTS

541-750	Plague of Justinian
c.570-632	Life of Muhammad
587	Reccared, Visigothic king, converts to Catholic Christianity
590	Saint Columbanus arrives on the Continent
590-604	Pope Gregory the Great
597	Augustine arrives at the court of King Ethelbert
607-630	Sasanid-Byzantine wars
622	Hijra; Muhammad's migration from Mecca to Medina
624	Battle of Badr
633	Beginning of Islamic conquests outside of Arabia
661	Death of Ali
661-750	Umayyad caliphate
664	Synod of Whitby
681	Bulgars enter Byzantine territory
711-715	Conquest of Spain by Islamic-led armies
726-787, 815-843	Iconoclasm at Byzantium

NOTES

1. *The Farmer's Law*, in *Reading the Middle Ages: Sources from Europe, Byzantium, and the Islamic World*, ed. Barbara H. Rosenwein (Peterborough, ON, 2006), p.73.
2. *The Life of St. Theodore of Sykeon*, in *Reading the Middle Ages*, p.77.

3. *The Synod of 754*, in *Reading the Middle Ages*, p.83.

4. From *Qur'an Suras*, in *Reading the Middle Ages*, pp.89-90.

5. John of Damascus, *On Holy Images*, in *Reading the Middle Ages*, p.80.

6. *Late Merovingian France: History and Hagiography 640-720*, ed. and trans. Paul Fouracre and Richard A. Gerberding (Manchester, 1996), quotations on pp.121-23.

7. Bede, *The Ecclesiastical History of the English People*, ed. Judith McClure and Roger Collins (Oxford, 1994), p.114.

8. The image of the "radiant throne" is from Eugenius of Toledo, quoted in Geneviève Bührer-Thierry, "'Just Anger' or 'Vengeful Anger'? The Punishment of Blinding in the Early Medieval West," in *Anger's Past: The Social Uses of an Emotion in the Middle Ages*, ed. Barbara H. Rosenwein (Ithaca, NY, 1998), p.79.

9. *The Lives of the Eighth-Century Popes (Liber Pontificalis): The Ancient Biographies of Nine Popes from AD 715 to AD 817*, trans. Raymond Davis, Translated Texts for Historians, 13 (Liverpool, 1992), pp.58-59.

FURTHER READING

Barford, P.M. *The Early Slavs: Culture and Society in Early Medieval Eastern Europe.* Ithaca, NY, 2001.

Bowersock, G.W. *Mosaics as History: The Near East from Late Antiquity to Islam.* Cambridge, MA, 2006.

Charles-Edwards, T.M. *Early Christian Ireland.* Cambridge, 2001.

Ephesos, Metropolis of Asia: An Interdisciplinary Approach to Its Archaeology, Religion, and Culture. Ed. Helmut Koester. Cambridge, MA, 1995.

Fowden, Garth. *Qusayr 'Amra: Art and the Umayyad Elite in Late Antique Syria.* Berkeley, 2004.

Haldon, J.F. *Byzantium in the Seventh Century: The Transformation of a Culture.* Cambridge, 1990.

Herrin, Judith. *Byzantium: The Surprising Life of a Medieval Empire.* Princeton, 2007.

Liebeschuetz, J.H.W.G. *The Decline and Fall of the Roman City.* Oxford, 2001.

Little, Lester K., ed., *Plague and the End of Antiquity: The Pandemic of 541-750.* Cambridge, 2006.

Mayr-Harting, Henry. *The Coming of Christianity to Anglo-Saxon England.* University Park, PA, 1991.

Nuseibeh, Saïd, and Oleg Grabar. *The Dome of the Rock.* New York, 1996.

Peters, F.E. *Muhammad and the Origins of Islam.* Albany, NY, 1994.

Robinson, Chase F. *'Abd al-Malik.* Oxford, 2005.

Wickham, Chris. *Framing the Early Middle Ages: Europe and the Mediterranean, 400-800.* Oxford, 2005.

Wood, Ian. *The Merovingian Kingdoms, 450-751.* London, 1994.

◆▷◆▷◆▷◆▷◆▷◆▷◆▷◆▷◆

**To test your knowledge of this chapter, please go to
www.rosenweinshorthistory.com
and click "Study Questions."**

THREE

CREATING NEW IDENTITIES
(c.750-c.900)

IN THE SECOND half of the eighth century the periodic outbreaks of the Plague of Justinian that had devastated half of the globe for two centuries came to an end. In its wake came a gradual but undeniable upswing in population, land cultivation, and general prosperity. At Byzantium an empress took the throne, in the Islamic world the Abbasids displaced the Umayyads, in Francia the Carolingians deposed the Merovingians. New institutions of war and peace, learning, and culture developed, giving each state —Byzantium, the Islamic caliphate, Francia— its own characteristic identity (though with some telling similarities).

BYZANTIUM: FROM TURNING WITHIN TO CAUTIOUS EXPANSION

In 750 Byzantium was a state with its back to the world. Its iconoclasm isolated it from other Christians, its theme structure focused its military operations on internal defense, its abandonment of classical learning set it apart from its past. By 900, all this had changed. Byzantium was iconophile (icon-loving), aggressive, and cultured.

New Icons, New Armies, New Territories

Within Byzantium, iconoclasm sowed dissension. In the face of persecution and humiliation, men and women continued to venerate icons, even in the very bedrooms of the imperial palace. The tide turned in 780 when Leo IV died and his widow, Irene, in effect became head of the Byzantine state as regent for her son Constantine VI. Long a secret iconophile, Irene immediately moved to replace important iconoclast bishops. Then she called a council at Nicaea (787), the first there since the famous one of 325. The meeting went as planned, and the assembled bishops condemned iconoclasm. But iconoclastic fervor still lingered, and a partial ban on icons was put into effect between 815 and 843. The issue remained incendiary: even in the mid-850s, when Photius, the Patriarch of Constantinople, wrote to the Bulgar Khan, he fulminated about the indignities that iconoclasts had inflicted on images: "They mistreated them with their feet, with their murderous hands, and their profane lips."[1]

At first the end of iconoclasm displeased the old guard in the army, but soon a new generation was in charge. Already before Irene's rule Byzantium's militia had been reformed and the theme organization supplemented by an even more responsive force. In the mid-eighth century, Emperor Constantine V (r.741-775) had created new crack regiments, the *tagmata* (sing. *tagma*). These were mobile troops, not tied to any theme. Many were composed of cavalry, the elite of fighting men; others—infantry, muleteers—provided necessary backup. At first deployed largely around Constantinople itself to shore up the emperors, the *tagmata* were eventually used in cautious frontier battles. Under the ninth- and tenth-century emperors, they helped Byzantium to expand.

To the west, in the Balkans, Emperor Nicephorus I (r.802-811) remodeled the old thematic territories and added new ones. Leading his army against the Slavs, he took the region around Serdica (today Sofia, Bulgaria). His successes prompted the Bulgarians to attack. To secure the area, Nicephorus uprooted thousands of families from Anatolia and sent them to settle in the Balkans. Reshaping old themes and adding new ones, Nicephorus created fortified centers to anchor the settlers. Although he intended to recreate an earlier Byzantium, his policies in fact ensured the future fission between Greek- and Slavic-speaking Balkan states.

Nicephorus's later foray into Bulgarian territory further north in the Balkans proved disastrous. Marshaling a huge army and escorted by the luminaries of his court, the emperor plundered the Bulgarian capital, Pliska, and then coolly made his way west. But the Bulgarians blockaded his army as it passed through a narrow river valley, fell on the imperial party, and killed the emperor. The toll on the fleeing soldiers and courtiers was immense, but even more memorable was the imperial humiliation. Krum, the Bulgarian khan (ruler), lined Nicephorus's skull with silver and used it as a ceremonial drinking cup. Further defeats in the region in the late ninth century led to yet more shuffling of themes. The end result may be seen in Map 3.1, to which Map 2.1 on p. 62 (Byzantium at its smallest) should be compared.

Another glance at the two maps reveals a second area of modest expansion, this time on Byzantium's eastern front. In the course of the ninth century the Byzantines had worked out a strategy of skirmish warfare in Anatolia. When Arab raiding parties attacked, the *strategoi* evacuated the population, burned the crops, and, while sending out a few troops to harass the invaders, largely waited out the raid within their local fortifications. But by 860, the threat of Arab invading armies—apart from raiding parties—was largely over (though the threat of Muslim navies—on Sicily and in southern Italy, for example—remained very real). In 900, Emperor Leo VI (r.886-912) was confident enough to go on the offensive, sending the *tagmata* in the direction of Tarsus. The raid was a success, and in its wake at least one princely family of Armenia, which was allied with the Arabs, was persuaded to enter imperial service and cede its principality to Byzantium. Reorganized as the theme of Mesopotamia, it was the first of a series of new themes that Leo created in an area that had been largely a no-man's-land between the Islamic and Byzantine worlds.

Map 3.1: The Byzantine Empire, *c.*917

But the rise of the *tagmata* eventually had the unanticipated consequence of downgrading the themes. The soldiers of the themes got the "grunt work"—the inglorious job of skirmish warfare with the Arabs, for example—without the honor and (probably) extra pay. The *tagmata* were the professionals, gradually taking over most of the fighting, especially as the need to defend the interior of Anatolia receded. By the same token, the troops of the themes became increasingly inactive.

Educating Without and Within

No longer turned in on itself, the Byzantine Empire brought many of the Slavic regions into its orbit, not (this time) with troops but via missionaries. The whole of the eastern and northern Balkans was ripe for conversion. Here Byzantium's competitors were the papacy and the Franks, who preached the Roman Catholic brand of Christianity. The Slavic principalities tried to manipulate the two sides—the Roman Catholics and the Orthodox Byzantines—to their own advantage, but in the end they were pulled into one world or the other.

The prince of Moravia (a new Slavic state bounded by Francia to the west and the Bulgarian khanate to the east) made a bid for autonomy from Frankish hegemony by calling on Byzantium for missionaries. The imperial court was ready. Two brothers, Constantine (later called Cyril) and Methodius, set out in 863, armed with translations of the Gospels and liturgical texts. Born in Thessalonica, they well knew about the Slavic languages, which had been purely oral. Constantine devised an alphabet using Greek letters to represent the sounds of one Slavic dialect (the "Glagolitic" alphabet), and then added Greek words and grammar where the Slavic lacked Christian vocabulary and suitable expressions. The resulting language, later called Old Church Slavonic, was an effective tool for conversion: "What man can tell all the parables/ Denouncing nations without their own books/ And who do not preach in an intelligible tongue?/ ...Whoever accepts these letters,/ To him Christ speaks wisdom" reads the prologue to Constantine/Cyril's translation of the Gospels.[2] However much Byzantium valued the Greek language, and however keen it was to control all matters from Constantinople, it was nevertheless willing at times to work with regional linguistic and cultural traditions. The Catholic church, by contrast, was more rigid, insisting that the Gospels and liturgy be in Latin. In the end, Moravia ended in the Catholic camp, but the Byzantine brand of Christianity prevailed in Bulgaria, Serbia, and later (see Chapter 4) Russia.

The creation of an alphabet in the mid-ninth century was one of many scholarly and educational initiatives. Constantinople had always had schools, books, and teachers, all dedicated most importantly to training civil servants. But in the eighth century the number of bureaucrats was dwindling, the schools were decaying, and the books, painstakingly written out on papyrus, were disintegrating. Ninth-century confidence reversed this trend, while fiscal stability and surplus wealth in the treasury greased the wheels. Emperor Theophilus (r.829-842) opened a public school in the palace, headed by Leo the Mathematician, a master of geometry, mechanics, medicine, and philosophy. Controversies over iconoclasm sent churchmen scurrying to the writings of the Church Fathers to find passages that supported their cause. With the end of iconoclasm, the monasteries, staunch defenders of icons, garnered renewed prestige and gained new recruits. Because their abbots insisted that they read Christian texts, the monks had to get new manuscripts in a hurry. Practical need gave impetus to the creation of a new kind of script: minuscule. This was made up of lower-case letters, written in cursive, the letters strung together. It was faster and easier to write than the formal capital uncial letters that had previously been used. Words were newly separated by spaces, making them easier to read. Papyrus was no longer easily available from Egypt, so the new manuscripts were made out of parchment—animal skins scraped and treated to create a good writing surface. Far more expensive than papyrus, parchment was nevertheless much more durable, making possible their preservation over the long haul.

A general cultural revival was clearly underway by the middle of the century. As a young man, Photius, whom we first met venting his spleen against iconoclasts, had already read hundreds of books, including works of history, literature, and philosophy. As patriarch of Constantinople (r.858-867, 877-886) he gathered a circle of scholars around him; wrote sermons, homilies, and theological treatises; and tutored Emperor Leo VI. For his own part, Constantine-Cyril, the future missionary to the Slavs, was reportedly such a brilliant student in Thessalonica that an imperial official invited him to the capital, where he met Photius:

> When he arrived at Constantinople, he was placed in the charge of masters to teach him. In three months he learned all the grammar and applied himself to other studies. He studied Homer and geometry and with Leo [the Mathematician] and Photius dialectic and all the teachings of philosophy, and in addition [he learned] rhetoric, arithmetic, astronomy, music, and all the other "Hellenic" [i.e., pagan Greek] teachings.[3]

The resurrection of "Hellenic" books helped inspire an artistic revival. As we have seen (Plate 2.1 on p. 69), even during the somber years of iconoclasm, artistic activity did not entirely end at Byzantium. But the new exuberance and sheer numbers of mosaics, manuscript illuminations, ivories, and enamels after 870 suggest a new era. Sometimes called the Macedonian Renaissance, after the ninth- and tenth-century

Plate 3.1: The Empress Eudocia and Her Sons, Homilies of Gregory Nazianzus (*c.*880). After the end of iconoclasm in 843, two distinct, but complementary, artistic styles flourished at Byzantium, easily seen by comparing this plate to Plate 3.2. The frontal, formal, hierarchical, and decorative style represented by this illumination harks back to late imperial work, such as that of the Hippodrome obelisk base in Plate 1.7 on p. 39 and the image of Justinian flanked by officials of church and state in Plate 1.11 on pp. 52-53.

Plate 3.2 (facing page): Ezekiel in the Valley of Dry Bones, Homilies of Gregory Nazianzus (*c.*880). Although painted in the same manuscript as Plate 3.1, this miniature's style is inspired by a different—classical—tradition. Compare the drapery and modeling of the figure of Ezekiel on the right-hand side of this miniature (where he stands next to an archangel) with the figure of the boy on the right-hand side of the Theseus wall-painting in Plate 1.2, on p. 34.

imperial dynasty that fostered it, the new movement found its models in both the abstract, transcendental style that was so important during the pre-iconoclastic period (see Plate 1.11 on pp. 52-53) and the natural, plastic style of classical art and its revivals (see Plate 1.2 on p. 34 and Plate 1.9 on p. 41).

These different styles did not clash; indeed, they were sometimes used in the same artifact. Consider a lavish manuscript of the Homilies of Gregory of Nazianzus, made c.880 at Constantinople. It begins with several pages that represent the imperial family of Basil I (r.867-886), the original recipient of the manuscript. Plate 3.1 shows one of these opening pages: the emperor's wife, Eudocia, is flanked by two of her sons, potential heirs to the throne. All of the figures are flat and weightless. They stare out at the viewer, isolated from one another. In the center is the empress, towering above her sons not because she was physically taller than they but to telegraph her higher status. The artist is far more interested in the patterns of the richly ornamented clothing than in delineating any body underneath. The entire miniature celebrates hierarchy, transcendence, and imperial power. Yet in the very same manuscript are pages that draw eagerly upon the classical heritage. In Plate 3.2, on the left, the prophet Ezekiel stands in a landscape of bones, the hand of God reaching toward him to tell him that the bones will rise and live again (Ezek. 37:1-11). On the right the prophet stands next to an archangel. All the figures have roundness and weight; they turn and interact. It is true that their drapery flutters and loops unnaturally, giving the scene a nonclassical excitement; and it is true that the angel "floats," one foot in front of the prophet, one arm a bit behind him. But it is in just this way that the Byzantines adapted classical traditions to their overriding need to represent transcendence.

Not surprisingly, the same period saw the revival of monumental architecture. Already Emperor Theophilus was known for the splendid palace that he built on the outskirts of Constantinople, and Basil I (r.867-886) was famous as a builder of churches. Rich men from the court and church imitated imperial tastes, constructing palaces, churches, and monasteries of their own.

THE SHIFT TO THE EAST IN THE ISLAMIC WORLD

Just as at Byzantium the imperial court determined both culture and policies, so too the Islamic world of the ninth century was centered on the caliph and his court. The Abbasids, who ousted the Umayyad caliphs in 750, moved their center of power to Iraq (part of the former Persia) and stepped into the shoes of the Sasanid king of kings, the "shadow of God on earth." Yet much of their time was spent less in imposing their will than in conciliating different interest groups.

The Abbasid Reconfiguration

Years of Roman rule had made Byzantium relatively homogeneous. Nothing was less true of the Islamic world, made up of regions wildly diverse in geography, language, and political, religious, and social traditions. Each tribe, family, and region had its own expectations and desires for a place in the sun. The Umayyads paid little heed. Their power base was Syria, formerly a part of Byzantium. There they rewarded their hard-core followers and took the lion's share of conquered land for themselves. They expected every other region to send its taxes to their coffers at Damascus. This annoyed regional leaders, even though they probably managed to keep most of the taxes that they raised. Moreover, with no claims to the religious functions of an *imam*, the Umayyads could never gain the adherence of the followers of Ali. Soon still other groups began to complain. Where was the equality of believers preached in the Qur'an? The Umayyads privileged an elite; Arabs who had expected a fair division of the spoils were disappointed. So too were non-Arabs who converted to Islam: they discovered that they had still to pay the old taxes of their non-believing days.

Map 3.2: The Islamic World, *c.*800

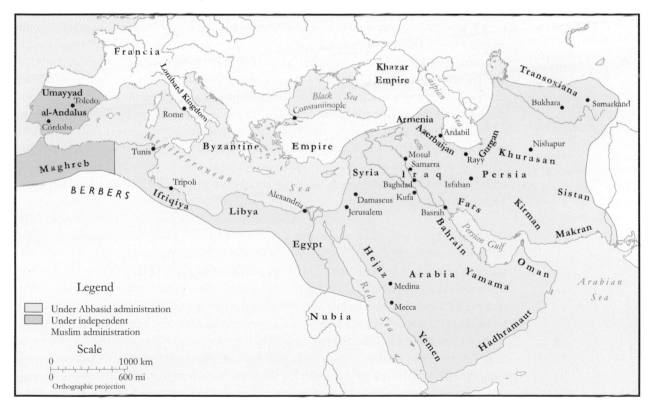

Plate 3.3 (facing page): Bowl from Iraq (9th cent.). Ceramicists in Iraq, inspired by Chinese white porcelains imported via bustling trade networks with the East, discovered a way to disguise the red-brown color of their clay with an opaque tin-based creamy-white glaze. Influenced by glass-decorating techniques, they also developed luster painting. This bowl reflects both innovations. First prepared with the white glaze, its elaborate floral design was created with metallic paints. Fired twice and polished with a soft cloth, the bowl glows with an iridescent sheen. Adorning the households of the Abbasid upper and middle classes, bowls such as this illustrate the luxurious tastes of the day.

The discontents festered, and two main centers of resistance emerged: Khurasan (today eastern Iran) and Iraq. (See Map 3.2.) Both had been part of the Persian Empire; the rebellion was largely a coming together of old Persian and newly "Persianized" Arab factions. In the 740s this defiant coalition at Khurasan decided to support the Abbasid family. This was an extended kin group with deep-rooted claims to the caliphate, tracing its lineage back to the very uncle who had cared for the orphaned Muhammad. With militant supporters, considerable money, and the backing of a powerful propaganda organization, the Abbasids organized an army in Khurasan and, marching it undefeated into Iraq, picked up more support there. In 749 they defeated the Umayyad governor at Kufa, and al-Saffah was solemnly named the first Abbasid caliph. Less than a year later the last Umayyad caliph, abandoned by almost everyone and on the run in Egypt, was killed in a short battle.

The new dynasty seemed to signal a revolution. (See list of Caliphs: The Abbasids on p. 363.) Most importantly, the Abbasids recognized the crucial centrality of Iraq and built their capital cities there: Baghdad became the capital in 762, Samarra in the 830s, in the aftermath of a bitter civil war. The Abbasids took the title of *imam* and even, at one point, wore the green color of the Shi'ites.

Yet as they became entrenched, the Abbasids in turn created their own elite, under whom other groups chafed. In the eighth century most of their provincial governors, for example, came from the Abbasid family itself. When building Baghdad, Caliph al-Mansur (r.754-775) allotted important tracts of real estate to his Khurasan military leaders. In the course of time, as Baghdad prospered and land prices rose, the Khurasani came to constitute a new, exclusive, and jealous elite. At the same time as they favored these groups, the Abbasids succeeded in centralizing their control even more fully than the Umayyads had done. This is clearest in the area of taxation. The Umayyads had demanded in vain that all taxes come to them. But the Abbasid caliph al-Mu'tasim (r.833-842) was able to control and direct provincial revenues to his court in Iraq.

Control, however, was uneven. Until the beginning of the tenth century, the Abbasid caliphs generally could count on ruling Iraq (their "headquarters"), Syria, Khurasan, and Egypt. But they never had the Iberian Peninsula; they lost Ifriqiya (today Tunisia) by about 800; and they never controlled the Berbers in the soft underbelly of North Africa. In the course of the tenth century, they would lose effective control even in their heartlands. That, however, was in the future (see Chapter 4).

Whatever control the Abbasids had depended largely on their armies. Unlike the Byzantines, the Abbasids did not need soldiers to stave off external enemies or to expand outwards. (The Byzantine strategy of skirmish warfare worked largely because the caliphs led raids to display their prowess, not to take territory. The serious naval wars that took Sicily from Byzantium were launched from Ifriqiya, independent of the caliphs.) Rather, the Abbasids needed troops to collect taxes in areas already conquered but weakly controlled.

Well into the ninth century the caliphs' troops were paid, but not mustered, by them. Generals recruited their own troops from their home districts, tribes, families, and clients. When the generals were loyal to the caliphs, this military system worked well. In the dark days of civil war, however, when two brothers fought over the caliphate (811–819), no one controlled the armies. After al-Ma'mun (r.813–833) won this civil war, he had no reliable army to back him up. His brother and successor, al-Mu'tasim, found the solution in a new-style, private army. He bought and trained his own slaves, many of them Turks and thus unrelated to other tribal groups. These men were given governorships as well as military posts. They were the reason that al-Mu'tasim was able to collect provincial taxes so effectively. He could not foresee that in time the Turks would come to constitute a new elite, one that would eventually help to overpower the caliphate itself.

With the Abbasids came wealth. The Mediterranean region had always been a great trade corridor. In the ninth century, Baghdad, at the crossroad of East and West, drew that trade into a wider network. All of Iraq participated in the commercial buoyancy. In the story *Sindbad the Sailor*, which is set in the time of Harun al-Rashid (r.786–809), the hero cannot resist the "irresistible longing to travel ... about the world and visit distant cities and islands in quest of profit and adventure."[4] He departs seven times from the port city of Basra, and every voyage yields untold riches. It is a fairy tale, of course, one of the stories in the collection known as *The Thousand and One Nights*, but it reflected a real economic boom. A treatise on commerce, probably from this period, listed Iraqi imports:

From India are imported tigers, panthers, elephants, panther skins, rubies, white sandal, ebony, and coconuts. From China are imported silk [textiles], [raw] silk, chinaware, paper, ink, peacocks, racing horses, saddles, felts, cinnamon, Greek unblended rhubarb ... racing horses, female slaves, knicknacks with human figures ... hydraulic engineers, expert agronomists, marble workers, and eunuchs. From Arabia: Arab horses, ostriches, pedigreed she-camels ... From Egypt: trotting donkeys, suits of fine cloth, papyrus, balsam, and — from its mines — topazes of superior quality. From the land of the Khazars [on the lower Volga River]: slaves of both sexes, coats of mail, [and] helmets.[5]

Brilliant porcelains from China inspired Islamic artisans to add tin to their own glazes to achieve a bright white color, over which they added decorative motifs (see Plate 3.3). Dining off of ornate plates and bowls was part of the newly luxurious lifestyle of the upper and middle classes: their clothes were made of richly woven fabrics, their homes furnished with fine rugs (on both floors and walls) and perfumed with elaborately carved censers.

With revenues from commerce and (above all) taxes from agriculture in their coffers, the caliphs paid their armies, salaried their officials (drawn from the many talented men — but, in this relentlessly male-dominated society, not women — in the Persian, Arab, Christian, and Jewish population), and presided over a cultural revival even more impressive than the one at Constantinople.

New Cultural Forms

Under the Abbasids (most spectacularly, under caliphs Harun al-Rashid and al-Ma'-mun), literature, science, law, and other forms of scholarship flourished. The caliphs launched scientific studies via a massive translation effort that brought the philosophical, medical, mathematical, and astrological treatises of the Indian and Greek worlds into Islamic culture. They encouraged new literary forms — the refined and learned prose and poetry of *adab* literature — as part of the education of gentlemen at court. Books of all sorts were relatively cheap (and therefore accessible) in the Islamic world because they were written on paper.

Shoring up the regime with astrological predictions; winning theological debates with the pointed weapons of Aristotle's logical and scientific works; understanding the theories of bridge-building, irrigation, and land-surveying with Euclid's geometry — these were just some of the motives behind the translations and original scientific works of the period. The movement had general support. Patrons of scientific writing included the caliphs, their wives, courtiers, generals, and ordinary people with practical interests. Al-Khwarizmi (*d*.850), author of a book on algebra (the word itself is from the Arabic *al-jabr*), explained that his subject was useful for "inheritances, bequests, tax assessments, legal verdicts, commercial transactions, land surveying, water rights, [the construction of buildings, and the digging of canals]."[6] The same scholar also wrote the first Arabic treatise on the Indian method of calculation—Indian numerals are what *we* call Arabic numerals—and the use of the zero, essential (to give one example) for distinguishing 100 from 1.

How should one live to be pleasing to God? This was the major question that inspired the treatises on law (*fiqh*) that began to appear in the early Abbasid period. In Abu Dawud al-Sijistani's compilation of the oral jurisprudential teachings of his revered teacher Ahmad ibn Hanbal, an attempt was made to cover all the possibilities that life might offer. Ought a Muslim man to marry a Christian or a Jew? Al-Sijistani provided the answer: "I heard Ahmad ... [say], 'There is no harm in it if [the women] are free, but if they are slaves, no.'" Might a Muslim man marry a Muslim slave? Ibn Hanbal replied, "The strongest opinion related concerning this matter is on the authority of Ibn 'Abbas," thus harking back to the words of a cousin of the Prophet Muhammad.[7] Ahmad ibn Hanbal belonged to a school of legal thought that tried to find legal precedents in the reported sayings of the Prophet and his Companions. Other legal schools, such as the one associated with Abu Hanifa (*d*.767), did not rely on reports about Muhammad, preferring more eclectic legal reasoning.

Thus, especially under Caliph al-Ma'mun (813–833), Muslim scholars debated the importance of Muhammad's example. Those who considered the Prophet's words and deeds crucial for right living worked to determine the authenticity of the many *hadith* that had sprung up—eyewitness accounts of the words of Muhammad as transmitted through a chain (*isnad*) of trustworthy sources. But others, like al-Ma'mun himself, while admitting the importance of the *hadith*, stressed the use of reason as well.

Even the Qur'an did not escape scholarly scrutiny. While some interpreters read it literally as the word of God and thus part of God, others viewed it as something (like humankind) created by God and therefore separate from Him. For al-Ma'mun, taking the Qur'an literally undermined the caliph's religious authority. Somewhat like the Byzantine Emperor Leo III (see p. 68), whose iconoclastic policies were designed to separate divinity from its representations, al-Ma'mun determined to make God greater than the Qur'an. In 833 he instituted the Mihna, or Inquisition, demanding that the literalists profess the Qur'an's createdness. But al-Ma'mun died before he could punish those who refused, and his immediate successors were relatively ineffective in pursing the project. The scholars on the other side—the literalists and those who looked to the *hadith*—carried the day, and in 848 Caliph al-Mutawakkil (*r*.847–861) ended the Mihna, emphatically reversing the caliphate's position on the matter.

Sunni Islam thus defined itself against the views of a caliph who, by asserting great power, lost much. The caliphs ceased to be the source of religious doctrine; that role went to the scholars, the *ulama*. It was around this time that the title "caliph" came to be associated with the phrase "deputy of the Prophet of God" rather than the "deputy of God." The designation reflected the caliphate's decreasing political as well as religious authority (see Chap. 4).

Yet through all of this turmoil the literary model of *adab* reigned supreme. It was practiced by both men and women and was patronized by many great families, though it was above all associated with the court of the caliph. *Adab* strove for beautiful, elegant, and witty expression, even concerning mundane or irreverent matters. For example, Abu Nuwas (*d.* 813)—a poet both patronized and imprisoned (at least once) by Harun al-Rashid—once punned about a singer: "Gorgeous one!—God has made your face a *qibla* [the direction of prayer] for me,/ So allow me to pray toward your face, and let's have a kiss [*qubla*]."[8]

Map 3.3 (facing page): Europe, *c.*814

The highest form of *adab* was poetry. When performed, it was sung and thus was closely tied to music. *Adab* poets wrote verses of praise, satire, nostalgia, suffering, deep religious feeling, worldly loves and hates, and wry comments on the human condition:

> She said, "I love you"; "you're a liar," I said,
> "cheat someone else who cannot scrutinize
> these words which I can't accept!
> For truly I say, no one loves an old man!
> It's like saying, 'We have tethered the wind,'
> or like saying, 'Fire is cold' or 'water is aflame.'"[9]

Al-Andalus: A Society in the Middle

The poet who wrote those lines was al-Ghazal (775–864), a great practitioner of *adab*—in Spain! In the eighth and ninth centuries, Islamic Spain was a miniature caliphate minus the caliph. In the mid-eighth century Abd al-Rahman I, an Umayyad prince on the run from the Abbasids, managed to gather an army, make his way to Iberia, defeat the provincial governor at Córdoba, and (in 756) proclaim himself "emir" (commander) of al-Andalus. His dynasty would govern Islamic Spain for two and a half centuries, and one of his descendants, Abd al-Rahman III (*r.*912–961) would even take the title caliph. Nevertheless, like the Abbasid caliphs, the Umayyad rulers of Spain headed a state poised to break into its regional constituents.

Al-Andalus under the emirs was hardly Muslim and even less Arab. As the caliphs came to rely on Turks, so the emirs relied on a professional standing army of non-

Norway

Sweden

North

Sea

Baltic Sea

Scotland

Ireland

Denmark

Haithabu

OBODRITES

York

Anglo-Saxon England

London

English Channel

Vistula

Frisia

St. Amand Meerssen

Herstal Aachen Hersfeld

Laon

Soissons

Cologne

Elbe

Saxony

Oder

Fulda

CZECHS

Würzburg

Regensburg

Passau

Moravian Empire

Dniester

Atlantic

Ocean

Quierzy

Paris

Attigny

Verdun

Austrasia

Neustria

Brittany

Seine

Orléans

Sens

Loire

Tours

Poitiers

Aquitaine

Garonne

Lyon

Vienne

F r a n c i a

Burgundy

Rhine

Main

Danube

Tisza

Prut

Bulgarian

Empire

Drava

Sava

CROATS

Danube

Kingdom of Asturias

Oviedo

León

Duero

Spanish March

Ebro

Barcelona

Milan

Turin

Genoa

Grasse

Aix-en-Provence

Marseille

Po

Verona

Kingdom of Italy

Venice

Ravenna

Spoleto

Duchy of Spoleto

Rome

Adriatic Sea

Byzantine

Empire

Benevento

Duchy of Benevento

Naples

al-Andalus

Tagus

Guadiana

Córdoba

Guadalquivir

M e d i t e r r a n e a n

Sea

M a g h r e b

I f r i q i y a

L i b y a

Legend

Carolingian Kingdom 768
Conquests of Charles the Great

Scale

0	500 km
0	300 mi

Arabs, the *al-khurs*, the "silent ones"—men who could not speak Arabic. They lived among a largely Christian—and partly Jewish—population; even by 900, only about 25 per cent of the people in al-Andalus were Muslims. This had its benefits for the regime, which taxed Christians and Jews heavily. Although, like Western European rulers, they did not have the land tax that the Byzantine emperors and caliphs could impose, the emirs did draw some of their revenue from Muslims, especially around their capital at Córdoba. (See Map 3.3.)

Money allowed the emirs to pay salaries to their civil servants and to sponsor a culture of science and literature of their own. Al-Ghazal was only one of the poets and musicians patronized by the court. Like the others, his poems—blunt and to the point—were not quite what a poet from, say, Baghdad would write. The culture of al-Andalus reflected its unique ethnic and religious mix. The Great Mosque in Córdoba is a good example. Begun under Abd al-Rahman I and expanded by his successors, it drew on the design of the Roman aqueduct at Mérida for its rows of columns connected by double arches. (See Plate 3.4.) For the shape of the arches, however, it borrowed a form—the "Visigothic" horseshoe arch—from the Christians. For the decorative motif of alternating light and dark stones, it looked to the Great Mosque of Damascus.

The cultural "mix" went beyond buildings and poems. Some Christians and Muslims intermarried; Muslim men took Christian wives (as we might anticipate from Ahmad's opinion in al-Sijistani's law treatise [see p. 113]). Even religious practices may have melded a bit. The Christians who lived in al-Andalus were called "Mozarabs"—"would-be Arabs"—by Christians elsewhere. It used to be thought that the martyrdom of 48 Christians at Córdoba between 850 and 859 was proof of implacable hostility between Christians and Muslims there. But recent research suggests that the story of the martyrs was hugely exaggerated by its idiosyncratic author, Eulogius. It is likely that Christians and Muslims on the whole got along fairly well. Christians dressed like Muslims, worked side-by-side with them in government posts, and used Arabic in many aspects of their life. At the time of the supposed martyrdoms, there were in the region of Córdoba alone at least four churches and nine monasteries.

Still, some Andalusian Christians were not content—Eulogius was one—and they were glad to have contact with the north. For to the north of al-Andalus, beyond the Duero River, were tiny Christian principalities. Partaking in the general demographic and economic growth of the period, they had begun to prosper a little. One, Asturias, became a kingdom. There Alfonso II (r.791-842) and his successors established a capital city—first at Oviedo, then, at the beginning of the tenth century, at León. They built churches, encouraged monastic foundations, collected relics, patronized literary efforts, and welcomed Mozarabs from the south. The kings themselves looked to models still further north—to Francia, where Charlemagne and his heirs ruled as kings "by grace of God."

Plate 3.4 (facing page): Great Mosque, Córdoba (785-787). The Great Mosque of Córdoba gave monumental identity to the new Umayyad rulers. Note the two tiers of arches, the first set on pre-Islamic columns despoiled from Roman and Visigothic buildings, the second springing from high piers. With their alternating red and white stones and repeated pattern, the arches suggest lively arcades leading from west to east.

Charlemagne

The most famous Carolingian king was Charles (*r.*768-814), called "the Great" ("le Magne" in Old French). Large, tough, wily, and devout, he was everyone's model king. Einhard (*d.*840), his courtier and scholar, saw him as a Roman emperor: he patterned his *Life of Charlemagne* on the *Lives of the Caesars*, written in the second century by the Roman biographer Suetonius. Alcuin (*d.*804), also the king's courtier and an even more famous scholar, emphasized Charlemagne's religious side, nicknaming him "David," the putative author of the psalms, victor over the giant Goliath, and king of Israel. Empress Irene at Constantinople saw Charlemagne as a suitable husband for herself (though the arrangement eventually fell through). An anonymous poet, possibly Einhard, emphasized Charlemagne's outsized celebrity, who "casts the light of his great name all the way to the stars."[13]

So great a name was achieved largely through warfare. While the Byzantine and Islamic rulers clung tightly to what they had, Charlemagne waged wars of plunder and conquest. He invaded Italy, seizing the Lombard crown and annexing northern Italy in 774. He moved his armies northward, fighting the Saxons for more than thirty years, forcibly converting them to Christianity, and annexing their territory. To the southeast, in a series of campaigns against the Avars, Charlemagne captured their strongholds, forced them to submit to his overlordship, and made off with cartloads of plunder. (Once they were defeated, around 800, the Bulgars and Moravians moved in.) His expedition to al-Andalus gained him a band of territory north of the Ebro River, a buffer between Francia and the Islamic world called the "Spanish March." Even his failures were the stuff of myth: a Basque attack on Charlemagne's army as it returned from Spain became the core of the epic poem *The Song of Roland*.

Ventures like these depended on a good army. Charlemagne's was led by his *fideles*, faithful aristocrats, and manned by free men, many the "vassals" (clients) of the aristocrats. The king had the *bannum*, the right to call his subjects to arms (and, more generally, to command, prohibit, punish, and collect fines when his ban was not obeyed). Soldiers provided their own equipment; the richest went to war on horseback, the poorest had to have at least a lance, shield, and bow. There was no standing army; men had to be mobilized for each expedition. No *tagmata*, themes, or Turkish slaves were to be found here! Yet, while the empire was expanding, it was a very successful system; men were glad to go off to war when they could expect to return enriched with booty.

By 800, Charlemagne's kingdom stretched 800 miles east to west, even more north to south when Italy is counted. (See Map 3.3.) On its eastern edge was a strip of "buffer regions" extending from the Baltic to the Adriatic; they were under Carolingian overlordship. Such hegemony was reminiscent of an empire, and Charlemagne began to act according to the model of Roman emperors, sponsoring building programs to symbolize his authority, standardizing weights and measures, and acting as a patron of intellectual and artistic enterprises. He built a capital "city"—a palace complex, in fact—at Aachen, complete with a chapel patterned on San Vitale, the church built by Justinian at Ravenna (see p. 54). So keen was Charlemagne on Byzantine models that he had columns, mosaics, and marbles from Rome and Ravenna carted up north to use in his own buildings.

Further drawing on imperial traditions, Charlemagne issued laws in the form of "capitularies," summaries of decisions made at assemblies held with the chief men of the realm. He appointed regional governors, called "counts," to carry out his laws, muster his armies, and collect his taxes. Chosen from Charlemagne's aristocratic supporters, they were compensated for their work by temporary grants of land rather than with salaries. This was not Roman; but Charlemagne lacked the fiscal apparatus of the Roman emperors (and of his contemporary Byzantine emperors and Islamic caliphs), so he made land substitute for money. To discourage corruption, he appointed officials called *missi dominici* ("those sent out by the lord king") to oversee the counts on the king's behalf. The *missi*, chosen from the same aristocratic class as bishops and counts, traveled in pairs across Francia. They were to look into the affairs—large and small—of the church and laity, ensuring, for example,

> that laymen should not be put in charge of monks.... That all who as the result of some crime are rebels against [the peace] should be brought to justice ... That the old established and lawful tolls should be exacted from traders on bridges, on water crossings and on sales.[14]

In this way, Charlemagne set up institutions meant to echo those of the Roman Empire. It was a brilliant move on the part of Pope Leo III (795–816) to harness the king's imperial pretensions to papal ambitions. In 799, accused of adultery and perjury by a hostile faction at Rome, Leo narrowly escaped blinding and having his tongue cut out. Fleeing northward to seek Charlemagne's protection, he returned home under escort, the king close behind. Charlemagne arrived in late November 800 to an imperial welcome orchestrated by Leo. On Christmas Day of that year, Leo put an imperial crown on Charlemagne's head, and the clergy and nobles who were present acclaimed the king "Augustus," the title of the first Roman emperor. In one stroke the pope managed to exalt the king of the Franks, downgrade Irene at Byzantium, and enjoy the role of "emperor maker" himself.

About twenty years later, when Einhard wrote about this coronation, he said that the imperial titles at first so displeased Charlemagne "that he declared that he would not have set foot in the church the day that they were conferred, although it was a

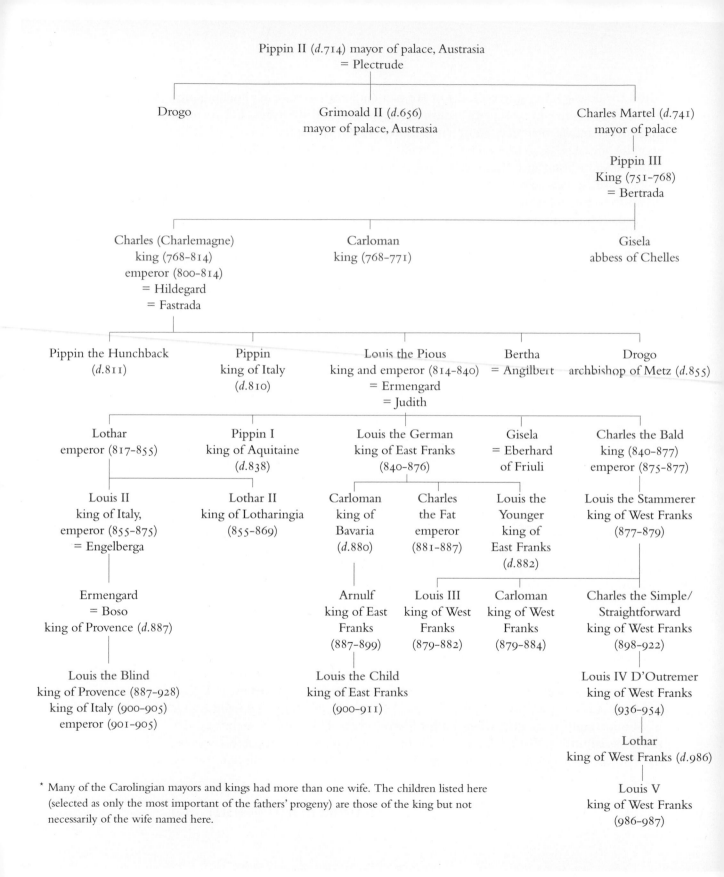

Pippin II (*d.*714) mayor of palace, Austrasia
= Plectrude

Drogo

Grimoald II (*d.*656)
mayor of palace, Austrasia

Charles Martel (*d.*741)
mayor of palace

Pippin III
King (751–768)
= Bertrada

Charles (Charlemagne)
king (768–814)
emperor (800–814)
= Hildegard
= Fastrada

Carloman
king (768–771)

Gisela
abbess of Chelles

Pippin the Hunchback
(*d.*811)

Pippin
king of Italy
(*d.*810)

Louis the Pious
king and emperor (814–840)
= Ermengard
= Judith

Bertha
= Angilbert

Drogo
archbishop of Metz (*d.*855)

Lothar
emperor (817–855)

Pippin I
king of Aquitaine
(*d.*838)

Louis the German
king of East Franks
(840–876)

Gisela
= Eberhard
of Friuli

Charles the Bald
king (840–877)
emperor (875–877)

Louis II
king of Italy,
emperor (855–875)
= Engelberga

Lothar II
king of Lotharingia
(855–869)

Carloman
king of
Bavaria
(*d.*880)

Charles
the Fat
emperor
(881–887)

Louis the
Younger
king of
East Franks
(*d.*882)

Louis the Stammerer
king of West Franks
(877–879)

Ermengard
= Boso
king of Provence (*d.*887)

Arnulf
king of East
Franks
(887–899)

Louis III
king of West
Franks
(879–882)

Carloman
king of West
Franks
(879–884)

Charles the Simple/
Straightforward
king of West Franks
(898–922)

Louis the Blind
king of Provence (887–928)
king of Italy (900–905)
emperor (901–905)

Louis the Child
king of East Franks
(900–911)

Louis IV D'Outremer
king of West Franks
(936–954)

Lothar
king of West Franks (*d.*986)

Louis V
king of West Franks
(986–987)

* Many of the Carolingian mayors and kings had more than one wife. The children listed here
(selected as only the most important of the fathers' progeny) are those of the king but not
necessarily of the wife named here.

great feast-day, had he foreseen the plan of the pope."[15] In fact, Charlemagne continued to use the title "king" for about a year; then he adopted a new one that was both long and revealing: "Charles, the most serene Augustus, crowned by God, great and peaceful emperor who governs the Roman Empire and who is, by the mercy of God, king of the Franks and the Lombards." According to this title, Charlemagne was not the Roman emperor crowned by the pope but rather God's emperor, who governed the Roman Empire along with his many other duties.

Charlemagne's Heirs

When Charlemagne died, only one of his sons remained alive: Louis, nicknamed "the Pious." (See Genealogy 3.1: The Carolingians.) Emperor he was (from 814 to 840), but over an empire that was a conglomeration of territories with little unity. He had to contend with the revolts of his sons, the depredations of outside invaders, the regional interests of counts and bishops, and above all an enormous variety of languages, laws, customs, and traditions, all of which tended to pull his empire apart. He contended with gusto, his chief unifying tool being Christianity. Calling on the help of the monastic reformer Benedict of Aniane, Louis imposed *The Benedictine Rule* on all the monasteries in Francia. Monks and abbots served as his chief advisors. Louis's imperial model was Theodosius I, who had made Christianity the official religion of the Roman Empire. Organizing inquests by the *missi*, he looked into allegations of exploitation of the poor, standardized the procedures of his chancery, and put all Frankish bishops and monasteries under his control.

Charlemagne had employed his sons as "sub-kings." Louis politicized his family still more. Early in his reign he had his wife crowned empress, named his first-born son, Lothar, emperor and co-ruler, and had his other sons, Pippin and Louis (later called "the German"), agree to be sub-kings under their older brother. It was neatly planned. But when Louis's first wife died he married Judith, daughter of a relatively obscure kindred (the Welfs) that would later become enormously powerful in Saxony and Bavaria. In 823 she and Louis had a son, Charles (later "the Bald"), and this (plus the death of Pippin in 838) upset the earlier division of the empire. A family feud turned into bitter civil war as brothers fought one another and their father for titles and kingdoms.

After Louis's death a peace was hammered out in the Treaty of Verdun (843). (See Map 3.4a.) The empire was divided into three parts, an arrangement that would roughly define the future political contours of Western Europe. The western third, bequeathed to Charles the Bald (r.840-877), would eventually become France, and the eastern third, given to Louis the German (r.840-876), would become Germany.

Genealogy 3.1 (facing page): The Carolingians*

The "Middle Kingdom," which became Lothar's portion (r.817-855) along with the imperial title, had a different fate: parts of it were absorbed by France and Germany, while the rest eventually coalesced into the modern states of Belgium, the Netherlands, and Luxembourg—the so-called Benelux countries—as well as Switzerland and Italy. All this was far in the future. As the brothers had their own children, new divisions were tried: one in 870 (the Treaty of Meerssen), for example, and another in 880. (See Maps 3.4b and 3.4c.) After the deposition of Emperor Charles the Fat (888), as one chronicler put it,

Map 3.4a:
Partition of 843
(Treaty of Verdun)

Map 3.4b:
Partition of 870
(Treaty of Meerssen)

Map 3.4c:
Partition of 880

> the kingdoms which had obeyed his will, as if devoid of a legitimate heir, were loosened from their bodily structure into parts and now awaited no lord of hereditary descent, but each set out to create a king for itself from its own inner parts.[16]

Dynastic problems were not the primary cause of the breakup of the Carolingian empire, however. Nor were the invasions by outsiders—Vikings, Muslims, and, start-

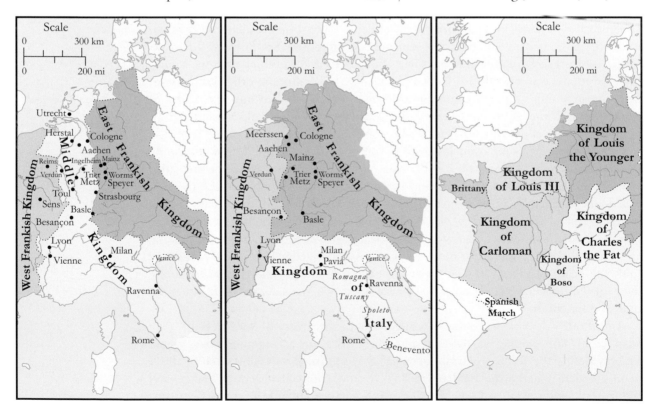

ing in 899, Magyars (Hungarians)—which harassed the Frankish Kingdom through-out the ninth century. These certainly weakened the kings: without a standing army, they were unable to respond to lightning raids, and what regional defense there was fell into the hands of local leaders, such as counts. The Carolingians lost prestige and money as they paid out tribute to stave off further attacks. But the invasions were not all bad; to some degree they even helped fortify the king. The Carolingian empire atomized because linguistic and other differences between regions—and familial and other ties within regions—were simply too strong to be overcome by directives from a central court. Even today a unified Europe is only a distant ideal. Anyway, as we shall see, fragmentation had its own strengths and possibilities.

The Wealth of a Local Economy

The Carolingian economy was based on plunder, trade, and agriculture. After the Carolingians could push no further, and the booty raids of Charlemagne's day came to an end, trade and land became the chief resources of the kingdom. To the north, in Viking trading stations such as Haithabu (see Map 3.3), archaeologists have found Carolingian glass and pots alongside Islamic coins and cloth, showing that the Carolingian economy meshed with that of the Abbasid caliphate. Silver from the Islamic world probably came north from the Caspian Sea, up the Volga River (through what is today Russia) to the Baltic Sea. (You can figure out the likely route from the map at the front of this book.) There the coins were melted down, the silver traded to the Carolingians in return for wine, jugs, glasses, and other manufactured goods. The Carolingians turned the silver into coins of their own, to be used throughout the empire for small-scale local trade. Baltic Sea emporia such as Haithabu supplemented those—Quentovic and Dorestad, for example (see Map 2.3 on p. 79)—that served the North Sea trade.

Nevertheless, the backbone of the Carolingian economy was land. A few written records, called *polyptyques*, document the output of the Carolingian great estates—"villae," as they were called in Latin, "manors," as we term them. On the far-flung and widely scattered manors of rich landowners—churches, monasteries, kings, and aristocrats—a major reorganization and rationalization was taking place. The most enterprising landlords instituted a three-field rather than a two-field cultivation system. It meant that two-thirds of the land rather than one-half was sown with crops each year, yielding a tidy surplus.

Consider Lambesc, near Aix-en Provence, one of the many manors belonging to the cathedral of St. Mary of Marseille. It was not a compact farm but rather a conglomeration of essential parts, with its lands, woods, meadows, and vineyards dotting the countryside. All were worked by peasant families, some legally free, some unfree, each settled on its own holding—here called a *colonica*; elsewhere often called a *mansus*, or "manse"—usually including a house, a garden, small bits of several fields, and so on. The peasants farmed the land that belonged to them and paid yearly dues to their lord—in this case the Church of St. Mary, which, in its *polyptyque*, kept careful track of what was owed:

> [There is a] holding [*colonica*] in Siverianis [a place-name within the manor of Lambesc]. Valerius, colonus [tenant]. Wife [is named] Dominica. Ducsana, a daughter 5 years old. An infant at the breast. It pays in tax: 1 pig; 1 suckling [pig]; 2 fattened hens; 10 chickens; 20 eggs.[17]

Valerius and his wife apparently did not work the *demesne*—the land, woods, meadows, and vineyards directly held by St. Mary—but other tenants had that duty. At Nidis, in the region of Grasse, Bernarius owed daily service, probably farming the *demesne*, and also paid a penny (1 denarius) in yearly dues. On many manors women were required to feed the lord's chickens or busy themselves in the *gynecaeum*, the women's workshop, where they made and dyed cloth and sewed garments.

Clearly the labor was onerous and the accounting system complex and unwieldy; but manors organized on the model of St. Mary made a profit. Like the Church of St. Mary and other lords, the Carolingian kings benefited from their own extensive manors. Nevertheless, farming was still too primitive to return great surpluses, and as the lands belonging to the king were divided up in the wake of the partitioning of the empire, Carolingian dependence on manors scattered throughout their kingdom proved to be a source of weakness.

The Carolingian Renaissance

With the profits from their manors, some monasteries and churches invested in books. These were not made of paper—a product which, although used in the Islamic world, did not reach the West until the eleventh century—but rather of parchment: animal skins soaked, scraped, and cut into sheets. Nor were Carolingian books printed, since the printing press was not invented until around 1450. Rather, they were manuscripts, written by hand in scribal workshops (*scriptoria*; sing. *scriptorium*). Consider the monastery of Saint-Amand, which made books both for its own use and for the needs of many other institutions: its *scriptorium* produced Gospels, works of the Church Fathers, grammars, and above all beautifully illustrated liturgical books.

Books for the liturgy—church services—required particular expertise, for they were becoming books of music as well as text. The development of written music was a response to royal policy. Before Charlemagne's day, the melodies used for the Mass and the Divine Office were not at all uniform. Various churches in different places sang the tunes as they had learned them; music was part of local oral traditions. But since Charlemagne's time the melodies used for the Mass and the Divine Office were required to be "Roman," not Frankish. This reform—the imposition of the so-called "Gregorian chant"—posed great practical difficulties. It meant that every monk and priest had to learn a year's worth of Roman music; but how? A few cantors were imported from Rome; but without a system of musical notation, it was easy to forget new tunes. The monks of Saint-Amand were part of a musical revolution: they invented one of the first systems of musical notation. In a Sacramentary (a set of texts for the Mass) that they produced, they added "neumes," precursors of "notes," above some lines of text to indicate the melodic pattern. On the manuscript leaf shown in Plate 3.5, the neumes hover over a few words in the first column, seven lines from the bottom of the page.

The same Sacramentary reveals another key development of the era: the use of minuscule writing. As at Byzantium, and at about the same time, the Carolingians experimented with letter forms that were quick to write and easy to read. "Caroline minuscule" lasted into the eleventh century, when it gave way to a more angular script, today called "Gothic." But the Carolingian letter forms were rediscovered in the fifteenth century—by scholars who thought that they represented ancient Roman writing!—and they became the model for modern lower case printed fonts.

Like monasteries, cathedrals too were centers of cultural production in the Carolingian period. Würzburg, for example, had a *scriptorium*, library, and school for young clerics. As enterprising about its books as St. Mary was about its manors, Würzburg made lists of its library's holdings. By the mid-ninth century these were substantial: Gospels, writings of the Church Fathers, liturgical manuscripts, grammars, biblical commentaries, and even books of canon (church) law. The bishops of Würzburg were avid collectors. When one of them wanted Hraban Maur's Bible commentaries, he sent his request for a copy along with a pile of blank parchment to the monastery of Fulda, where Hraban was abbot. Meanwhile, Würzburg helped Fulda and other places build their own libraries, lending Fulda, for example, a manuscript of Gregory the Great's Homilies so that the monks there could copy it.

The Carolingian court was behind much of this activity. Most of the centers of learning, scholarship, and book production began under men and women who at one time or another were part of the royal court. Alcuin, perhaps the most famous of the Carolingian intellectuals, was "imported" by Charlemagne from England—where, as we have seen (p. 89), monastic scholarship flourished—to head up the king's palace school. Chief advisor to Charlemagne and tutor to the entire royal family, Alcuin

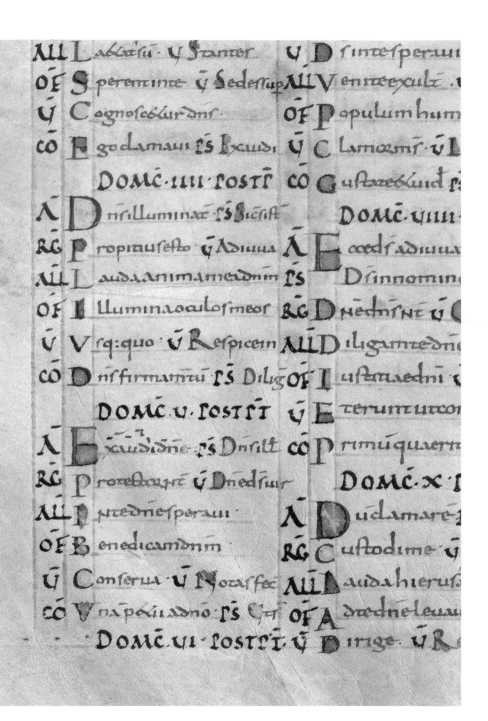

Plate 3.5: Sacramentary of Saint-Germain-des-Prés (early 9th cent.). The scribe of this list of incipits (the "first words") of mass chants provided a musical reminder of one (seven lines from the bottom, on the left) by adding neumes above the first words, "Exaudi Domine," "Hear, O Lord."

eventually became abbot of Saint-Martin of Tours, grooming a new generation of teachers, including Hraban Maur (*d.*856). More unusual but equally telling was the experience of Gisela, Charlemagne's sister. She too was a key royal advisor, the one who alerted the others at home about Charlemagne's imperial coronation at Rome in 800. She was also abbess of Chelles, a center of manuscript production in its own right. Chelles had a library, and its nuns were well educated. They wrote learned letters and composed a history (the "Prior Metz Annals") that treated the rise of the Carolingians as a tale of struggle between brothers, sons, and fathers eased by the wise counsel of mothers, aunts, and sisters.

Women and the poor make up the largely invisible half of the Carolingian Renaissance. But without doubt some were part of it. One of Charlemagne's capitularies ordered that the cathedrals and monasteries of his kingdom should teach reading and writing to all who could learn. There were enough complaints (by rich people) about upstart peasants who found a place at court that we may be sure that some talented sons of the poor were getting an education. A few churchmen expressed the hope that schools for "children" would be established even in small villages and hamlets. Were they thinking of girls as well as boys? Certainly one woman—admittedly noble—in the mid-ninth century in the south of France proves that education was available to some women. We would never know about Dhuoda had she not worried enough about her absent son to write a *Handbook for her Son* full of advice. Only incidentally does it become clear in the course of her deeply-felt moral text that Dhuoda was drawing on an excellent education: she clearly knew the Bible, writings of the Church Fathers, Gregory the Great, and "moderns," like Alcuin. Her Latin was fluent and sophisticated. And she understood the value of the written word:

> My great concern, my son William, is to offer you helpful words. My burning, watchful heart especially desires that you may have in this little volume what I have longed to be written down for you, about how you were born through God's grace.[18]

The original manuscript of Dhuoda's text is not extant. Had it survived, it would no doubt have looked like other "practical texts" of the time: the "folios" (pages) would have been written in Caroline minuscule, each carefully designed to set off the poetry—Dhuoda's own and quotes from others—from the prose; the titles of each chapter (there are nearly a hundred, each very short) would have been enlivened with delicately colored capital letters. The manuscript would probably not have been illuminated; fancy books were generally made for royalty, for prestigious ceremonial occasions, or for books that were especially esteemed, such as the Gospels.

There were, however, many such lavish productions. In fact, Carolingian art and

Following pages:

Plate 3.6: Saint Mark, Soissons Gospels (800-810). Compare this "author portrait" of Saint Mark with that of Saint Luke in Plate 2.4 on p. 91. Consider the different elements that each artist has used to render the portraits both figural and decorative.

Plate 3.7: First Text Page, Gospel of Saint Mark, Soissons Gospels (800-810). Compare this Carolingian first text page of the Gospel of Mark with the first text page of the Anglo-Saxon Gospel of Luke in Plate 2.6 on p. 93. In the Carolingian text, the letter forms are resolutely Roman looking, as if cut in stone. This classical allusion is reinforced by the artist's lavish use of purple (the Roman imperial color) and gold leaf. This is a manuscript meant for an emperor—Charlemagne.

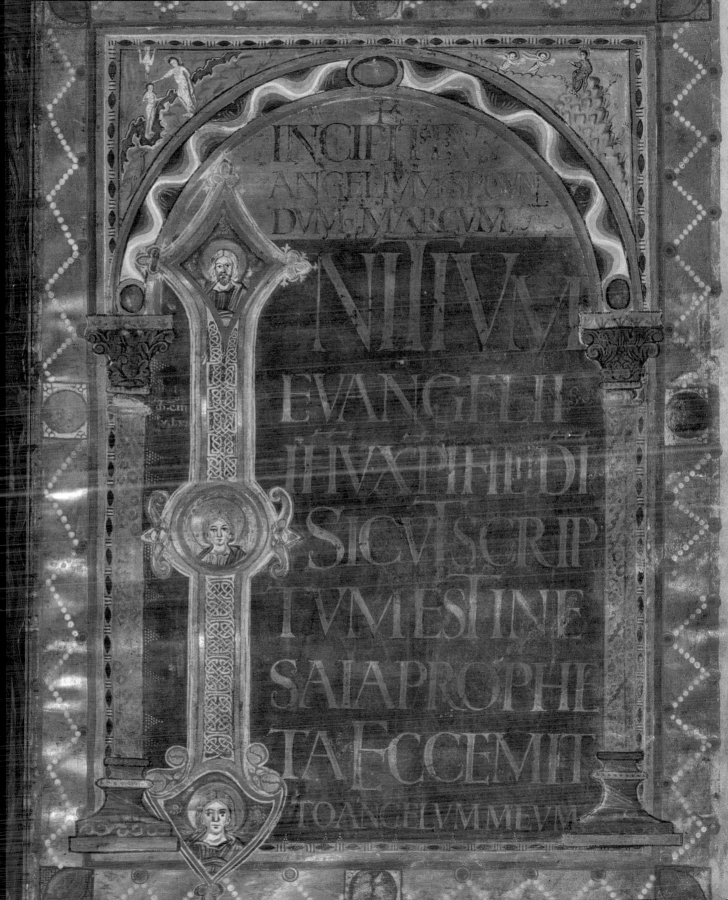

INCIPIT E
ANGELIVM SCVNL
DVM MARCVM
NITIVM
EVANGELII
IHV XPI FIE DI
SICVI SCRIP
TVM EST INE
SAIA PROPHE
TA ECCE MIT
TO ANGELVM MEVM

Plate 3.8: Saint Mark, Coronation Gospels (*c*.800). Two portraits of Saint Mark (this and the one in Plate 3.6), done at about the same time, and in about the same place, could hardly be in more disparate styles. They attest to the eclectic and wide-ranging artistic endeavors of the Carolingians.

architecture mark a turning point. For all its richness, Merovingian culture had not stressed artistic expression, though some of the monasteries inspired by Saint Columbanus produced a few illuminated manuscripts. By contrast, the Carolingians, admirers and imitators of Christian Rome, vigorously promoted a vast, eclectic, and ideologically motivated program of artistic work. They were reviving the Roman Empire. We have already seen how Charlemagne brought the very marble of Rome and Ravenna home to Aachen to build his new palace complex. A similar impulse inspired Carolingian art.

As with texts, so with pictures: the Carolingians revered and imitated the past while building on and changing it. Their manuscript illuminations were inspired by a vast repertory of models: from the British Isles (where, as we have seen, a rich synthesis of decorative and representational styles had a long tradition), from late-antique Italy (which yielded its models in old manuscripts), and from Byzantium (which may have inadvertently provided some artists, fleeing iconoclasm, as well as manuscripts).

In Plates 3.6 and 3.7, facing pages from a Carolingian manuscript made in the early ninth century, the artist has borrowed from the Anglo-Saxons by pairing his evangelist portrait of Mark with the beginning of Mark's Gospel text. The interlace motif of the large I in Plate 3.7 is also insular. But insofar as the figure of Saint Mark is sturdy, with clothes clinging to a body of convincing roundness, the artist has used a late Roman or Byzantine model. And yet the real inspiration for this Mark is entirely original. The evangelist's lively twist—his attention caught by the lion (Mark's symbol) about to give him the Word—and the bright, exuberant colors and designs that frame him are pure Carolingian invention. Like the artist of the Lindisfarne Gospels, the anonymous Mark artist has synthesized figural and decorative elements to suit the flat pages of a book; but the two syntheses are nothing alike.

Quite different, yet equally characteristic of Carolingian art, is the Saint Mark of Plate 3.8, made in the late eighth century. Here is a somber, utterly corporeal evangelist. He sits between mountains, with tinted sky above, light playing on his face. Were it not for his halo, he would be simply a man with a scroll. The colors are soft, the drapery subdued. No one was producing art like this outside of Francia. Its closest comparison is with Pompeiian wall paintings (see Plates 1.1 and 1.2 on pp. 33 and 34).

Both of these styles, the first richly decorative, the second subtly naturalistic, would have long lives in the West. It may even be said that they are the direct ancestors of the entire Western artistic tradition. One more model with a long life must be added: the Utrecht Psalter (Plate 3.9), a book containing all 150 psalms and 16 other songs known as canticles. Fleeting precedents for this extraordinary manuscript of narrative art exist. For example, Plate 3.7 has lithe figures in the top corners to illustrate Bible stories: on the left is the baptism of Christ, on the right angels minister to Christ after the Temptation. The Utrecht Psalter, produced *c.*820–835, takes this impulse to its

CIRCUMDABITTE
ETPROPTERHANCINALTU
REGREDERE DNSIUDI
CATPOPULOS
IUDICAMIDNISECUN
DUIUSTITIAMMEA ET
SECUNDUMINNOCEN
TIAMMEAMSUPERME
CONSUMMETURNEQUITI
APECCATORUETDIRI
GESIUSTUM ETSCRUTANS
CORDAETRENESDS
IUSTUMADIUTORIUM
MEUMADNO QUISAL
VIII INFINEM

UOSFACITRECTOSCORDE
DSIUDEXIUSTUSETFORTIS
ETPATIENS NUMQUIDI
RASCETURPERSINGU
LOSDIES
NISICONUERSIFUERITIS
GLADIUMSUUMUIBRA
BITARCUMSUUMTE
TENDITETPARAUITILLU
ETINEOPARAUITUASA
MORTIS SAGITTASSU
ASARDENTIBUSEFFECIT
ECCEPARTURITINIUS
TITIAM CONCEPITDO
PROTORCOLARIBUS

LORISMETPEPERITINIQUI
TATEM
LACUMAPERUITETEFFODIT
EUM ETINCIDITINFOUE
AMQUAMFECIT
CONUERTETURDOLOR
EIUSINCAPUTEIUS ET
INUERTICEMIPSIUSINI
QUITASEIUSDESCENDET
CONFITEBORDNO SECUN
DUMIUSTITIAMEIUS
ETPSALLAM NOMINI
DNIALTISSIMI;

PSALMUSDAUID

DNENOSTER
QUAMADMIRABILE
ESTNOMENTUUM
INUNIUERSATERRA
QNMELEUATAESTMAG
NIFICENTIATUA SU
PERCAELOS
EXOREINFANTIUMETLAC

TANTIUM PERFECISTI
LAUDEMPROPTERINI
MICOSTUOS UTDESTRU
ASINIMICUMETULTORE
QNMUIDEBOCAELOSTU
OSOPERADIGITORU
TUORUM LUNAMEIS
TELLASQUAETUFUNDASTI

QUIDESTHOMOQUOD
MEMORESHIUS AUT
FILIUSHOMINIS QUO
NIAMUISITASEUM
MINUISTIEUMPAULOMI
NUSABANGELIS GLO
RIAETHONORECORO
NASTIEUM ETCONS

logical conclusion. It precedes each poem with drawings that depict its important elements in unified composition. In Plate 3.9, the illustration for Psalm 8, the artist has, for example, sketched sheep and oxen on the bottom left, birds flying and fish swimming on the bottom right, to render literally verses 8 and 9:

> Thou hast subjected all things under his feet, all sheep and oxen: moreover the beasts also of the fields. / The birds of the air, and the fishes of the sea, that pass through the paths of the sea.

The ambition, style, wit, and narrative thrust of the Utrecht Psalter inspired much art in the Middle Ages and beyond.

★   ★   ★   ★

In the course of the eighth and ninth centuries, the three heirs of Rome established clearly separate identities, each largely bound up with its religious affiliation. Byzantium saw itself as the radiating center of Orthodox faith; the caliphate first asserted itself as the guarantor of Islam, then ceded that position to the *ulama*; Francia and the papacy cooperated and vied for the leadership of Catholic Europe. From this perspective, there were few commonalities. Yet today we are struck more by the similarities than the differences. All were centralizing monarchies shored up by military might. All had a bit of wealth, though the East certainly had more than the West. All had pretensions to God-given power. And all used culture and scholarship to give luster and expression to their political regimes. All may also have known, without explicitly admitting it, how strong were the forces of dissolution.

Plate 3.9 (facing page): Utrecht Psalter (*c.*820–835). Never completed, the Utrecht Psalter was commissioned by Archbishop Ebbo of Reims and executed at a nearby monastery. Providing a visual "running commentary" on every psalm, it may have been meant for Emperor Louis the Pious and his wife Queen Judith.

732	Charles Martel's victory over Muslim-led army near Poitiers
750	Abbasid caliphate begins
751	Deposition of last Merovingian king; Pippin III elevated to kingship and anointed
756	"Donation of Pippin"
756	Emirate of Córdoba established
762	Baghdad founded as the Abbasid capital city
768-814	Reign of Charlemagne (Charles the Great)
787	Second Council of Nicaea; end of the first phase of iconoclasm
c.790-c.900	Carolingian Renaissance
c.790-c.1050	Renaissance in Islamic world
800	Charlemagne crowned emperor
814-840	Reign of Louis the Pious
833-848	The Mihna, pursued by the caliphs and rationalists
843	End of iconoclasm in Byzantine Empire
843	Treaty of Verdun
c. 860	Arab invasions of Byzantium end
863	Missionary expedition of Constantine (Cyril) and Methodius begins
c.870-c.1025	Macedonian Renaissance at Byzantium

NOTES

1. Photius, *Letter to the Bulgar Khan*, in *Reading the Middle Ages: Sources from Europe, Byzantium, and the Islamic World*, ed. Barbara H. Rosenwein (Peterborough, ON, 2006), p.145.

2. Constantine/Cyril, *Prologue to the Gospel*, in *Reading the Middle Ages*, p.147.

3. *The Life of Constantine-Cyril*, quoted in *Byzantium: Church, Society, and Civilization Seen through Contemporary Eyes*, ed. Deno John Geanakoplos (Chicago, 1984), p.409.

4. *Sindbad the Sailor*, in *Reading the Middle Ages*, p.163.

5. "Imports of Iraq," in *Medieval Trade in the Mediterranean World: Illustrative Documents,* trans. Robert S. Lopez and Irving W. Raymond (New York, 1997), p.28.

6. Quoted in Michael Cooperson, *Al-Ma'mun* (Oxford, 2005), p.99.

7. Abu Dawud al-Sijistani, *Compilation of the Jurisprudential Responses of Ahmad ibn Hanbal*, in *Reading the Middle Ages*, p.158.

8. Quoted in Philip F. Kennedy, *Abu Nuwas: A Genius of Poetry* (Oxford, 2005), pp.22–23.

9. Quoted in Salma Khadra Jayyusi, "Andalusi Poetry: The Golden Period," in *The Legacy of Muslim Spain* (Leiden, 1994), 1:327.

10. *The Fourth Book of the Chronicle of Fredegar with its Continuations*, trans. J.M. Wallace-Hadrill (London, 1960), p.91.

11. Quoted in Thomas F.X. Noble, *The Republic of St. Peter: The Birth of the Papal State, 680–825* (Philadelphia, 1984), p.263.

12. *The Donation of Constantine*, in *Reading the Middle Ages*, p.176.

13. *Once Again my Burdened Anchor*, in *Reading the Middle Ages*, p.177.

14. *Double Capitulary of Thionville for the* missi, in *Reading the Middle Ages*, pp.183–84.

15. "Einhard's *Life of Charlemagne*," in *Carolingian Civilization: A Reader*, ed. Paul Dutton, 2nd ed. (Peterborough, ON, 2004), p.44.

16. "Regino's Reasons for the End of the Carolingian Line," in *Carolingian Civilization*, p.541.

17. *Polyptyque of the Church of Saint Mary of Marseille*, in *Reading the Middle Ages*, p.131.

18. Dhuoda, *Handbook for her Son*, in *Reading the Middle Ages*, p.187.

FURTHER READING

Barford, P.M. *The Early Slavs: Culture and Society in Early Medieval Eastern Europe*. Ithaca, NY, 2001.

Becher, Matthias. *Charlemagne*. Trans. David S. Bachrach. New Haven, CT, 2003.

Bloom, Jonathan M. *Paper before Print: The History and Impact of Paper in the Islamic World*. New Haven, CT, 2001.

Brubaker, Leslie. *Vision and Meaning in Ninth-Century Byzantium: Image as Exegesis in the Homilies of Gregory of Nazianzus*. Cambridge, 1999.

Cooperson, Michael. *Al-Ma'mun*. Oxford, 2005.

Goldberg, Eric J. *Struggle for Empire: Kingship and Conflict under Louis the German, 817–876*. Ithaca, NY, 2006.

Fouracre, Paul. *The Age of Charles Martel*. Harlow, Essex, 2000.

Hallaq, Wael B. *The Origins and Evolution of Islamic Law*. Cambridge, 2005.

Herrin, Judith. *Women in Purple: Rulers of Medieval Byzantium*. Princeton, 2002.

Holmes, Catherine. *Basil II and the Governance of Empire (976-1025)*. Oxford, 2005.

James, Edward. *Britain in the First Millennium*. London, 2001.

Kennedy, Philip F. *Abu Nuwas: A Genius of Poetry*. Oxford, 2005.

McCormick, Michael. *Origins of the European Economy: Communications and Commerce, AD 300-900*. Cambridge, 2001.

McKitterick, Rosamond, ed. *Carolingian Culture: Emulation and Innovation*. Cambridge, 1994.

—. *The Carolingians and the Written Word*. Cambridge, 1989.

Nelson, Janet L. *Charles the Bald*. London, 1992.

—. *The Frankish World, 750-900*. London, 1996.

Treadgold, Warren. *The Byzantine Revival, 780-842*. Stanford, 1988.

Verhulst, Adriaan. *The Carolingian Economy*. Cambridge, 2002.

Whittow, Mark. *The Making of Byzantium, 600-1025*. Berkeley, 1996.

◄►◄►◄►◄►◄►◄►◄►

**To test your knowledge of this chapter, please go to
www.rosenweinshorthistory.com
and click "Study Questions."**

FOUR

POLITICAL COMMUNITIES REORDERED (c.900-c.1050)

The large-scale centralized governments of the ninth century dissolved in the tenth. The fission was least noticeable at Byzantium, where, although important landowning families emerged as brokers of patronage and power, the primacy of the emperor was never effectively challenged. Quite the opposite happened in the Islamic world, where new dynastic groups established themselves as regional rulers. In Western Europe, Carolingian kings ceased to control land and men, while new political entities — some extremely local and weak, others quite strong and unified—emerged in their wake. Everywhere political reordering brought new military elites to the fore.

BYZANTIUM: THE STRENGTHS AND LIMITS OF CENTRALIZATION

By 1025 the Byzantine Empire once again shadowed the Danube and touched the Euphrates. To the north it had a new and restless neighbor: Kievan Rus. The emperors at Constantinople maintained the traditional cultural importance of the capital city by carefully orchestrating the radiating power of the imperial court. Nevertheless, the centralized model of the Byzantine state was challenged by powerful men in the countryside, who gobbled up land and dominated the peasantry.

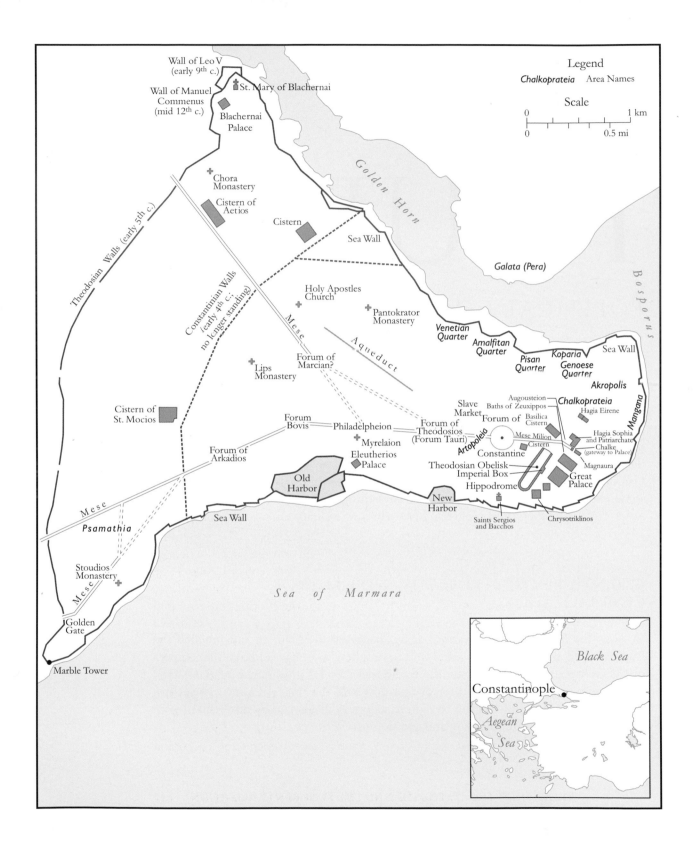

Legend

Chalkoprateia   Area Names

Scale

0 ——————————— 1 km

0 ——————————— 0.5 mi

Wall of Leo V
(early 9th c.)

St. Mary of Blachernai

Wall of Manuel
Commenus
(mid 12th c.)

Blachernai
Palace

Golden Horn

Theodosian Walls (early 5th c.)

Chora
Monastery

Cistern of
Aetios

Cistern

Sea Wall

Galata (Pera)

Bosporus

Constantinian Walls
(early 4th c.;
no longer standing)

Holy Apostles
Church

Pantokrator
Monastery

*Venetian
Quarter*

*Amalfitan
Quarter*

*Pisan
Quarter*

Koparia

Sea Wall

*Genoese
Quarter*

Mese

Aqueduct

Forum of
Marcian?

Lips
Monastery

Akropolis

Mangana

Slave
Market

Augousteion

Baths of Zeuxippos

Chalkoprateia

Hagia Eirene

Cistern of
St. Mocios

Forum
Bovis

Philadelpheion

Forum of
Theodosios
(Forum Tauri)

Forum of
Constantine

Basilica
Cistern

Mese Milion

Cistern

Hagia Sophia
and Patriarchate

Chalke
(gateway to Palace)

Artopoleia

Forum of
Arkadios

Myrelaion

Eleutherios
Palace

Old
Harbor

Theodosian Obelisk

Imperial Box

Hippodrome

Magnaura

Great
Palace

Mese

New
Harbor

Saints Sergios
and Bacchos

Chrysotriklinos

Psamathia

Sea Wall

Sea of Marmara

Stoudios
Monastery

Mese

Golden
Gate

Marble Tower

Black Sea

Constantinople

*Aegean
Sea*

The Imperial Court

The Great Palace of Constantinople, a sprawling building complex begun under Constantine, was expanded, redecorated, and fortified under his successors. (See Map 4.1.) It was more than the symbolic emplacement of imperial power; it was the central command post of the empire. Servants, slaves, and grooms; top courtiers and learned clergymen; cousins, siblings, and hangers-on of the emperor and empress lived within its walls. Other courtiers—civil servants, officials, scholars, military men, advisers, and other dependents—lived as near to the Palace as they could manage. They were "on call" at every hour. The emperor had only to give short notice and all were to assemble for impromptu but nevertheless highly choreographed ceremonies. These were in themselves instruments of power; the emperors manipulated courtly formalities to indicate new favorites or to signal displeasure.

The court was mainly a male preserve, but there were women's quarters at the Great Palace as well—and sometimes powerful women. Consider Zoe (*d.*1050), the daughter of Constantine VIII. Contemporaries acknowledged her right to rule through her imperial blood. But they were happier when she was married, her blood-right legitimizing the rule of her husband. In most cases, though, the emperors themselves boasted the hereditary bloodline, and their wives were the ones to marry into the imperial family. In that case the empress normally could exercise power only as a widow acting on behalf of her children.

There was also a "third gender" at the Great Palace: eunuchs—men who had been castrated, normally as children, and raised to be teachers, doctors, or guardians of the women at court. Their status began to rise in the tenth century. Originally foreigners, they were increasingly recruited from the educated upper classes in the Byzantine Empire itself. In addition to their duties in the women's quarter, some of them accompanied the emperor during his most sacred and vulnerable moments—when he removed his crown; when he participated in religious ceremonies; even when he dreamed, at night. They hovered by his throne, like the angels in Mary's icon in Plate 1.12 on p. 55. No one, it was thought, was as faithful, trustworthy, or spiritually pure as a eunuch. Small wonder that in the tenth century Basil the Nothos, the castrated bastard son of one emperor, rose to become grand chamberlain (responsible for internal affairs) at the court of another.

About a century later, the grand chamberlain was not a eunuch but rather a professor, Michael Psellus (1018-*c.*1092). The Macedonian Renaissance, which had begun in the ninth century, continued apace in the tenth and eleventh, bringing people like Psellus to the fore. Under his direction a new school of philosophy at Constantinople, founded by Constantine IX (*r.*1042-1055), began to flourish. Beyond his philosophical interests, Psellus was a moralist, keen to explore the character and emotional

Map 4.1 (facing page): Constantinople, *c.*1100

life of powerful men and women. In his hands, a new sort of historical writing was born: not a universal chronicle covering Creation to the present, as had been the style, but rather an opinionated account of recent events, personalities, and well-oiled political networks:

> [Basil II] surrounded himself with favorites who were neither remarkable for brilliance of intellect, nor of noble lineage, nor too learned. To them were entrusted the imperial rescripts [laws written in response to particular cases], and with them he was accustomed to share the secrets of State.[1]

The impression that Psellus gives of a self-indulgent emperor presiding over a frivolous court is only part of the story, however. As Psellus himself recognized, Basil was a successful centralizer, amassing enormous wealth through taxes, confiscations, and tribute. Above all—something that Psellus only hinted at—Basil was a tough military man whose rule reshaped the geography of Byzantium.

Map 4.2: The Byzantine Empire, *c.*1025

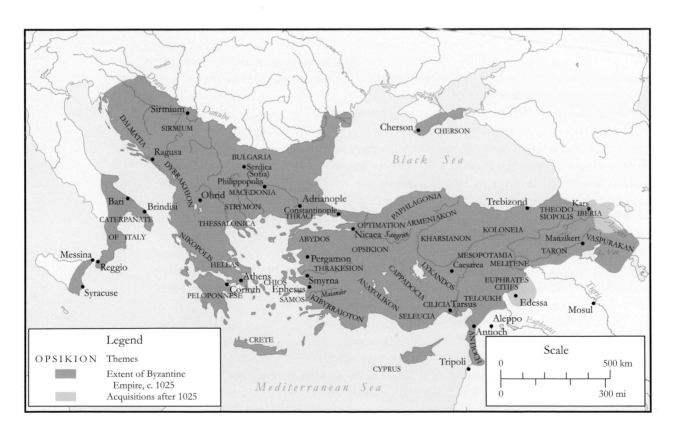

A Wide Embrace and Its Tensions

The expansion of the Byzantine Empire, so cautiously begun in the ninth century, quickened under the tenth-century soldier-emperors Nicephorus Phocas and John Tzimisces. (See Map 4.2.) Crete, lost to the Muslims in the ninth century, was retaken in 961; Cyprus was reconquered in 965; Antioch, portal to Syria, in 969. Most importantly, under Basil II (r.963-1025), Bulgaria, a thorn in Byzantium's side since the seventh century, was at last definitively defeated (1018). The entire region was put under Byzantine rule, its territory divided into themes.

Certainly Basil's nickname, the "Bulgar Slayer," was apt. Nevertheless, it hid the fact that the same emperor was also busy setting up protectorates against the Muslims on his eastern front and that at the end of his life he was preparing an expedition to Sicily. By 1025 the Byzantine army was no longer focused on the interior but was rather mobilized at the peripheries of the empire.

This empire was no longer the tight fist centered on Anatolia that it had been in the dark days of the eighth century. On the contrary, it was an open hand: sprawling, multi-ethnic, and multilingual. To the east it embraced Armenians, Syrians, and Arabs; to the north it included Slavs and Bulgarians (by now themselves Slavic speaking) as well as Pechenegs, a Turkic group that had served as allies of Bulgaria; to the west, in the Byzantine toe of Italy, it contained Lombards, Italians, and Greeks. There must have been Muslims right in the middle of Constantinople: a mosque was built for them there in 1027. Russian soldiers from the region of Kiev formed the backbone of Basil's "Varangian Guard," his elite troops; by the mid-eleventh century, Byzantine mercenaries included "Franks" (mainly from Normandy), Arabs, and Bulgarians as well. In spite of ingrained prejudices, Byzantine princesses had occasionally been married to foreigners before the tenth century, but in Basil's reign this happened to a sister of the emperor himself.

All this openness went only so far, however. In the tenth century, the emperors expelled the Jews from Constantinople, severely curtailing their participation in the silk trade (their traditional profession), and forcing them into the degrading labor of tanners. Some of these restrictions were lifted in the course of the eleventh century, but Jews were never integrated into Byzantine society. Similarly, the annexation of Armenia did not lead to the assimilation of Armenians, who kept their Monophysite beliefs (see p. 29), heretical to many Orthodox Byzantines.

Ethnic diversity was in part responsible for new regional political movements that threatened centralized imperial control. More generally, however, regional revolts were the result of the rise of a new class of wealthy provincial landowners, the *dynatoi* (sing. *dynatos*), "powerful men." Benefiting from a general quickening in the economy and the rise of new urban centers, they took advantage of unaccustomed wealth, buying

Scale

0 ⊢ 500 km

0 ⊢ 300 mi

Lake Ladoga

Gulf of Finland

Kingdom of Sweden

Kingdom of Denmark

Baltic Sea

Novgorod

Lake Ilmen

Volga

Vladimir

Suzdal

Western Dvina

Polatsk

Kievan Rus

Smolensk

LITHUANIANS

Vistula

PRUSSIANS

Kolobrzeg

Wolin

Radgošč

Poznań

Gniezno

Plock

Poland

Oder

Bautzen

Wroclaw

Chernigov

Cracow

Czerwien

Volodymyr

Kiev

Pereiaslav

Dnieper

PECHENEGS

Przemyśl

Halych

Vienna

Nitra

Dniester

Esztergom

Székesfehérvár

Hungary

Zagreb

Kalocsa

PECHENEGS

Pannonia

Sea of Azov

Croatia

Split

Doclea
(Serbian Kgdm)

Ragusa
(Dubrovnik)

Duklja

Danube

Black Sea

Adriatic Sea

Bari

Serdica

Preslav

Odessos

Brindisi

Dyrrhachium

Philippopolis

Byzantine Empire

land from still impoverished peasants as yet untouched by the economic upswing. In his *Novel* (New Law) of 934, Emperor Romanus I Lecapenus (*r.*920-944) bewailed the "intrusion" of the rich

> into a village or hamlet for the sake of a sale, gift, or inheritance.... For the domination of these persons has increased the great hardship of the poor ... [and] will cause no little harm to the commonwealth unless the present legislation puts an end to it first. For the settlement of the population demonstrates the great benefit of its function—contribution of taxes and fulfillment of military obligations—which will be completely lost should the common people disappear.[2]

Map 4.3 (facing page): Kievan Rus, *c.*1050

The *dynatoi* also made military men their clients (even if they were not themselves military men) and often held positions in government. The Dalasseni family was fairly typical of this group. The founder of the family was an army leader and governor of Antioch at the end of the tenth century. One of his sons, Theophylact, became governor of "Iberia"—not Spain but rather a theme on the very eastern edge of the empire. Another, Constantine, inherited his father's position at Antioch. With estates scattered throughout Anatolia and a network of connections to other powerful families, the Dalasseni at times could defy the emperor and even coordinate rebellions against him. From the end of the tenth century, imperial control had to contend with the decentralizing forces of provincial *dynatoi* such as these. But the emperors were not dethroned, and a man like Basil II could triumph over the families that challenged his reign to emerge even stronger than before.

The rise of the provincial aristocracy and the prestige of the soldier emperors worked a change in Byzantine culture: from civilian to military ideals. The emperor had long ceased to be "declared" by his troops; but in the eleventh century artists insisted on portraying the emperor hoisted on a shield, symbol of military power. Military saints, such as George, became increasingly popular, especially in their roles as arms-wielding knights on horseback. An epic poem, *Digenis Akritis*, begun in the tenth century and probably put into its final form in the twelfth, depicts Digenis Akritis, a twin-blooded hero (half Greek, half Muslim), winning single-handed battles on the Byzantine frontier.

The Formation of Rus

Digenis plied his trade in Anatolia, but his talents would have served equally well to the north. There, well before the ninth century, fur traders from Scandinavia—in the

West known as Vikings—had settled east of the Gulf of Finland, in the regions of Lake Ladoga and Lake Ilmen (see Maps 4.3 and 4.5). Once settled, they took advantage of river networks and other trade routes that led as far south as Iraq and as far west as Austria. Other peoples in the region were doing the same, above all the Khazars, whose powerful state straddling the Black and Caspian Seas dominated part of the silk road. (See Map 3.2 on p. 109 for the location of the Khazar Empire.) A Turkic-speaking group whose elites converted to Judaism in the ninth century, the Khazars were ruled by a khagan, much like the Avars and the Bulgars. Scandinavians had no khagans, but they were influenced enough by Khazar culture to adopt the title for the ruler of their own fledgling ninth-century state at Novgorod, the first Rus polity.

Soon northern Rus had an affiliate in the south—in the region of Kiev—very close to the Khazars, to whom it likely at first paid tribute. While on occasion attacking both Khazars and Byzantines, Rus rulers saw their greatest advantage in good relations with the Byzantines, who wanted their fine furs, wax, honey, and—especially—slaves. In the course of the tenth century, with the blessing of the Byzantines, Rus brought the Khazar Empire to its knees.

Nurtured through trade and military agreements, good relations between Rus and Byzantium were sealed through religious conversion. In the mid-tenth century quite a few Christians lived in Rus (indeed, one Rus princess converted, calling herself Helena, after Constantine's mother). But the conversion of Rus to Christianity was ultimately the work of Vladimir (r.c.978-1015). Ruler of Rus by force of conquest (though from a princely family), Vladimir was anxious to court the elites of both Novgorod and Kiev. He did so through wars with surrounding peoples that brought him and his troops plunder and tribute—but never enough to satisfy. Losing faith in the traditional gods, Vladimir sought something better. In 988, wooed by the Byzantines, he adopted the Byzantine form of Christianity, took the name "Basil" in honor of Emperor Basil II, and married Anna, the emperor's sister. Christianization of the general population seems to have followed quickly. In any event, the *Russian Primary Chronicle*, a twelfth-century text based in part on earlier materials, reported that under Vladimir's son Yaroslav the Wise (r.1019-1054), "the Christian faith was fruitful and multiplied, while the number of monks increased, and new monasteries came into being."[3]

Vladimir's conversion was part of a larger movement of the tenth and eleventh centuries in which most of the remaining non-monotheistic peoples of the western Eurasian land mass adopted one of the four dominant monotheisms: Islam, Roman Catholicism, Byzantine Orthodoxy, or Judaism. Given its geographic location, it was anyone's guess which way Rus would go. On its western flank was Poland, where in 966, Mieszko I (r.963-992), leader of the tribe known as the Polanians, accepted baptism into the Roman Catholic faith. Eventually (in 991) he placed his realm under the protection of the pope. The experience of Hungary, just south of Poland, was similar: there Géza (*r.c.*972-997) converted to Roman Catholicism and, according to a potent legend, his son, Stephen I (*r.*997-1038), accepted a royal crown from the pope in the year 1000 or 1001. Further north the Scandinavians were also turning to Catholic Christianity: the king of the Danes, for example, was baptized around 960. But to the east Rus had other models: the Khazars, as we have seen, were Jewish; the Volga Bulgars converted to Islam in the early tenth century. Why, then, did Vladimir choose the Byzantine form of Christianity? Perhaps because he could drive the hardest bargain with Basil, who badly needed troops from Rus for his Varangian Guard.

That momentary decision left lasting consequences. Rus, ancestor of Russia, became the heir of the Byzantine church, customs, art, and political ideology. Choosing Christianity linked Russia to the West, but choosing the Byzantine form guaranteed that Russia would always stand apart from Western Europe.

DIVISION AND DEVELOPMENT IN THE ISLAMIC WORLD

While at Byzantium the forces of decentralization were feeble, they carried the day in the Islamic world. Where once the caliph at Baghdad or Samarra could boast collecting taxes from Kabul (today in Afghanistan) to Benghazi (today in Libya), in the eleventh century a bewildering profusion of regional groups and dynasties divided the Islamic world. Yet this was in general a period of prosperity and intellectual blossoming.

The Emergence of Regional Powers

The Muslim conquest had never eliminated all local powers or regional affiliations. It had simply papered over them. While the Umayyad and Abbasid caliphates remained strong, they imposed their rule through their governors and army. But when the caliphate became weak, as it did in the tenth and eleventh centuries, old and new regional interests came to the fore.

A glance at a map of the Islamic world *c.*1000 (Map 4.4) shows, from east to west, the main new groups that emerged: the Samanids, Buyids, Hamdanids, Fatimids, and Zirids. But the map hides the many territories dominated by smaller independent rulers. North of the Fatimid Caliphate, al-Andalus had a parallel history. Its Umayyad ruler took the title of caliph in 929, but in the eleventh century, he too was unable to stave off political fragmentation.

The key cause of the weakness of the Abbasid caliphate was lack of revenue. When landowners, governors, or recalcitrant military leaders in the various regions of the Islamic world refused to pay taxes into the treasury, the caliphs had to rely on the rich farmland of Iraq, long a stable source of income. But a deadly revolt lasting from 869 to 883 by the Zanj—black slaves from sub-Saharan Africa who had been put to work to turn marshes into farmland—devastated the Iraqi economy. Although the revolt was put down and the head of its leader was "displayed on a spear mounted in front of [the winning general] on a barge," there was no chance for recovery.[4] In the tenth century the Qaramita (sometimes called the "Carmathians"), a sect of Shi'ites based in Arabia, found Iraq easy prey. The result was decisive: the caliphs could not pay their troops. New men—military leaders with their own armies and titles like "commander of commanders"—took the reins of power. They preserved the Abbasid line, but they reduced the caliph's political authority to nothing.

The new rulers represented groups that had long awaited their new power. The Buyids, for example, belonged to ancient warrior tribes from the mountains of Iran. Even in the tenth century, most were relatively new converts to Islam. Bolstered by long-festering local discontent, one of them became "commander of commanders" in 945. Thereafter, the Buyids, with the help from their own Turkish mercenaries,

Map 4.4: Fragmentation of the Islamic World, *c.*1000

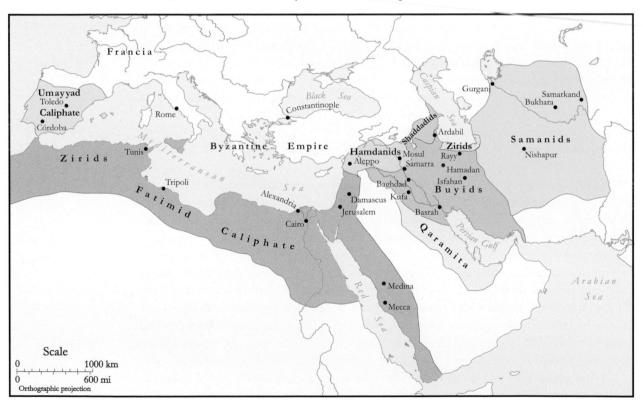

dominated the region south of the Caspian Sea, including Baghdad (once again the home of the caliphs) itself. Yet already by the end of the tenth century, their own power was challenged by still more local men, in a political process—the progressive regionalization and fragmentation of power—echoed elsewhere in the Islamic world and in parts of Western Europe as well.

The most important of the new regional rulers were the Fatimids. They, like the Qaramita (and, increasingly in the course of time, the Buyids), were Shi'ites, taking their name from Muhammad's daughter Fatimah, wife of Ali. The Fatimid leader claimed to be not only the true *imam*, descendant of Ali, but also the *mahdi*, the "divinely guided" messiah, come to bring justice on earth. Because of this, the Fatimids were proclaimed "caliphs" by their followers—the true "successors" of the Prophet. (See the list of Fatimid caliphs on p. 363.) Allying with the Berbers in North Africa, the Fatimids established themselves as rulers by 909 in what is today Tunisia and Libya. Within a half-century they had moved eastward (largely abandoning the Maghreb to the Zirids), to rule Egypt, southern Syria, and the western edge of the Arabian Peninsula.

The Fatimids looked east rather than west because the east was rich and because the west was dominated by Sunnis, hostile to Shi'ite rule. The most important of the Sunni rulers were the Umayyads at Córdoba. Abd al-Rahman III (r.912–961) took the title caliph in 929 as a counterweight to the Fatimids, although he claimed to rule only all of al-Andalus, not the whole Islamic world. An active military man backed by an army made up mainly of Slavic slaves, al-Rahman defeated his rivals and imposed his rule not only on southern Iberia (as his predecessors had done) but also in northern regions (near the Christian kingdoms) and in the Maghreb. Under al-Rahman and his immediate successors, al-Andalus became a powerful centralized state. But regional Islamic rulers there worked to undermine the authority of the Umayyads, so that between 1009 and 1031 bitter civil war undid the dynasty's power. After 1031, al-Andalus was split into small emirates called *taifas*, ruled by local strongmen.

Thus in the Islamic world, far more decisively than at Byzantium, newly powerful regional rulers came to the fore. Nor did the fragmentation of power end at the regional level. To pay their armies, rulers often resorted to granting their commanders *iqta*—lands and villages from which the *iqta*-holder was expected to gather revenues and pay their troops. As we shall see, this was a bit like the Western institution of the fief. It meant that even minor commanders could act as local governors, tax-collectors, and military leaders. But there was a major difference between this institution and the system of fiefs and vassals in the West: while vassals were generally tied to one region and one lord, the troops under Islamic local commanders were often foreigners and former slaves, unconnected to any particular place and easily wooed by rival commanders.

At Byzantium the ascendancy of the military classes led poets and artists to praise warriors in general. In the Islamic world as well, a few writers proudly portrayed old Persian and Bedouin heroes as model fighting men. In the *Shahnama* (*Book of Kings*) by the poet Firdawsi (*c*.935–*c*.1020), the hero slays demons and saves kings. But on the whole, poets and writers continued to laud "civilian" life and to embroider the old themes of *adab* literature.

Cultural Unity, Religious Polarization

In fact, the emergence of local strongmen meant not the end of Arab court culture but a multiplicity of courts, each attempting to out-do one another in brilliant artistic, scientific, theological, and literary productions. Consider Cairo, for example, which was founded by the Fatimids. Already by 1000 it was a huge urban complex. Imitating the Abbasids, the Fatimid caliphs built mosques and palaces, fostered court ceremonials, and turned Cairo into a center of intellectual life. One of the Fatimid caliphs, al-Hakim (*r*.996–1021), founded the *dar al-ilm*, a sort of theological college plus public library.

Even more impressive was the Umayyad court at Córdoba, the wealthiest and showiest city of the West. It boasted 70 public libraries in addition to the caliph's private library of perhaps 400,000 books. The Córdoban Great Mosque was a center for scholars from the rest of the Islamic world (the caliph paid their salaries), while nearly 30 free schools were set up throughout the city.

Córdoba was noteworthy not only because of the brilliance of its intellectual life but also because of the role women played in it. Elsewhere in the Islamic world there were certainly a few unusual women associated with cultural and scholarly life. But at Córdoba this was a general phenomenon: women not only were doctors, teachers, and librarians but also worked as copyists for the many books so widely in demand.

Male scholars were, however, everywhere the norm, and they moved easily from court to court. Ibn Sina (980–1037), known to the West as Avicenna, began his career serving the ruler at Bukhara in Central Asia, and then moved westward to Gurganj, Rayy, and Hamadan before ending up for thirteen years at the court of Isfahan in Iran. Sometimes in favor and sometimes decidedly not so (he was even briefly imprisoned), he nevertheless managed to study and practice medicine and write numerous books on the natural sciences and philosophy. His pioneering systematization of Aristotle laid the foundations of future philosophical thought in the field of logic:

> There is a method by which one can discover the unknown from what is known. It is the science of logic. Through it one may know how to obtain

the unknown from the known. This science is also concerned with the different kinds of valid, invalid, and near valid inferences.[5]

Despite its political disunity, then, the Islamic world of the tenth and eleventh centuries remained in many ways an integrated culture. This was partly due to the model of intellectual life fostered by the Abbasids, which even in decline was copied by the new rulers, as we have just seen. It was also due to the common Arabic language, the glue that bound the astronomer at Córdoba to the philosopher at Cairo. Finally, integration was the result of open trade networks. With no national barriers to commerce and few regulations, merchants regularly dealt in far-flung, various, and sometimes exotic goods. From England came tin, while salt and gold were imported from Timbuktu in west-central Africa; from Russia came amber, gold, and copper; slaves were wrested from sub-Saharan Africa, the Eurasian steppes, and Slavic regions.

Although Muslims dominated these trade networks, other groups were involved in commerce as well. We happen to know a good deal about one Jewish community living at Fustat, about two miles south of Cairo. It observed the then-common custom of depositing for eventual ritual burial all worn-out papers containing the name of God. For good measure, the Jews in this community included everything written in Hebrew letters: legal documents, fragments of sacred works, marriage contracts, doctors' prescriptions, and so on. By chance, the materials that they left in their *geniza* (depository) at Fustat were preserved rather than buried. These sources reveal a cosmopolitan, middle-class society. Many were traders, for Fustat was the center of a vast and predominately Jewish trade network that stretched from al-Andalus to India. Consider the Tustari brothers, Jewish merchants from southern Iran. By the early eleventh century, the brothers had established a flourishing business in Egypt. Informal family networks offered them many of the same advantages as branch offices: friends and family in Iran shipped the Tustaris fine textiles to sell in Egypt, while they exported Egyptian fabrics back to Iran.

Only Islam, ironically, pulled Islamic culture apart. In the tenth century the split between the Sunnis and Shiʿites widened to a chasm. At Baghdad, al-Mufid (*d.*1022) and others turned Shiʿism into a partisan ideology that insisted on publicly cursing the first two caliphs, turning the tombs of Ali and his family into objects of veneration, and creating an Alid caliph by force. Small wonder that the Abbasid caliphs soon became ardent spokesmen for Sunni Islam, which developed in turn its own public symbols. Many of the new dynasties—the Fatimids and the Qaramita especially—took advantage of the newly polarized faith to bolster their power.

THE WEST: FRAGMENTATION AND RESILIENCE

Fragmentation was the watchword in Western Europe in many parts of the shattered Carolingian Empire. Historians speak of "France," "Germany," and "Italy" in this period as a shorthand for designating broad geographical areas. But there were no national states, only regions with more or less clear borders and rulers with more or less authority. In some places—in parts of "France," for example—regions as small as a few square miles were under the control of different lords who acted, in effect, as independent rulers. Yet this same period saw both England and Scotland become unified kingdoms. And to the east, in Saxony, a powerful royal dynasty, the Ottonians, emerged to rule an empire stretching from the North Sea to Rome.

Map 4.5 (facing page): Viking, Muslim, and Hungarian Invasions, Ninth and Tenth Centuries

The Last Invaders of the West

Three groups invaded Western Europe during the ninth and tenth centuries: the Vikings, the Muslims, and the Magyars (called Hungarians by the rest of Europe). (See Map 4.5.) In the short run, they wreaked havoc on land and people. In the long run, they were absorbed into the European population and became constituents of a newly prosperous and aggressive European civilization.

THE VIKINGS

At the same time as they made their forays into Russia, the Vikings were raiding the coasts of France, England, Scotland, and Ireland. In their longships—often traveling as families with husbands, wives, children, and slaves—they crossed the Atlantic, making themselves at home in Iceland and Greenland and, in about 1000, touching on the North American mainland. They settled as well in Ireland, Scotland, England, and Normandy (giving their name to the region: Norman = Northman, or Viking).

In Ireland, where the Vikings settled in the east and south, the newcomers added their own claims to rule an island already fragmented among four or five competing dynasties. In Scotland, however, in the face of Norse settlements in the north and west, the natives drew together under kings who—in a process we have seen elsewhere—allied themselves with churchmen and other powerful local leaders. Cináed mac Ailpín (Kenneth I MacAlpin) (*d.*858) established a hereditary dynasty of kings that ruled over two hitherto separate native peoples. By *c.*900, the separate identities were gone, and most people in *Alba*, the nucleus of the future Scotland, shared a common sense of being Scottish.

England underwent a similar process of unification. Initially divided into small

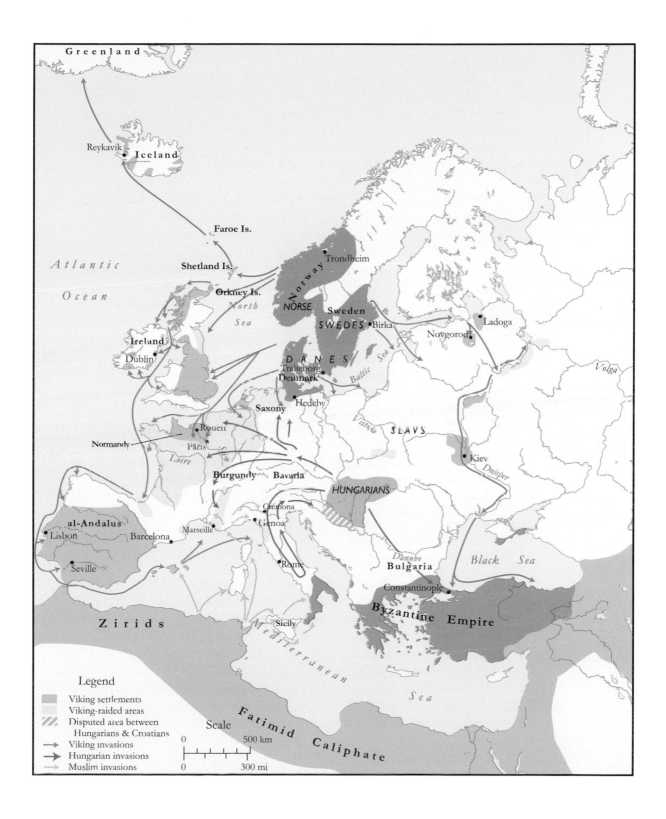

Greenland

Reykavik · **Iceland**

Atlantic

Ocean

Faroe Is.

Shetland Is.

North
Sea

Orkney Is.

Ireland
Dublin

Norway
Trondheim ·

NORSE

Sweden
SWEDES · Birka

Ladoga

Novgorod

Volga

D A N E S
Trelleborg
Denmark
· Hedeby

Saxony

Baltic Sea

Vistula

S L A V S

Rouen ·
Normandy
Paris ·
Loire
Seine

Burgundy **Bavaria**

HUNGARIANS

· Kiev
Dnieper

al-Andalus
· Lisbon   Barcelona

Marseille ·

Crémona ·
Genoa ·

· Rome

Danube

Bulgaria

Black   Sea

· Seville

Z i r i d s

Sicily

Constantinople ·

Byzantine   Empire

Mediterranean

Sea

F a t i m i d   C a l i p h a t e

Legend

▨ Viking settlements
▨ Viking-raided areas
▨ Disputed area between
   Hungarians & Croatians
→ Viking invasions
→ Hungarian invasions
→ Muslim invasions

Scale

0   500 km

0   300 mi

competing kingdoms, it was weak prey in the face of invasion. By the end of the ninth century, the Vikings were plowing fields in eastern England and living in accordance with their own laws. In Wessex, the southernmost English kingdom, King Alfred the Great (r.871–899) bought time and peace by paying a tribute with the income from a new tax, later called the Danegeld. (It eventually became the basis of a relatively lucrative taxation system in England.) Even more importantly, in 878 he mustered an army and, as his biographer, Asser, put it,

> gained the victory through God's will. He destroyed the Vikings with great slaughter, and pursued those who fled as far as the stronghold, hacking them down; he seized everything which he found outside the stronghold—men (whom he killed immediately), horses, and cattle—and boldly made camp in front of the gates of the Viking stronghold with all his army. When he had been there for fourteen days the Vikings, thoroughly terrified by hunger, cold and fear, and in the end by despair, sought peace.[6]

Thereafter the pressure of invasion eased as Alfred reorganized his army, set up strongholds of his own (called *burhs*), and created a fleet of ships—a real navy. An uneasy stability was achieved, with the Vikings dominating the east of England and Alfred and his successors gaining control over most of the rest.

On the Continent, too, the invaders came to stay, above all in Normandy. The new inhabitants of the region were integrated into the political system when, in 911, their leader Rollo converted to Christianity and received Normandy as a duchy from the Frankish king Charles the Simple (or Straightforward). Although many of the Normans adopted sedentary ways, some of their descendants in the early eleventh century ventured to the Mediterranean, where they established themselves as rulers of petty principalities in southern Italy. By mid-century they had their eyes on Sicily.

MUSLIMS

Sicily, once Byzantine, was the rich and fertile plum of the conquests achieved by the Muslim invaders of the ninth and tenth centuries. That they took the island attests to the power of a new Muslim navy developed by the dynasty that preceded the Fatimids in Ifriqiya. After 909, Sicily came under Fatimid rule, but by mid-century it was controlled by independent Islamic princes, and Muslim immigrants were swelling the population.

Elsewhere the new Muslim presence in western Europe was more ephemeral. In the first half of the tenth century, Muslim raiders pillaged southern France, northern Italy, and the Alpine passes. But these were quick expeditions, largely attacks on churches and monasteries. Some of these Muslims did establish themselves at La

Garde-Freinet, in Provence, becoming landowners in the region and lords of Christian serfs. They even hired themselves out as occasional fighters for the wars that local Christian aristocrats were waging against one another. But they made the mistake of capturing for ransom the holiest man of his era, Abbot Majolus of Cluny. Outraged, the local aristocracy finally came together and ousted the Muslims from their midst.

HUNGARIANS

By contrast, a new kingdom was created by the Hungarians. ("Magyar" was and remains their name for themselves, but the rest of Europe called them "Hungarians," from the Slavonic for "Onogurs," a people already settled in the Danube basin in the eighth and ninth centuries.) The Hungarians were originally nomads who raised (and rode) horses, speaking a language unrelated to any other in Europe (except Finnish). Known as effective warriors, they were employed by Arnulf, king of the East Franks (887–899), during his war against the Moravians and by the Byzantine emperor Leo VI (886–912) during his struggle against the Bulgars. In 894, taking advantage of their position, the Hungarians conquered much of the Danube basin for themselves.

From there, for over fifty years, the Hungarians raided into Germany, Italy, and even southern France. At the same time, however, they worked for various western rulers. Until 937 they spared Bavaria, for example, because they were allies of its duke. Gradually they made the transition from nomads to farmers, and their polity coalesced into the Kingdom of Hungary. This is no doubt a major reason for the end of their attacks. At the time, however, the cessation of their raids was widely credited to the German king Otto I (r.936–973), who won a major victory over a Hungarian marauding party at the battle of Lechfeld in 955.

Polytheists at the time of their entry into the West, the majority of the Hungarians were peasants, initially specializing in herding but soon busy cultivating vineyards, orchards, and grains. Above them was a warrior class, and above the warriors were the elites, whose richly furnished graves reveal the importance of weapons, jewelry, and horses to this society. Originally organized into tribes led by dukes, by the mid-tenth century the Hungarians recognized one ruling house—that of Géza.

Determined to put his power on a new footing, Géza accepted baptism, probably by a bishop from Germany, and pledged to convert all his subjects. His son, Stephen I, consolidated the change to Christianity: he built churches and monasteries, and required everyone to attend church on Sundays. Establishing his authority as sole ruler, Stephen had himself crowned king in the year 1000 (or possibly 1001). Around the same time, "governing our monarchy by the will of God and emulating both ancient and modern caesars [emperors]," he issued a code of law that put his kingdom in step with other European powers.[7]

Public Power and Private Relationships

The invasions left new political arrangements in their wake. Unlike the Byzantines and Muslims, Western rulers had no mercenaries and no salaried officials. They commanded others by ensuring personal loyalty. The Carolingian kings had had their *fideles*—their faithful men. Tenth-century rulers were even more dependent on ties of dependency: they needed their "men" (*homines*), their "vassals" (*vassalli*). Whatever the term, all were armed retainers who fought for a lord. Sometimes these subordinates held land from their lord, either as a reward for their military service or as an inheritance for which services were due. The term for such an estate, fief (*feodum*), gave historians the word "feudalism" to describe the social and economic system created by the relationships among lords, vassals, and fiefs. Some recent historians argue that the word "feudalism" has been used in too many different and contradictory ways to mean anything at all: is it a mode of exploiting the land that involves lords and serfs? A state of anarchy and lawlessness? Or a state of ordered gradations of power, from the king on down? All of these definitions have been given. Ordinarily we may dispense with the word feudalism, though it can be very useful as a "fuzzy category" when contrasting, for example, the political, social, and economic organization of Antiquity with that of the Middle Ages.

LORDS AND VASSALS

The key to tenth- and eleventh-century society was personal dependency. This took many forms. Of the three traditional "orders" recognized by writers in the ninth through eleventh centuries—those who pray (the *oratores*), those who fight (the *bellatores*), and those who work (the *laboratores*)—the top two were free. The pray-ers (the monks) and the fighters (the nobles and their lower-class cousins, the knights) participated in prestigious kinds of subordination, whether as vassals, lords, or both. Indeed, they were usually both: a typical warrior was lord of several vassals and the vassal of another lord. Monasteries normally had vassals to fight for them, while their abbots in turn were vassals of a king or other lord. At the low end of the social scale, poor vassals looked to their lords to feed, clothe, house, and arm them. At the upper end, vassals looked to their lords to enrich them with still more fiefs.

Some women were vassals, and some were lords (or, rather, "ladies," the female counterpart). Many upper-class laywomen participated in the society of warriors and monks as wives and mothers of vassals and lords and as landowners in their own right. Others entered convents and became *oratores* themselves. Through its abbess or a man standing in for her, a convent was itself often the "lord" of vassals.

Vassalage was voluntary and public. In some areas, it was marked by a ceremony:

the vassal-to-be knelt and, placing his hands between the hands of his lord, said, "I promise to be your man." This act, known as "homage," was followed by the promise of "fealty"—fidelity, trust, and service—which the vassal swore with his hand on relics or a Bible. Then the vassal and the lord kissed. In an age when many people could not read, a public moment such as this represented a visual and verbal contract, binding the vassal and lord together with mutual obligations to help one another. On the other hand, these obligations were rarely spelled out, and a lord with many vassals, or a vassal with many lords, needed to satisfy numerous conflicting claims. "I am a loser only because of my loyalty to you," Hugh of Lusignan told his lord, William of Aquitaine, after his expectations for reward were continually disappointed.[8]

LORDS AND PEASANTS

At the lowest end of the social scale were those who worked: the peasants. In many regions of Europe, as power fell into the hands of local rulers, the distinction between "free" and "unfree" peasants began to blur; many peasants simply became "serfs," dependents of lords. This was a heavy dependency, without prestige or honor. It was hereditary rather than voluntary: no serf did homage or fealty to his lord; no serf and lord kissed.

Indeed, the upper classes barely noticed the peasants—except as sources of labor and revenue. In the tenth century, the three-field system became more prevalent, and the heavy moldboard plows that could turn wet, clayey northern soils came into wider use. Such plows could not work around fences, and they were hard to turn: thus was produced the characteristic "look" of medieval agriculture—long, furrowed strips in broad, open fields. (Peasants knew very well which strips were "theirs" and which belonged to their neighbors. See the late medieval lands of Toury in Map 7.7 on p. 298.) A team of oxen was normally used to pull the plow, but horses (more efficient than oxen) were sometimes substituted. The result was surplus food and a better standard of living for nearly everyone.

In search of still greater profits, some lords lightened the dues and services of peasants temporarily to allow them to open up new lands by draining marshes and cutting down forests. Other lords converted dues and labor services into money payments, providing themselves with ready cash. Peasants benefited from these rents as well because their payments were fixed despite inflation. As the prices of agricultural products went up, peasants became small-scale entrepreneurs, selling their chickens and eggs at local markets and reaping a profit.

In the eleventh century, and increasingly so in the twelfth, peasant settlements gained boundaries and focus: they became real villages. (For the example of Toury, see Map 7.6 on p. 297.) The parish church often formed the center, around which was the cemetery. Then, normally crowded right onto the cemetery itself, were the houses, barns, animals, and tools of the living peasants. Boundary markers—sometimes simple stones, at other times real fortifications—announced not only the physical limit of the village but also its sense of community. This derived from very practical concerns: peasants needed to share oxen or horses to pull their plows; they were all dependent on the village craftsmen to fix their wheels or shoe their horses.

Variety was the hallmark of peasant society for this period of history across the regions of Europe. In Saxony and other parts of Germany free peasants prevailed. In France and England most were serfs. In Italy peasants ranged from small independent landowners to leaseholders; most were both, owning a parcel in one place and leasing another nearby.

Where the power of kings was weak, peasant obligations became part of a larger system of local rule. As landlords consolidated their power over their manors, they collected not only dues and services but also fees for the use of their flour mills, bake houses, and breweries. In some regions—parts of France and in Catalonia, for example—some lords built castles and exercised the power of the "ban": the right to collect taxes, hear court cases, levy fines, and muster men for defense. These lords were "castellans." Guillem Guifred, a castellan in Catalonia (and a bishop, too, for good measure), for example, received "half of the revenue of the courts [at Sanahuja], without deceit. From the market, half.... Of the oven, half. Of rights on minting, half."[9]

Warriors and Bishops

Although the developments described here did not occur everywhere simultaneously (and in some places hardly at all), in the end the social, political, and cultural life of the West came to be dominated by landowners who saw themselves as both military men and regional leaders. These men and their armed retainers shared a common lifestyle, living together, eating in the lord's great hall, listening to bards sing of military exploits, hunting for recreation, competing with one another in military games. They fought in groups as well—as cavalry, riding on horses. In the month of May, when the grasses were high enough for their mounts to forage, the war season began. To be sure, there were powerful vassals who lived on their own fiefs and hardly ever saw their lord—except for perhaps forty days out of the year, when they owed him military duty. But they themselves were lords of knightly vassals who were not married and who lived and ate and hunted with them.

The marriage bed, so important to the medieval aristocracy from the start, now took on new meaning. Long before, in the seventh and eighth centuries, aristocratic families had been large, diffuse, loosely organized kin groups. (Historians often use the German word *Sippe*—clan—to refer to them.) These families were not tied to any particular estate, for they had numerous estates, scattered all about. With wealth enough to go around, the rich practiced partible inheritance, giving land (though not in equal amounts) to all of their sons and daughters. The Carolingians "politicized" these family relations. As some men were elevated to positions of dazzling power, they took the opportunity to pick and choose their "family members," narrowing the family circle. They also became more conscious of their male line, favoring sons over daughters. In the eleventh century, family definitions tightened even further. The claims of one son, often the eldest, overrode all else; to him went the family inheritance. (This is called "primogeniture"; but there were regions in which the youngest son was privileged, and there were also areas in which more equitable inheritance practices continued in place.) The heir in the new system traced his lineage only through the male line, backward through his father and forward through his own eldest son.

What happened to the other sons? Some of them became knights, others monks. Nor should we forget that some became bishops. In many ways the interests of bishops and lay nobles were similar: they were men of property, lords of vassals, and faithful to patrons, such as kings, who appointed them to their posts. In some cities, bishops wielded the powers of a count or duke. We have seen that Bishop Guillem Guifred was a castellan at Sanahuja—and that was only one of his properties. Nevertheless, bishops were also "pastors," spiritual leaders charged with shepherding their flock. The "flock" included the priests and monks in the diocese, a district that gained clear definition in the eleventh century. The flock also included the laity, among them the very warriors from whose class the bishops came.

As episcopal power expanded and was clarified in the course of the eleventh century, some bishops in southern France sought to control the behavior of the knightly class through a movement called the "Peace of God," which developed apace from 989 onwards. Their forum was the regional church council, where the bishops galvanized popular opinion, attracting both lords and peasants to their gatherings. There, drawing upon bits and pieces of defunct Carolingian legislation, the bishops declared the Peace, and knights took oaths to observe it. At Bourges a particularly enthusiastic archbishop took the oath himself: "I Aimon ... will wholeheartedly attack those who steal ecclesiastical property, those who provoke pillage, those who oppress monks, nuns, and clerics."[10] In the Truce of God, which soon supplemented the Peace, warfare between armed men was prohibited from Lent to Easter, while at other times of the year it was forbidden on Sunday (because that was the Lord's Day), on Saturday (because that was a reminder of Holy Saturday), on Friday (because it symbolized Good Friday), and on Thursday (because it stood for Holy Thursday).

The bishops who promulgated the Peace were ambivalent about warriors. There were the bad ones who broke the Peace, but there were also others who were righteous upholders of church law. Soon the Peace and Truce were taken up by powerful lay rulers, eager to sanctify their own warfare and control that of others.

The new importance of the fighting man in the West gave rise to a military ethos mirrored in art and literature. In *The Battle of Maldon* the hero, Byrhtnoth, inspires the English to face the Danes:

Then Byrhtnoth began to martial his men.
He rode about, issuing instructions
As to how they should stand firm, not yielding an inch,
And how they should tightly grip their shields
Forgetting their qualms and pangs of fear.[11]

The parallels with developments in the Byzantine and Islamic worlds are striking: everywhere a military class, more or less local, rose to power.

Equally important, however, are the differences: in no place but Europe were overlapping lordships the rule. Nowhere else was fealty so important. Nowhere else were rural enclaves the normal centers of power.

CITIES AND MERCHANTS

Though ruralism was the norm in the West, it was not invariable. In Italy the power structure reflected, if feebly, the political organization of ancient Rome. Whereas in France great landlords built their castles in the countryside, in Italy they often constructed their family seats within the walls of cities. From these perches the nobles, both lay and religious, dominated the *contado*, the rural area around the city.

In Italy, most peasants were renters, paying cash to urban landowners. Peasants depended on city markets to sell their surplus goods; their customers were not only bishops and nobles but also middle-class shopkeepers, artisans, and merchants. At Milan, for example, the merchants were prosperous enough to own houses in both the city center and the *contado*.

Rome, although exceptional in size, was in some ways a typical Italian city. Large and powerful families built their castles within its walls and controlled the churches and monasteries in the vicinity. The population depended on local producers for their food, and merchants brought their wares to sell within its walls. Yet Rome was special apart from its size: it was the "see"—the seat—of the pope, the most important bishop in the West. The papacy did not control the church, but it had great prestige, and powerful families at Rome fought to place one of their sons at its head.

Outside of Italy cities were less prevalent in the West. Yet even so we can see the rise of a new mercantile class. This was true less in the heartland of the old Carolingian empire than on its fringes. In the north, England, northern Germany, Denmark, and the Low Countries bathed in a sea of silver coins; commercial centers such as

Haithabu reached their grandest extent in the mid-tenth century. Here merchants bought and sold slaves, honey, furs, wax, and pirates' plunder. Haithabu was a city of wood, but a very rich one indeed.

In the south of Europe, beyond the Pyrenees, Catalonia was equally commercialized, but in a different way. It imitated the Islamic world of al-Andalus (which was, in effect, in its backyard). The counts of Barcelona minted gold coins just like those at Córdoba. The villagers around Barcelona soon got used to selling their wares for money, and some of them became prosperous. They married into the aristocracy, moved to Barcelona to become city leaders, and lent money to ransom prisoners of the many wars waged to their south.

New-style Kingships

In such a world, what did kings do? At the least, they stood for tradition; they served as symbols of legitimacy. At the most, they united kingdoms and maintained a measure of law and order. (See Map 4.6.)

England

Alfred was a king of the second sort. In the face of the Viking invasions, he developed new mechanisms of royal government, creating institutions that became the foundation of strong English kingship. We have already seen his military reforms: the system of *burhs* and the creation of a navy. Alfred was interested in religious and intellectual reforms as well. These were closely linked in his mind: the causes of England's troubles (in his view) were the sins — many due to ignorance — of its people. Alfred intended to educate "all free-born men." He brought scholars to his court and embarked on an ambitious program to translate key religious works from Latin into Anglo-Saxon (or Old English). This was the vernacular, the spoken language of the people. As Alfred wrote in his prose preface to the Anglo-Saxon translation of *The Pastoral Care* of Gregory the Great,

> I recalled how the Law was first composed in the Hebrew language, and thereafter, when the Greeks learned it, they translated it all into their own language, and all other books as well. And so too the Romans, after they had mastered them, translated them all through learned interpreters into their own language.... Therefore it seems better to me ... that we too should turn into the language that we can all understand certain books which are the most necessary for all men to know.[12]

Scale

0   500 km

0   300 mi

*North
Sea*

Scotland

*Atlantic
Ocean*

Ireland

England

Wales

• Durham

London

• Haithabu

N O R W A Y   S w e d e n

D e n m a r k

Frisia   S a x o n y
                          Magdeburg •
              Hildesheim •

Lower   • Cologne   G E R M A N
Lotharingia
                 Franconia
Flanders
Montreuil   Picardy   Bohemia
Ponthieu   Trier   Moravia
        Vermandois   Upper   • Worms
Beauvais   Lotharingia   K i n g d o m
Normandy Vexin   Alsace
          Paris • Troyes   Swabia   Bavaria
Brittany   Maine Île-de-France
          Blois
Anjou   Gatinais   Burgundy   Carinthia
    Touraine Auxerre •
          Nevers • Autun •
      Bourges •
Châteauroux •   Cluny •
          Kingdom
Aquitaine   of
                 Burgundy
Auvergne
                            I t a l y   Venice •
        Gevaudan   Venice •

Gascony   Marseille •

Santiago de Compostela •
                    Navarre
L e ó n   Aragon
          Castile   Barcelona
                 Barcelona •

I s l a m i c

T a i f a s

Córdoba •

B a l t i c
S e a

P o l a n d

H u n g a r y

C r o a t i a   Byzantine Empire

Doclea

A d r i a t i c
S e a

Toulouse

Corsica
(Pisan
c.1020)

Pisa •
          Patrimony of St. Peter
                    Spoleto
          Rome •   South Italian
                       principalities

Sardinia
(Pisan
c.1050)

M e d i t e r r a n e a n

S e a

Those "certain books" included the Psalter and writings by the Church Fathers—Gregory the Great and Saint Augustine—as well as Boethius. Soon Anglo-Saxon was being used in England not only for literature but for official administrative purposes as well, in royal "writs" that kings and queens directed to their officials. England was not alone in its esteem for the vernacular: in Ireland, too, the vernacular language was a written one. But the British Isles *were* unusual by the standards of Continental Europe, where Latin alone was the language of scholarship and writing.

As Alfred harried the Danes who were pushing south and westward, he gained recognition as king of all the English not under Viking rule. His law code, issued in the late 880s or early 890s, was the first by an English king since 695. Unlike earlier codes, which had been drawn up for each separate kingdom, Alfred's contained laws from and for all the English kingdoms in common. The king's inspiration was the Mosaic law of the Bible. Alfred believed that God had made a new covenant with the victors over the Vikings; as leader of his people, Alfred, like the Old Testament patriarch Moses, should issue a law for all.

His successors, beneficiaries of that covenant, rolled back the Viking rule in England. (See Genealogy 4.1: Alfred and His Progeny.) "Then the Norsemen made off in their nailed boats,/ Saddened survivors shamed in battle," wrote one poet about a battle lost by the Vikings in 937.[13] But, as we have seen, many Vikings remained. Converted to Christianity, their great men joined Anglo-Saxons to attend the English king at court. The whole kingdom was divided into districts called "shires" and "hundreds," and in each shire, the king's reeve—the sheriff—oversaw royal administration.

Alfred's grandson Edgar (r.c.959–975) commanded all the possibilities early medieval kingship offered. The sworn lord of all the great men of the kingdom, he also controlled appointments to the English church and sponsored monastic reform. In 973, following the Continental fashion, he was anointed. Master of *burhs* and army, Edgar asserted hegemony over many of the non-Anglo-Saxon rulers in Britain. He extended Alfred's legal reforms by proclaiming certain crimes—arson and theft—to be under royal jurisdiction.

From the point of view of control, however, Edgar had nowhere near the power over England that, say, Basil II had over Byzantium at about the same time. The *dynatoi* might sometimes chafe at the emperor's directives and rebel, but the emperor had his Varangian guard to put them down and an experienced, professional civil service to do his bidding. The king of England depended less on force and bureaucracy than on consensus. The great landowners adhered to the king because they found it in their interest to do so. When they did not, the kingdom easily fragmented, becoming prey to civil war. Disunity was exacerbated by new attacks from the Danes. One Danish king, Cnut (or Canute), even became king of England for a time (r.1016–1035). Yet under Cnut, English kingship did not change much. He kept intact much

Map 4.6 (facing page): Europe, c.1050

of the administrative, ecclesiastical, and military apparatus already established. By Cnut's time, Scandinavia had been Christianized and its traditions had largely merged with those of the rest of Europe. The Vikings were no longer an alien culture.

GERMANY

The king of Germany was as effective as the English king—and additionally worked with a much wider palette of territories, institutions, and possibilities. It is true that at first Germany seemed ready to disintegrate into duchies: five emerged in the late Carolingian period, each held by a military leader who exercised quasi-royal powers. But, in the face of their own quarrels and the threats of outside invaders, the dukes needed and wanted a strong king. With the death in 911 of the last Carolingian king in Germany, Louis the Child, they crowned one of themselves. Then, as attacks by the Hungarians increased, the dukes gave the royal title to their most powerful member,

Genealogy 4.1: Alfred and His Progeny

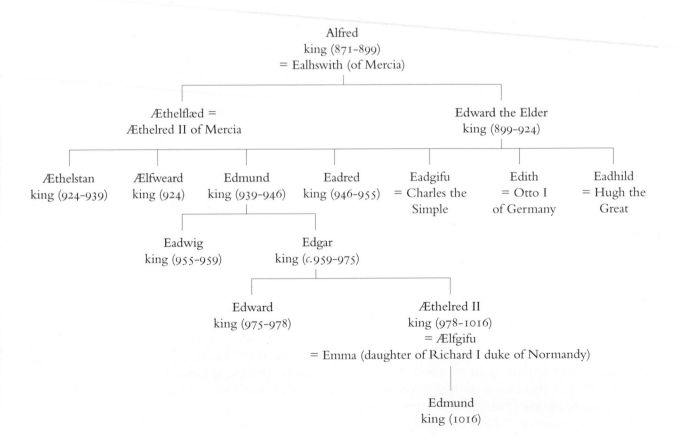

Alfred
king (871-899)
= Ealhswith (of Mercia)

Æthelflæd =
Æthelred II of Mercia

Edward the Elder
king (899-924)

Æthelstan
king (924-939)

Ælfweard
king (924)

Edmund
king (939-946)

Eadred
king (946-955)

Eadgifu
= Charles the
Simple

Edith
= Otto I
of Germany

Eadhild
= Hugh the
Great

Eadwig
king (955-959)

Edgar
king (c.959-975)

Edward
king (975-978)

Æthelred II
king (978-1016)
= Ælfgifu
= Emma (daughter of Richard I duke of Normandy)

Edmund
king (1016)

the duke of Saxony, Henry I (*r.*919-936), who proceeded to set up fortifications and reorganize his army, crowning his efforts with a major defeat of the Hungarians in 933.

Henry's son Otto I (*r.*936-973) defeated rival family members, rebellious dukes, and Slavic and Hungarian armies soon after coming to the throne. Through astute marriage alliances and appointments, he was eventually able to get his family members to head up all of the duchies. In 951, Otto marched into Italy and took the Lombard crown. He was thus king of Germany and Italy, and soon (in 962) he received the imperial crown that recognized his far-flung power. Both to himself and to contemporaries he recalled the greatness of Charlemagne. Meanwhile, Otto's victory at Lechfeld in 955 (see p. 155) ended the Hungarian threat. In the same year, Otto defeated a Slavic incursion, and for about a half-century the Slavs of central and eastern Europe came under German hegemony.

Victories such as these brought tribute, plum positions to disburse, and lands to give away, ensuring Otto a following among the great men of the realm. His successors,

Genealogy 4.2: The Ottonians

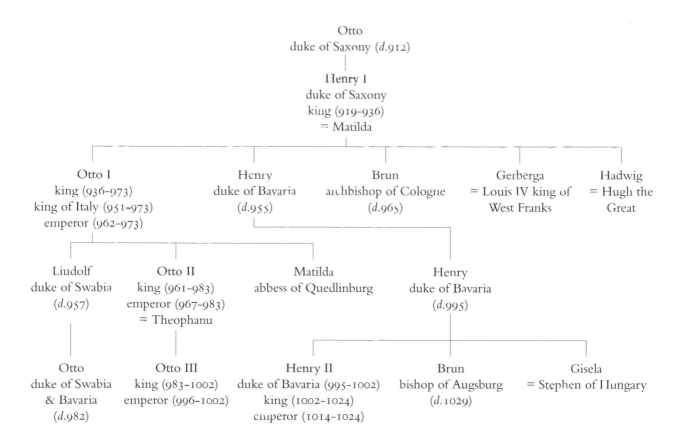

Otto II, Otto III—hence the dynastic name "Ottonians"—and Henry II, built on his achievements. (See Genealogy 4.2: The Ottonians.) Granted power by the magnates, they gave back in turn: they gave away lands and appointed their aristocratic supporters to duchies, counties, and bishoprics. Always, however, their decisions were tempered by hereditary claims and plenty of lobbying by influential men at court and at the great assemblies that met with the king to hammer out policies. The role of kings in filling bishoprics and archbishoprics was particularly important because, unlike counties and duchies, these positions could not be inherited. Otto I created a ribbon of new bishoprics in newly converted regions along his eastern border, endowing them with extensive lands and subjecting the local peasantry to episcopal overlordship. Throughout Germany bishops gained the power of the ban, with the right to collect revenues and call men to arms. Once the king chose the bishop (usually with at least the consent of the clergy of the cathedral over which he was to preside), he "invested" the new prelate in his post by participating in the ceremony that installed him into office. Bishop Thietmar of Merseburg, for example, reported on his own experience:

> The archbishop [Tagino of Magdeburg, Thietmar's sponsor] led me to Bishop Bruno's chapel [Bruno was the king's brother], where the king [Henry II] awaited him. After preparing for the celebration of the mass, he commended me into the hands of the king. I was elected by those who were present, and the king committed the pastoral office to me with the staff.[14]

With wealth coming in from their eastern tributaries, Italy, and the silver mines of Saxony (discovered in the time of Otto I), the Ottonians presided over a brilliant intellectual and artistic efflorescence. As in the Islamic world, much of this was dispersed; in Germany the centers of culture included the royal court, the great cathedral schools, and women's convents.

The most talented young men crowded the schools at episcopal courts at Trier, Cologne, Magdeburg, Worms, and Hildesheim. Honing their Latin, they studied classical authors such as Cicero and Horace as well as Scripture, while their episcopal teachers wrote histories, saints' lives, and works on canon law. One such was the *Decretum* (*c.*1020) by Burchard, bishop of Worms, a widely influential collection that (much like the compilations of *hadith* produced about a century before in the Islamic world) winnowed out the least authoritative canons and systematized the contradictory ones. The men at the cathedral schools were largely in training to become courtiers, administrators, and bishops themselves.

Bishops appreciated art as well as scholarship. Some, such as Egbert, archbishop of Trier (*r.*977–993), patronized artists and fine craftsworkers. Plate 4.1, an illustration of the Raising of Lazarus from the Egbert Codex (named for its patron) is a good example of

Plate 4.1 (facing page): The Raising of Lazarus, Egbert Codex (977–993). This miniature is one of 51 gospel illustrations in a Pericopes, a book of readings arranged for the liturgical year. The story of the Raising of Lazarus, which is recounted in John 11:1–45, is read during the week before Easter. Of the many elements of this story, the artist chose a few important moments, arranging them into a unified scene.

Plate 4.2: Christ Asleep, Hitda Gospels (*c.*1000–1020). The moral of the story (which is told in Matt. 8:23–26) is right in the picture: as the apostles look anxiously toward the mast to save them from the stormy sea, one (in the exact center) turns to rouse the sleeping Christ, the real Savior.

what is called the "Ottonian style" at the end of the tenth century. Drawing above all on the art of the late antique "Renaissance" (see p. 40 and Plate 1.9) nevertheless, the Egbert Codex artists achieved an effect all their own. Utterly unafraid of open space, which was rendered in otherworldly pastel colors, their focus was on the figures, who gesture like actors on a stage. In Plate 4.1 the apostles are on the left-hand side, their arms raised and hands wide open with wonder at Christ. He has just raised the dead Lazarus from the tomb, and one of the Jews, on the right, holds his nose. Two women—Mary and Martha, the sisters of Lazarus—fall at Christ's feet, completing the dramatic tableau.

At around the same time, in convents that provided them with comfortable private apartments, noblewomen were writing books and (in the case of Hrotsvitha of Gandersheim) Roman-style plays. Ottonian noblewomen also supported other artists and scholars. Plate 4.2 is from a manuscript made at Cologne between c.1000 and c.1020 for Abbess Hitda of Meschede. It draws on Byzantine and Carolingian models as well as the palette of the Egbert Codex to produce a calm Christ, asleep during a wild storm on the Sea of Galilee that ruffles the sails of the ship and seems to toss it into sheer air. The marriage of Otto II to a Byzantine princess, Theophanu, helps account for the Byzantine influence.

Among the most active patrons of the arts were the Ottonian kings themselves. In a Gospel book made for Otto III—a work fit for royal consumption—the full achievement of Ottonian culture is made clear. Plate 4.3 shows one of 29 full-page miniatures in this manuscript, whose binding alone—set with countless gems around a Byzantine carved ivory—was worth a fortune. The figure of the evangelist Luke emerges from a pure gold-leaf background, while the purple of his dress and the columns that frame him recall imperial majesty. At the same time, Luke is clearly of another world, and his Gospels have here become a theological vision.

FRANCE

By contrast with the English and German kings, those in France had a hard time coping with invasions. Unlike the English kings, who started small and built slowly, the French kings had half an empire to defend. Unlike the Ottonians, who asserted their military prowess in decisive battles such as the one at Lechfeld, the French kings generally had to let local men both take the brunt of the attacks and reap the prestige and authority that came with military leadership. Nor did the French kings have the advantage of Germany's tributaries, silver mines, or Italian connections. Much like the Abbasid caliphs at Baghdad, the kings of France saw their power wane. During most of the tenth century, Carolingian kings alternated on the throne with kings from a family that would later be called the "Capetians." At the end of that century

FONSPATRU DUCTAS BOSAGNISELICIT UNDA.

Plate 4.3 (facing page):
Saint Luke, Gospel Book of Otto III (998–1001)

This is a complicated picture. How can we tease out its meaning? We know that the main subject is the evangelist Saint Luke, first because this illustration precedes the text of the Gospel of Saint Luke in the manuscript, and second because of the presence of the ox (who is labeled "Luc"). Compare Plate 2.4 on p. 91, which shows the same symbol and also includes the label "Agios Lucas"—Saint Luke. In that plate, Luke is writing his gospel. Here Luke is doing something different. But what?

An important hint is at the bottom of the page: the Latin inscription there says, "From the fountain of the Fathers, the ox draws water for the lambs." So Luke (the ox) draws water, or nourishment, from the Fathers for the "lambs," who are in fact shown drinking from the stream. Who are the lambs? In the same manuscript, the page depicting the evangelist Saint Matthew, which precedes his own Gospel, shows men, rather than lambs, drinking from the streams: clearly the lambs signify the Christian people.

Above Luke's head are the "Fathers." They are five of the Old Testament prophets, each provided with a label; the one to Luke's right, for example, is "Abacuc"—Habakkuk. Behind each prophet is an angel (David, at the very top, is accompanied by two), and each is surrounded by a cloud of glory, giving off rays of light that appear like forks jutting into the sky. The artist was no doubt thinking of Paul's Epistle to the Hebrews (12:1) where, after naming the great Old Testament prophets and their trials and tribulations, Paul calls them a "cloud of witnesses over our head" who help us to overcome our sins. But the artist must also have had in mind Christ's Second Coming, when, according to Apoc. 4:2–3, Christ will be seated on a "throne set in heaven" with "a rainbow round about the throne." In our plate, Luke sits in the place of Christ.

Thus this picture shows the unity of the Gospel of Luke with both the Old Testament and the final book of the Bible, the Apocalypse. Luke is the continuator and the guardian of the prophets, whose books are piled on his lap.

There is more. The figure of Luke forms the bottom half of a cross, with the ox in the center. The lamb and the ox were both sacrificial animals, signifying Christ himself, whose death on the cross redeemed mankind. Thus Luke not only "draws water for the lambs" from the Fathers, but he prefigures the Second Coming of Christ himself, the moment of salvation. The mandorla—the oval "halo" that surrounds him—was frequently used to portray Christ in glory.

Why would Emperor Otto III want to own a Gospel book of such theological sophistication? It is very likely because he saw *himself* as part of the divine order. He called himself the "servant of Jesus Christ," and he appears in one manuscript within a mandorla, just like Luke. (See the illustration below.) In this depiction, the symbols of the evangelists hold up the scarf of heaven that bisects the emperor: his feet touch the ground (note the cringing figure of Earth holding him up), while his head touches the cross of Christ, whose hand places a crown on his head.

Otto III Enthroned, Aachen Gospels (c.996).
Otto III saw himself—much like Christ (and Luke)—as mediating between the people and God.

Further Reading
Mayr-Harting, Henry. *Ottonian Book Illumination: An Historical Study.* 2nd rev. ed. London, 1999.
Nees, Lawrence. *Early Medieval Art.* Oxford, 2002.

the most powerful men of the realm, seeking to stave off civil war, elected Hugh Capet (*r.*987-996) as their king. The Carolingians were displaced, and the Capetians continued on the throne until the fourteenth century. (See Genealogy 5.4: The Capetian Kings of France, on p. 202.)

The Capetians' scattered but substantial estates lay in the north of France, in the region around Paris. Here the kings had their vassals and their castles. This "Ile-de-France" (which was all there was to "France" in the period; see Map 4.6) was indeed an "island," surrounded by independent castellans. In the sense that he, too, had little more military power than a castellan, Hugh Capet and his eleventh-century successors were similar to local strongmen. But the Capetian kings had the prestige of their office. Anointed with holy oil, they represented the idea of unity and God-given rule inherited from Charlemagne. Most of the counts and dukes—at least those in the north of France—swore homage and fealty to the king, a gesture, however weak, of personal support. Unlike the German kings, the French could rely on vassalage to bind the great men of the realm to them.

★   ★   ★   ★

Political fragmentation did not mean chaos. It simply betokened a new order. At Byzantium, in any event, even the most centrifugal forces were focused on the center; the real trouble for Basil II, for example, came from *dynatoi* who wanted to be emperors, not from people who wanted to be independent regional rulers. In the Islamic world fragmentation largely meant replication, as courts patterned on or competitive with the Abbasid model were set up by Fatimid caliphs and other rulers. In the West, the rise of local rulers was accompanied by the widespread adoption of forms of personal dependency—vassalage, serfdom—which could be (and were) manipulated even by kings, such as the Capetians, who seemed to have lost the most from the dispersal of power.

The *real* fragmentation was among the former heirs of the Roman Empire. They did not speak the same language, they were increasingly estranged by their religions, and they knew almost nothing about one another. In the next century, Christian Europeans, newly prosperous and self-confident, would go on the offensive. Henceforth, without forgetting about the Byzantine and Islamic worlds, we shall focus on this aggressive and dynamic new society.

NOTES

1. Michael Psellus, *Portrait of Basil II*, in *Reading the Middle Ages: Sources from Europe, Byzantium, and the Islamic World*, ed. Barbara H. Rosenwein (Peterborough, ON, 2006), pp.228–29.

2. Romanus Lecapenus, *Novel*, in *Reading the Middle Ages*, pp.205–6.

3. *The Russian Primary Chronicle*, in *Reading the Middle Ages*, p.237.

4. Al-Tabari, *The Defeat of the Zanj Revolt*, in *Reading the Middle Ages*, p.204.

5. Ibn Sina (Avicenna), *Treatise on Logic*, in *Reading the Middle Ages*, p.235.

6. "Asser's Life of King Alfred," in *Alfred the Great: Asser's "Life of King Alfred" and Other Contemporary Sources*, trans. Simon Keynes and Michael Lapidge (Harmondsworth, 1983), pp.84–85.

7. King Stephen, *Laws*, in *Reading the Middle Ages*, p.239.

8. *Agreements between Count William of the Aquitanians and Hugh of Lusignan*, in *Reading the Middle Ages*, p.215.

9. *Charter of Guillem Guifred*, in *Reading the Middle Ages*, p.221.

10. Andrew of Fleury, *The Miracles of St. Benedict*, in *Reading the Middle Ages*, p.220.

11. *Battle of Maldon*, in *Reading the Middle Ages*, p.258.

12. *Prefaces to Gregory the Great's Pastoral Care*, in *Reading the Middle Ages*, p.257.

13. *The Battle of Brunanburh*, in *The Battle of Maldon and Other Old English Poems*, trans. Kevin Crossley-Holland, ed. Bruce Mitchell (London & New York, 1966), p.42.

14. *Ottonian Germany: The Chronicon of Thietmar of Merseburg*, trans. David A. Warner (Manchester, 2001), p.265.

FURTHER READING

Abels, Richard. *Alfred the Great: War, Kingship and Culture in Anglo-Saxon England*. Harlow, Essex, 1998.

Berkey, Jonathan P. *The Formation of Islam: Religion and Society in the Near East, 600-1800*. Cambridge, 2003.

Bowman, Jeffrey A. *Shifting Landmarks: Property, Proof, and Dispute in Catalonia around the Year 1000*. Ithaca, NY, 2004.

Engel, Pál. *The Realm of St. Stephen: A History of Medieval Hungary, 895-1526*. Trans. Tamás Pálosfalvi. London, 2001.

Franklin, Simon, and Jonathan Shepard. *The Emergence of Rus, 750-1200*. London, 1996.

Jayyusi, Salma Khadra, ed. *The Legacy of Muslim Spain*. 2 vols. Leiden, 1994.

Kazhdan, A.P., and Ann Wharton Epstein. *Change in Byzantine Culture in the Eleventh and Twelfth Centuries*. Berkeley, 1985.

Lev, Yaacov. *State and Society in Fatimid Egypt*. Leiden, 1991.

Maguire, Henry, ed. *Byzantine Court Culture from 829 to 1204*. Washington, 1997.

Moore, R.I. *The First European Revolution, c. 970-1215*. Oxford, 2000.

Neville, Leonora. *Authority in Byzantine Provincial Society, 950-1100*. Cambridge, 2004.

Reuter, Timothy. *Germany in the Early Middle Ages, c. 800-1056*. London, 1991.

Reynolds, Susan. *Fiefs and Vassals: The Medieval Evidence Reinterpreted*. Oxford, 1994.

Richards, Julian D. *The Vikings: A Very Short Introduction*. Oxford, 2005.

Ringrose, Kathryn M. *The Perfect Servant: Eunuchs and the Social Construction of Gender in Byzantium*. Chicago, 2003.

Stafford, Pauline. *Unification and Conquest: A Political and Social History of England in the Tenth and Eleventh Centuries*. London, 1989.

Walter, Christopher. *The Warrior Saints in Byzantine Art and Tradition*. Aldershot, 2003.

◆►◄◆◇◄◆◇◄◆◇◄◆◇◄◆◇►◄◆

To test your knowledge of this chapter, please go to www.rosenweinshorthistory.com and click "Study Questions."

PART II
THE
EUROPEAN
TAKE-OFF

FIVE

THE EXPANSION OF EUROPE
(c.1050-c.1150)

Europeans gained muscle in the second half of the eleventh century. They built cities, reorganized the church, created new varieties of religious life, expanded their intellectual horizons, pushed aggressively at their frontiers, and even waged war over 1400 miles away, in what they called the Holy Land. Expanding population and a vigorous new commercial economy lay behind all this. So, too, did the weakness, disunity, and beckoning wealth of their neighbors, the Byzantines and Muslims.

THE SELJUKS

In the eleventh century the Seljuk Turks, a new group from outside the Islamic world, entered and took over its eastern half. Eventually penetrating deep into Anatolia, they took a great bite out of Byzantium. Soon, however, the Seljuks themselves split apart, and the Islamic world fragmented anew under the rule of dozens of emirs.

From the Sultans to the Emirs

Pastoralists on horseback, the Turkish peoples called the "Seljuks" (after the name of their most enterprising leader) crossed from the region east of the Caspian Sea into

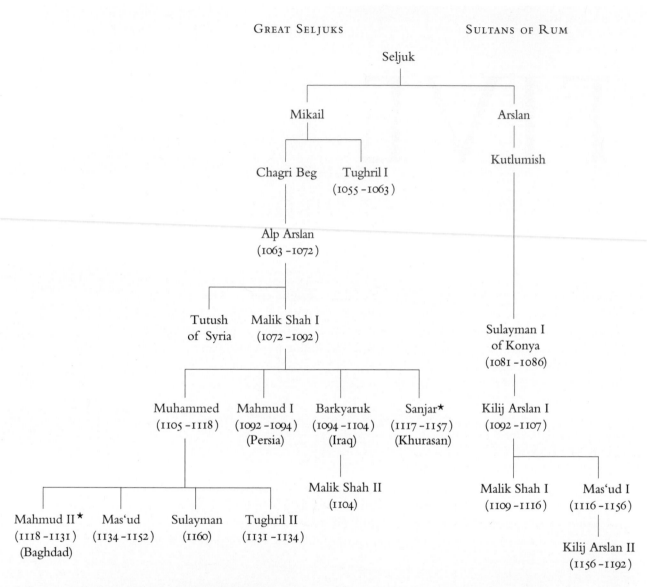

GREAT SELJUKS   SULTANS OF RUM

Seljuk

Mikail   Arslan

Chagri Beg   Tughril I
(1055-1063)

Kutlumish

Alp Arslan
(1063-1072)

Tutush   Malik Shah I
of Syria   (1072-1092)

Sulayman I
of Konya
(1081-1086)

Muhammed   Mahmud I   Barkyaruk   Sanjar★
(1105-1118)   (1092-1094)   (1094-1104)   (1117-1157)
          (Persia)   (Iraq)   (Khurasan)

Kilij Arslan I
(1092-1107)

Malik Shah II
(1104)

Mahmud II★   Mas'ud   Sulayman   Tughril II
(1118-1131)   (1134-1152)   (1160)   (1131-1134)
(Baghdad)

Malik Shah I   Mas'ud I
(1109-1116)   (1116-1156)

Kilij Arslan II
(1156-1192)

★ Sanjar and Mahmud II contested the Sultanate.

Iran in about the year 1000. Within a little over fifty years, they had allied themselves with the caliphs as upholders of Sunni orthodoxy, defeated the Buyids, taken over the cities, and started collecting taxes. Between 1055 and 1092, a succession of formidable Seljuk leaders — Tughril I, Alp Arslan, and Malik Shah (see Genealogy 5.1: The Early Seljuks) — proclaimed themselves rulers, "sultans," of a new state. Bands of herdsmen followed in their wake, moving their sheep into the very farmland of Iran (disrupting agriculture there), then continuing westward, into Armenia, which had been recently annexed by Byzantium. Meanwhile, under Alp Arslan (r. 1063-1072), the Seljuk army (composed precisely of such herdsmen but also, increasingly, of other Turkish tribesmen recruited as slaves or freemen) harried Syria. This was Muslim territory, but it was equally the back door to Byzantium. Thus the Byzantines got involved, and throughout the 1050s and 1060s they fought numerous indecisive battles with the Seljuks. Then in 1071 a huge Byzantine force met an equally large Seljuk army at Manzikert (today Malazgirt, in Turkey). The battle ended with the Byzantines defeated and Anatolia open to a flood of militant nomads. (See Map 5.1.)

The Seljuks of Anatolia set up their own sultanate and were effectively independent

Genealogy 5.1 (facing page): The Early Seljuks

Map 5.1: The Byzantine Empire and the Seljuk World, *c*. 1090

of the Great Seljuks who ruled (and disputed among themselves) elsewhere. The Anatolian Seljuks did not so much declare themselves rulers of the region as simply take it over; for them this once-central Byzantine province was Rum, "Rome." Meanwhile, other Seljuks took off on their own, hiring themselves out (as Turks long had done) as military leaders. Atsiz ibn Uwaq is a good example. For a while he worked for Alp Arslan, but in 1070 he was called in by the Fatimid caliph at Egypt to help shore up the crumbling rule of the Fatimids against their own military leaders. Seizing his chance, Atsiz turned the tables to become emir himself of a region that stretched from Jerusalem to Damascus.

Atsiz was the harbinger of a new order. After the death of Malik Shah I in 1092, the Seljuks could no longer maintain any sort of centralized rule over the Islamic world, even though they still were valued, if only to confer titles like "emir" on local rulers who craved legitimacy. Nor could the Fatimids prevent their own territories from splintering into tiny emirates, each centered on one or a few cities. Some emirs were from the Seljuk family; others were military men who originally served under them. We shall see that the tiny states set up by the crusaders who conquered the Levant in 1099 were, in size, not so very different from their neighboring Islamic emirates.

In the western part of North Africa, the Maghreb, Berber tribesmen (camel breeders rather than sheep herders) forged a state similar to that of the Seljuks. Fired (as the Seljuks had been) with religious fervor on behalf of Sunni orthodoxy, the Berber Almoravids took over north-west Africa in the 1070s and 1080s. In 1086, invited by the ruler of Seville to help fight Christian armies from the north, they sent troops into al-Andalus. This military "aid" soon turned into conquest. By 1094 all of al-Andalus not yet conquered by the Christians was under Almoravid control. Their hegemony over the western Islamic world ended only in 1147, with the triumph of the Almohads, a rival Berber group.

Together the Seljuks and Almoravids rolled back the Shi'ite wave. They kept it back through a system of schools, the *madrasas*. These centers of higher learning, which were attached to mosques, were places where young men attended lessons in religion, law, and literature. Sometimes visiting scholars arrived to debate at lively public displays of intellectual brilliance. More regularly, teachers and students carried on a quiet regimen of classes on the Qur'an and other texts. In the face of Sunni retrenchment, some Shi'i scholars modified their teachings to be more palatable to the mainstream. The conflicts between the two sects receded as Muslims drew together to counter the crusaders.

Byzantium: Bloodied but Unbowed

There would have been no crusaders if Byzantium had remained strong. But the once triumphant state of Basil II was unable to sustain its successes in the face of Turks and Normans. We have already discussed the triumph of the Turks in Anatolia; meanwhile, in the Balkans, the Turkic Pechenegs raided with ease. The Normans, some of whom (as we saw on p. 154) had established themselves in southern Italy, began attacks on Byzantine territory there (see Map 4.2 on p. 142), conquering its last stronghold, Bari, in 1071. Ten years later Norman knights were making penetrating attacks on Byzantine territory in the Balkans. In 1130 the Norman Roger II became king of a territory that ran from southern Italy to Palermo—the Kingdom of Sicily. It was a persistent thorn in Byzantium's side.

Clearly the Byzantine army was no longer very effective. Few themes were still manned with citizen-soldiers, and the emperor's army was also largely made up of mercenaries—Turks and Russians, as had long been the case, and increasingly Normans and Franks as well. But the Byzantines were not entirely dependent on armed force; in many instances they turned to diplomacy to confront the new invaders. When Emperor Constantine IX Monomachos (r.1042–1055) was unable to prevent the Pechenegs from entering the Balkans, he shifted policy, welcoming them, administering baptism, conferring titles, and settling them in depopulated regions. Much the same process took place in Anatolia, where the emperors at times welcomed the Turks to help them fight rival *dynatoi*. Here the invaders were sometimes also welcomed by Christians who did not adhere to Byzantine orthodoxy; the Monophysites of Armenia and Syria (see p. 143) were glad to have new Turkish overlords. The Byzantine grip on its territories loosened and its frontiers became nebulous, but Byzantium still stood.

There were changes at the imperial court as well. The model of the "public" emperor ruling alone with the aid of a civil service gave way to a less costly, more "familial" model of government. To be sure, for a time competing *dynatoi* families swapped the imperial throne. But Alexius I Comnenus (r.1081–1118), a Dalassenus on his mother's side, managed to bring most of the major families together through a series of marriage alliances. (The Comneni remained on the throne for about a century; see Genealogy 5.2: The Dynasty of Comnenus.) Until her death in c.1102, Anna Dalassena, Alexius's mother, held the reins of government while Alexius occupied himself with military matters. At his revamped court, which he moved to the Blachernai palace area, at the northwestern tip of the city (see Map 4.1 on p. 140), his relatives held the highest positions. Many of them received *pronoiai* (sing. *pronoia*), temporary grants of imperial lands that they administered and profited from.

Altogether, Byzantine rulers were becoming more like European ones, holding a relatively small amount of territory, handing some of it out in grants that worked a bit

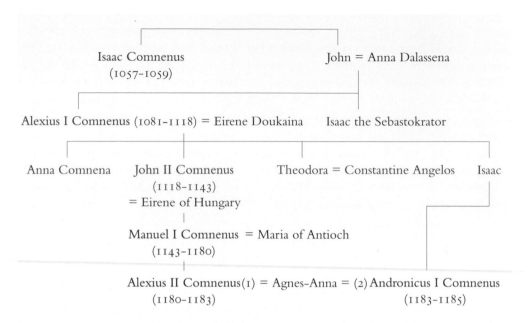

like fiefs, spending most of their time in battle to secure a stronghold here, a city
there. Meanwhile, Western rulers were becoming less regional in focus, muscling
their way, for example, into Byzantine territory and (as we shall see) attacking the
Islamic world as well.

THE QUICKENING OF THE EUROPEAN ECONOMY

Behind the new European expansion was a new economy. Draining marshes, felling
trees, setting up dikes: this was the backbreaking work that brought new land into
cultivation. With their heavy, horse-drawn plows, peasants were able to reap greater
harvests; using the three-field system, they raised more varieties of crops. Great
landowners, the same "oppressors" against whom the Peace of God fulminated (see p.
159), could also be efficient economic organizers. They set up mills to grind grain,
forced their tenants to use them, and then charged a fee for the service. It was in their
interest that the peasants produce as much grain as possible. Some landlords gave
peasants special privileges to settle on especially inhospitable land: the bishop of
Hamburg was generous to those who came from Holland to work soil that was
"uncultivated, marshy, and useless."[1]

As the countryside became more productive, people became healthier, their fertility increased, and there were more mouths to feed. Even so, surprising surpluses made possible the growth of old and the development of new urban centers. Within a generation or two, city dwellers, intensely conscious of their common goals, elaborated new instruments of commerce, self-regulating organizations, and forms of self-government.

Towns and Cities

Around castles and monasteries in the countryside or at the walls of crumbling ancient towns, merchants came with their wares and artisans set up shop. At Bruges (today in Belgium; for all the places mentioned in this section, see Map 5.3), it was the local lord's castle that served as a magnet. As one late medieval chronicler put it,

> To satisfy the needs of the people in the castle at Bruges, first merchants with luxury articles began to surge around the gate; then the wine-sellers came; finally the inn-keepers arrived to feed and lodge the people who had business with the prince.... So many houses were built that soon a great city was created.[2]

Churches and monasteries were the other centers of town growth. Recall Tours as it had been in the early seventh century (Map 1.4 on p. 46), with its semi-permanent settlements around the church of Saint-Martin, out in the cemetery, and its lonely cathedral nestling against one of the ancient walls. By the twelfth century (see Map 5.2), Saint-Martin was a monastery, the hub of a small town dense enough to boast eleven parish churches, merchant and artisan shops, private houses, and two markets. To the east, the episcopal complex was no longer alone: a market had sprung up outside the old western wall, and private houses lined the street leading to the bridge. Smaller than the town around Saint-Martin, the one at the foot of the old city had only two parish churches, but it was big and rich enough to warrant the construction of a new set of walls to protect it.

Early cities developed without prior planning, but some later ones were "chartered," that is, declared, surveyed, and plotted out. A marketplace and merchant settlement were already in place at Freiburg im Breisgau when the duke of Zähringen chartered it, promising each new settler there a house lot of 5000 square feet for a very small yearly rent. The duke had fair hopes that commerce would flourish right at his back door and yield him rich revenues.

The look and feel of medieval cities varied immensely from place to place. Nearly all included a marketplace, a castle, and several churches. Most were ringed by walls.

(See Map 7.4, p. 271, for the successive walls of Piacenza, evidence of the growth of population there.) Within the walls lay a network of streets—narrow, dirty, dark, smelly, and winding—made of packed clay or gravel. Most cities were situated near waterways and had bridges; the one at Tours was built in the 1030s. Many had to adapt to increasingly crowded conditions. At the end of the eleventh century in Winchester, England, city plots were still large enough to accommodate houses parallel to the street; but soon those houses had to be torn down to make way for narrow ones, built at right angles to the street. The houses at Winchester were made of wattle and daub—twigs woven together and covered with clay. If they were like the stone houses built in the late twelfth century (about which we know a good deal), they had two stories: a shop or warehouse on the lower floor and living quarters above. Behind this main building were the kitchen, enclosures for livestock, and a garden. Even city dwellers clung to rural pursuits, raising much of their food themselves.

Although commercial centers developed throughout Western Europe, they grew fastest and most densely in regions along key waterways: the Mediterranean coasts of Italy, France, and Spain; northern Italy along the Po River; the river system of Rhône-Saône-Meuse; the Rhineland; the English Channel; the shores of the Baltic Sea. During the eleventh and twelfth centuries, these waterways became part of a single, interdependent economy. At the same time, new roads through the countryside linked urban centers to rural districts and stimulated the growth of fairs (regular, short-term, often lively markets). (See Map 7.3 on p. 268 for a depiction of the trade routes and urban centers of a somewhat later period.)

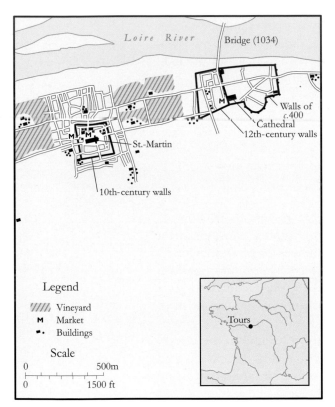

Map 5.2: Tours in the Eleventh and Twelfth Centuries

Legend

//// Vineyard
M   Market
•-• Buildings

Scale
0   500m
0   1500 ft

Tours

Business Arrangements

The revival of urban life and the expansion of trade, together dubbed the "commercial revolution" by historians, was sustained and invigorated by merchants. They were a varied lot. Some were local traders, like one monk who supervised a manor twenty miles south of his monastery and sold its surplus horses and grain at a local market. Others—mainly Jews and Italians—were long-distance traders, much in demand because they supplied fine wines, spices, and fabrics to the aristocracy. Some Jews had long been involved at least part time in long-distance trade as vintners. In the eleventh century, as lords reorganized the countryside, Jewish landowners were driven out and forced into commerce and urban trades full time. Other long-distance traders came from Italy. The key players were from Genoa, Pisa, Amalfi, and Venice. Regular merchants at Constantinople, their settlements were strung like pearls along the Golden Horn (see Map 4.1 on p. 140).

Italian traders found the Islamic world nearly as lucrative as the Byzantine. Establishing bases at ports such as Tunis, they imported Islamic wares — ceramics, textiles, metalwork — into Europe. Near Pisa, for example, the façade of the cathedral of San Miniato (Plate 5.1) was decorated with shiny bowls (Plate 5.2) imported by Pisan traders from North African artisans. In turn, merchants from the West exported wood, iron, and woolen cloth to the East.

Merchants invented new forms of collective enterprises to pool their resources and finance large undertakings. The Italian *commenda*, for example, was a partnership established for ventures by sea. A *compagnia* was created by investing family property in trade. Contracts for sales, exchanges, and loans became common, with the interest on loans hidden in the fiction of a penalty for "late payment" in order to avoid the church's ban on usury.

Pooled resources made large-scale productive enterprises possible. A cloth industry began, powered by water mills. New deep-mining technologies provided Europeans with hitherto untapped sources of metals. Forging techniques improved, and iron was for the first time regularly used for agricultural tools and plows, enhancing food production.

Whether driven by machines or handwork, the new economy was sustained by the artisans, financiers, and merchants of the cities. They formed guilds to regulate and protect themselves. In these social, religious, and economic associations, guild members prayed for and buried one another, agreed on quality standards for their products, and regulated their work hours, materials, and prices. Guilds guaranteed their members — mostly male — a place in the market by controlling production within each city. They represented the social and economic counterpart to urban walls, giving their members protection, shared identity, and recognized status.

The political counterpart to the walls was the "commune" — town self-government. City dwellers — keenly aware of their special identity in a world dominated by knights and peasants — recognized their mutual interest in reliable coinage, laws to facilitate commerce, freedom from servile dues and services, and independence to buy and sell as the market dictated. They petitioned the political powers that ruled them — bishops, kings, counts, castellans, dukes — for the right to govern themselves.

Collective movements for urban self-government were especially prevalent in Italy, France, and Germany. Already Italy's political life was city-centered; communes

there were attempts to substitute the power of one group (the citizens) for another (the nobles and bishops). At Milan in the second half of the eleventh century, for example, popular discontent with the archbishop, who effectively ruled the city, led to numerous armed clashes that ended, in 1097, with the transfer of power from the archbishop to a government of leading men of the city. Outside of Italy movements for urban independence—sometimes violent, as at Milan, at other times peaceful—took place within a larger political framework. For example, King Henry I of England (r. 1100–1135) freed the citizens of London from numerous customary taxes while granting them the right to "appoint as sheriff from themselves whomsoever they may choose, and [they] shall appoint from among themselves as justice whomsoever they choose to look after the pleas of my crown."[3] The king's law still stood, but it was carried out by the Londoners' officials.

Plate 5.1 (facing page): San Miniato (late 12th cent.). The façade of San Miniato was once decorated with *bacini*, bowls that sparkled in the Italian sun. In this picture you can see the small round cavities where they once belonged. The *bacino* in Plate 5.2 was slightly above and just to the left (from the viewer's point of view) of the oculus (the round window). The *bacini* were, in effect, cheap and attractive substitutes for marble or mosaics.

Plate 5.2: Bowl, North Africa (late 12th cent.). This earthenware bowl (*bacino*), imported from North Africa, and decorated with pseudo Arabic writing, once adorned the façade of San Miniato. Such bowls, evidence of lively trade between the Islamic world and the West, were in great demand by Italians, not only for the façades of their churches but also for their kitchens. (See Plate 3.3, p. 111, for a far more sophisticated bowl from the Abbasid period.)

CHURCH REFORM AND ITS AFTERMATH

Disillusioned citizens at Milan denounced their archbishop not only for his tyranny but also for his impurity; they wanted their pastors to be untainted by sex and by money. In this they were supported by a new-style papacy, keen on reform in the church and society. The "Gregorian Reform," as this movement came to be called, broke up clerical marriages, unleashed civil war in Germany, changed the procedure for episcopal elections, and transformed the papacy into a monarchy. It began as a way to free the church from the world; but in the end the church was deeply involved in the new world it had helped to create.

The Coming of Reform

Freeing the church from the world: what could it mean? In 910 the duke and duchess of Aquitaine founded the monastery of Cluny with some unusual stipulations. They endowed the monastery with property (normal and essential if it were to survive), but then they gave it and its worldly possessions to Saints Peter and Paul. In this way they put control of the monastery into the hands of the two most powerful heavenly saints. They designated the pope, as the successor of Saint Peter, to be the monastery's worldly protector if anyone should bother or threaten it. The whole notion of "freedom" at this point was very vague. But Cluny's prestige was great because of the influence of its founders, the status of Saint Peter, and the fame of the monastery's elaborate round of prayers. The Cluniac monks fulfilled the role of "those who pray" in dazzling manner. Through their prayers, they seemed to guarantee the salvation of all Christians. Rulers, bishops, rich landowners, and even serfs (if they could) gave Cluny donations of land, joining their contributions to the land of Saint Peter. Powerful men and women called on the Cluniac abbots to reform new monasteries along the Cluniac model.

The abbots of Cluny came to see themselves as reformers of the world as well as the cloister. They believed in clerical celibacy, preaching against the prevailing norm in which parish priests and even bishops were married. They also thought that the laity could be reformed, become more virtuous, and cease its oppression of the poor. In the eleventh century, the Cluniacs began to link their program to the papacy. When they disputed with bishops or laypeople about lands and rights, they called on the popes to help them out.

The popes were ready to do so. A parallel movement for reform had entered papal circles via a small group of influential monks and clerics. Mining canon (church) law for their ammunition, these churchmen emphasized two abuses: nicolaitism (clerical marriage) and simony (buying church offices). The new patrilineal family taught them the importance of limiting offspring; in their eyes, celibate priests had higher status than men who procreated. The new profit economy sensitized them to the crass commercial meanings of gifts; in their eyes, churchmen should not give gifts in return for their offices.

Initially, the reformers got imperial backing. In the view of German king and emperor Henry III (r.1039-1056), as the anointed of God he was responsible for the well-being of the church in the empire. (For Henry and his dynasty, see Genealogy 5.3: The Salian Kings and Emperors.) Henry denounced simony and personally refused to accept money or gifts when he appointed bishops to their posts. He presided over the Synod of Sutri which, in 1046, deposed three papal rivals and elected another. When that pope and his successor died, Henry appointed Bruno of Toul, a member of the royal family, seasoned courtier, and reforming bishop. Taking the name Leo IX (1049-1054), the new pope surprised his patron: he set out to reform the church under papal, not imperial, control.

Leo revolutionized the papacy. He had himself elected by the "clergy and people" to satisfy the demands of canon law. Unlike earlier popes, Leo left Rome often to preside over church councils and make the pope's influence felt outside Italy, especially in France and Germany. To the papal curia Leo brought the most zealous church reformers of his day: Peter Damian, Hildebrand (later Pope Gregory VII), and Humbert of Silva Candida. They put new stress on the passage in Matthew's gospel

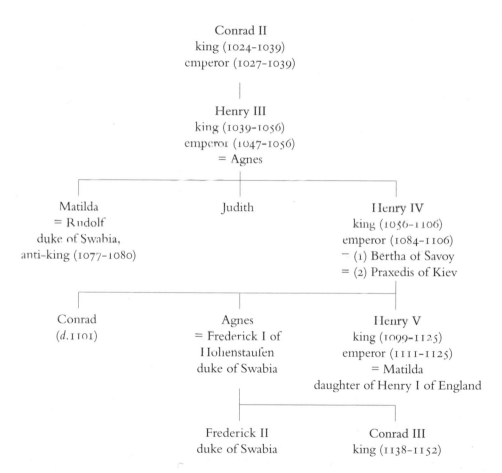

Genealogy 5.3: The Salian Kings and Emperors

Conrad II
king (1024-1039)
emperor (1027-1039)

Henry III
king (1039-1056)
emperor (1047-1056)
= Agnes

Matilda
= Rudolf
duke of Swabia,
anti-king (1077-1080)

Judith

Henry IV
king (1056-1106)
emperor (1084-1106)
= (1) Bertha of Savoy
= (2) Praxedis of Kiev

Conrad
(d. 1101)

Agnes
= Frederick I of
Hohenstaufen
duke of Swabia

Henry V
king (1099-1125)
emperor (1111-1125)
= Matilda
daughter of Henry I of England

Frederick II
duke of Swabia

Conrad III
king (1138-1152)

(Matt. 16:19) in which Christ tells Peter that he is the "rock" of the Church, with the keys to heaven and the power to bind (impose penance) and loose (absolve from sins). As the successor to the special privileges of Saint Peter, the Roman church, headed by the pope, was "head and mother of all churches." What historians call the doctrine of "papal supremacy" was thus announced.

Its impact was soon felt at Byzantium. On a mission at Constantinople in 1054 to forge an alliance with the emperor against the Normans and, at the same time, to "remind" the patriarch of his place in the church hierarchy, Humbert ended by excommunicating the patriarch and his followers. In retaliation, the patriarch excommunicated Humbert and his fellow legates. Clashes between the Roman and Byzantine churches had occurred before and had been patched up, but this one, though not recognized as such at the time, marked a permanent schism. After 1054, the Roman Catholic and Greek Orthodox churches largely went their separate ways.

More generally, the papacy began to wield new forms of power. It waged unsuccessful war against the Normans in southern Italy and then made the best of the situation by granting them parts of the region—and Sicily as well—as a fief, turning former enemies into vassals. It supported the Christian push into the *taifas* of al-Andalus, transforming the "*reconquista*"—the conquest of Islamic Spain—into a holy war: Pope Alexander II (1061–1073) forgave the sins of the Christians on their way to the battle of Barbastro.

The Investiture Conflict and its Effects

The papal reform movement is associated particularly with Pope Gregory VII (1073–1085), hence the term "Gregorian reform." A passionate advocate of papal primacy (the theory that the pope is the head of the church), Gregory was not afraid to clash directly with the king of Germany, Henry IV (r.1056–1106), over church leadership. In Gregory's view—an astonishing one at the time, given the religious and spiritual roles associated with rulers—kings and emperors were simple laymen who had no right to meddle in church affairs. Henry, on the other hand, brought up in the traditions of his father, Henry III, considered it part of his duty to appoint bishops and even popes to ensure the well-being of church and empire together.

The pope and the emperor first clashed over the appointment of the archbishop of Milan. Gregory disputed Henry's right to "invest" the archbishop (put him into his office). In the investiture ritual, the emperor or his representative symbolically gave the church and the land that went with it to the bishop or archbishop chosen for the job. This was, for example, the role that Henry II played in Thietmar of Merseburg's episcopal installation (see above, p. 166.) In the case of Milan, two rival candidates for archiepiscopal office (one supported by the pope, the other by the emperor) had been at loggerheads for several years when, in 1075, Henry invested his own candidate. Gregory immediately called on Henry to "give more respectful attention to the master of the Church," namely Peter and his living representative — Gregory himself.[4] In reply, Henry and the German bishops called on Gregory, that "false monk," to resign. This was the beginning of what historians delicately call the "Investiture Conflict" or "Investiture Controversy." In fact it was war. In February of 1076, Gregory called a synod that both excommunicated Henry and suspended him from office:

> I deprive King Henry [IV], son of the emperor Henry [III], who has rebelled against [God's] Church with unheard-of audacity, of the government over the whole kingdom of Germany and Italy, and I release all Christian men from the allegiance which they have sworn or may swear to him, and I forbid anyone to serve him as king.[5]

The last part of this decree gave it real punch: anyone in Henry's kingdom could rebel against him. The German "princes" — the aristocrats — seized the moment and threatened to elect another king. They were motivated partly by religious sentiments — many had established links with the papacy through their support of reformed monasteries — and partly by political opportunism, as they had chafed under strong German kings who had tried to keep their power in check. Some bishops, too, joined with Gregory's supporters, a major blow to Henry, who needed the troops that they supplied.

Attacked from all sides, Henry traveled in the winter of 1077 to intercept Gregory, barricaded in a fortress at Canossa, high in the Appennines (see Map 5.3). It was a refuge provided by the staunchest of papal supporters, Countess Matilda of Tuscany. In an astute and dramatic gesture, the king stood outside the castle (in cold and snow) for three days, barefoot, as a penitent. Gregory was forced, as a pastor, to lift his excommunication and to receive Henry back into the church, precisely as Henry intended. For his part, the pope had the satisfaction of seeing the king humiliate himself before the papal majesty. Although it made a great impression on contemporaries, the whole episode solved nothing. The princes elected an anti-king, and bloody civil war continued intermittently until 1122.

The Investiture Conflict ended with a compromise. The Concordat of Worms (1122) relied on a conceptual distinction between two parts of investiture — the spiritual (in which the bishop-to-be received the symbols of his office) and the secular (in which he received the symbols of the material goods that would allow him to function). Under the terms of the Concordat, the ring and staff, symbols of church office, would be given by a churchman in the first part of the ceremony. Then the

emperor or his representative would touch the bishop with a scepter, signifying the land and other possessions that went with his office. Elections of bishops in Germany would take place "in the presence" of the emperor—that is, under his influence. In Italy, the pope would have a comparable role.

In the end, then, secular rulers continued to matter in the appointment of churchmen. But just as the new investiture ceremony broke the ritual into spiritual and secular halves, so too it implied a new notion of kingship separate from the priesthood. The Investiture Conflict did not produce the modern distinction between church and state—that would develop only very slowly—but it set the wheels in motion. At the time, its most important consequence was to shatter the delicate balance among political and ecclesiastical powers in Germany and Italy. In Germany, the princes consolidated their lands and powers at the expense of the king. In Italy, the communes came closer to their goals: it was no accident that Milan gained its independence in 1097. And everywhere the papacy gained new authority: it had become a "papal monarchy."

Map 5.3 (facing page): Western Europe, c.1100

Papal influence was felt at every level. At the abstract level of canon law, papal primacy was enhanced by the publication c.1140 of the *Decretum*, written by a teacher of canon law named Gratian. Collecting nearly two thousand passages from the decrees of popes and councils as well as the writings of the Church Fathers, Gratian set out to demonstrate their essential agreement. In fact, the book's original title was *Harmony of Discordant Canons*. If he found any "discord" in his sources, Gratian usually imposed the harmony himself by arguing that the conflicting passages dealt with different situations. A bit later another legal scholar revised and expanded the *Decretum*, adding Roman law to the mix. At a more local level, papal denunciations of married clergy made inroads on family life. At Verona, for example, "sons of priests" disappeared from the historical record in the twelfth century. At the mundane level of administration, the papal claim to head the church helped turn the curia at Rome into a kind of government, complete with its own bureaucracy, collection agencies, and law courts. It was the teeming port of call for litigious churchmen disputing appointments and for petitioners of every sort.

The First Crusade

On the military level, the papacy's proclamations of holy wars led to bloody slaughter, tragic loss, and tidy profit. We have already seen how Alexander II encouraged the *reconquista* in Spain; it was in the wake of his call that the *taifa* rulers implored the Almoravids for help. An oddly similar chain of events took place at the other end of the Islamic world. Ostensibly responding to a request from the Byzantine Emperor Alexius for mercenaries to help retake Anatolia from the Seljuks, Pope Urban II

(1088-1099) turned the enterprise into something new: a pious pilgrimage to the Holy Land to be undertaken by an armed militia—one commissioned like those of the Peace of God, but thousands of times larger—under the leadership of the papacy. "Enter upon the road to the Holy Sepulcher," Urban exhorted the crowd at Clermont in 1095, "Wrest that land from the wicked race, and subject it to yourselves." On all sides the cry went up: "God wills it!"[6]

The event that historians call the First Crusade (1096-1099) mobilized a force of some 50,000-60,000 combatants, not counting women, children, old men, and hangers-on. The armies were organized not as one military force but rather as separate militias, each authorized by the pope and commanded by a different individual.

Several motley bands were not authorized by the pope. Though called collectively the "Peasants' (or People's) Crusade," these irregular armies included nobles. They were inspired by popular preachers, especially the eloquent Peter the Hermit, who was described by chroniclers as small, ugly, barefoot, and—partly because of those very characteristics—utterly captivating. Starting out before the other armies, the Peasants' Crusade took a route to the Holy Land through the Rhineland in Germany.

This indirect route was no mistake. The crusaders were looking for "wicked races" closer to home: the Jews. Under Henry IV many Jews had gained a stable place within the cities of Germany, particularly along the Rhine River. The Jews received protection from the local bishops (who were imperial appointees) in return for paying a tax. Living in their own neighborhoods, the Jews valued their tightly-knit communities focused on the synagogue, which was a school and community center as well as a place of worship. Nevertheless, Jews also participated in the life of the larger Christian community. For example, Archbishop Anno of Cologne made use of the services of the Jewish money-lenders in his city, and other Jews in Cologne were allowed to trade their wares at the fairs there.

Although officials pronounced against the Jews from time to time, and although Jews were occasionally (temporarily) expelled from some Rhineland cities, they were not persecuted systematically until the First Crusade. Then the Peasants' Crusade, joined by some local nobles and militias from the region, threatened the Jews with forced conversion or death. Some relented when the Jews paid them money; others, however, attacked. Beleaguered Jews occasionally found refuge with bishops or in the houses of Christian friends, but in many cities—Metz, Speyer, Worms, Mainz, and Cologne—they were massacred:

> Oh God, insolent men have risen against me
> They have sorely afflicted us from our youth
> They have devoured and destroyed us in their wrath against us
> Saying, let us take their inheritance for ourselves.[7]

So wrote Rabbi Eliezer ben Nathan, mourning and celebrating the Jewish martyrs who perished at the hands of the crusaders.

Leaving the Rhineland, some of the irregular militias disbanded, while others sought out the Holy Land via Hungary, at least one stopping off at Prague to massacre more Jews there. Only a handful of these armies continued on to Anatolia, where most of them were quickly slaughtered.

From the point of view of Emperor Alexius at Constantinople, even the "official" crusaders were potentially dangerous. One of the crusade's leaders, the Norman Bohemond, had, a few years before, tried to conquer Byzantium itself. Hastily forcing oaths from Bohemond and the other lords that any previously Byzantine lands conquered would be restored to Byzantium, Alexius shipped the armies across the Bosporus.

The main objective of the First Crusade—to conquer the Holy Land—was accomplished largely because of the disunity of the Islamic world and its failure to consider the crusade a serious military threat. Spared by the Turks when they first arrived in Anatolia, the crusaders first made their way to the Seljuk capital, Nicaea. Their armies were initially uncoordinated and their food supplies uncertain, but soon they organized themselves, setting up a "council of princes" that included all the great crusade leaders, while the Byzantines supplied food at a nearby port. Surrounding Nicaea and besieging it with catapults and other war machines, the crusaders took the city on June 18, 1097, dutifully handing it over to Alexius in accordance with their oath.

Gradually, however, the crusaders forgot their oath to the Byzantines. While most went toward Antioch, which stood in the way of their conquest of Jerusalem, one leader went off to Edessa, where he took over the city and its outlying area, creating the first of the Crusader States: the County of Edessa. Meanwhile the other crusaders remained stymied before the thick and heavily fortified walls of Antioch for many months. Then, in a surprise turn-around, they entered the town but found themselves besieged by Muslim armies from the outside. Their mood grim, they rallied when a peasant named Peter Bartholomew reported that he had seen in many visions the Holy Lance that had pierced Christ's body—it was, he said, buried right in the main church in Antioch. (Antioch had a flourishing Christian population even under Muslim rule.) After a night of feverish digging, the crusaders believed that they had discovered the Holy Lance, and, fortified by this miracle, they defeated the besiegers.

From Antioch, it was only a short march to Jerusalem, though disputes among the leaders delayed that next step for over a year. One leader claimed Antioch. Another eventually took charge—provisionally—of the expedition to Jerusalem. His way was eased by quarrels among Muslim rulers, and an alliance with one of them allowed free passage through what would have been enemy territory. In early June 1099, a large crusading force amassed before the walls of Jerusalem and set to work to build siege engines. In mid-July they attacked, breaching the walls and entering the city. "The Franks slaughtered more than 70,000 people .... [they] stripped the Dome of the Rock of more than forty silver candelabra," dryly noted a later Islamic historian looking back on the event.[8]

RULERS WITH CLOUT

While the papacy was turning into a monarchy, other rulers were beginning to turn their territories into states. They discovered ideologies to justify their hegemony, hired officials to work for them, found vassals and churchmen to support them. Some of these rulers were women.

The Crusader States

In the Holy Land, the leaders of the crusade set up four tiny states, European colonies in the Levant. Two (Tripoli and Edessa) were counties, Antioch was a principality, Jerusalem a kingdom. (See Map 5.4.) The region was habituated (as we have seen) to multi-ethnic and multi-religious territories ruled by a military elite; apart from the religion of that elite, the Crusader States were no exception. Yet, however much they engaged with their neighbors, the Europeans in the Levant saw themselves as a world apart, holding on to their western identity through their political institutions and the old vocabulary of homage, fealty, and Christianity.

The states won during the First Crusade lasted—tenuously—until 1291, though many new crusades had to be called in the interval to shore them up. Created by conquest, these states were treated as lordships. The new rulers carved out estates to give as fiefs to their vassals, who, in turn, gave portions of their holdings in fief to their own men. The peasants continued to work the land as before, and commerce boomed as the new rulers encouraged lively trade at their coastal ports. Italian merchants—the Genoese, Pisans, and Venetians—were the most active, but others—Byzantines and Muslim traders—participated as well. Enlightened lordship dictated that the mixed population of the states—Muslims, to be sure, but also Jews, Greek Orthodox Christians, Monophysite Christians, and others—be tolerated for the sake of production and trade. Most Europeans had gone home after the First Crusade; those left behind were obliged to maintain the inhabitants that remained.

The main concerns of the Crusader States' rulers were military, and these could be guaranteed as well by a woman as by a man. Thus Melisende (r.1131-1152), oldest daughter of King Baldwin II of Jerusalem, was declared ruler along with her husband, Fulk, formerly count of Anjou, and their infant son. Taking the reins of government into her own hands after Fulk's death, she named a constable to lead her army and made sure that the greatest men in the kingdom sent her their vassals to do military service. Vigorously asserting her position as queen, she found supporters in the church, appointed at least one bishop to his see, and created her own chancery, where her royal acts were drawn up.

But vassals alone, however well commanded, were not sufficient to defend the fragile Crusader States, nor were the stone castles and towers that bristled in the countryside. Knights had to be recruited from Europe from time to time, and a new and militant kind of monasticism developed in the Levant: the Knights Templar. Vowed to poverty and chastity, the Templars at the same time devoted themselves to war. They defended the town garrisons of the Crusader States and ferried money from Europe to the Holy Land. Even so, they could not prevent a new Seljuk leader, Zengi, from taking Edessa in 1144. The slow but steady shrinking of the Crusader States began at that moment. The Second Crusade (1147-1149), called in the wake of Zengi's victory, came to a disastrous end. After only four days of besieging the walls of Damascus, the crusaders, whose leaders could not keep the peace among themselves, gave up and went home.

Map 5.4: The Crusader States, *c.*1140

England under Norman Rule

Anglo-Saxon England was early linked to the Continent by the Vikings, who settled in England's eastern half. In the eleventh century it was further tied to Scandinavia under the rule of Cnut (*r.*1016-1035), king of a state that extended from England to Denmark, Norway, and part of Sweden. But it was with its conquest by William, duke of Normandy, that England was drawn inextricably into the Continental orbit. (See Map 5.3.)

William the Conqueror, duke of Normandy, carried a papal banner with him when he left his duchy in 1066 to dispute the crown of the childless King Edward the Confessor. The one-day battle of Hastings was decisive, and William was crowned the first Norman king of England. (See Genealogy 6.1: The Norman and Angevin Kings of England, on p. 224.) Treating his conquest like booty (as the crusader leaders would do a few decades later in the Levant), he kept about 20 per cent of the land for himself and divided the rest, distributing it in large but scattered fiefs to a relatively small number of his barons—his elite followers—and family members, lay and ecclesiastical, as well as to some lesser men, such as personal servants and soldiers. In turn, these men maintained their own vassals; they owed the king military service (and the service of a fixed number of their vassals) along with certain dues, such as reliefs (money paid upon inheriting a fief) and aids (payments made on important occasions).

These were noble obligations; William expected their servile counterparts from the peasantry. In 1086, he ordered a survey of the land and landholders of England. Quickly dubbed "Domesday Book" because, like the records of people judged at doomsday, it provided facts that could not be appealed, it was the most extensive inventory of land, livestock, taxes, and people that had ever been compiled anywhere in medieval Europe. According to a chronicler of the time, William

> sent his men over all England into every shire and had them find out how many hundred hides [a measure of land] there were in the shire, or what land and cattle the king himself had in the country, or what dues he ought to receive every year from the shire.... So very narrowly did he have the survey to be made that there was no single hide nor a yard of land, nor indeed .... one ox or one cow or one pig left out.[9]

The surveys were made by the king's men by consulting Anglo-Saxon tax lists and by taking testimony from local jurors, men sworn to answer a series of formal questions truthfully. Summarized in Domesday, the answers gave William what he needed to know about his kingdom and the revenues—including the Danegeld, which was now in effect a royal tax—that could be expected from it.

Communication with the Continent was constant. The Norman barons spoke a brand of French; they talked more easily with the peasants of Normandy (if they bothered) than with those tilling the land in England. They maintained their estates on the Continent and their ties with its politics, institutions, and culture. English wool was sent to Flanders to be turned into cloth. The most brilliant intellect of his day, Saint Anselm of Bec (or Canterbury; 1033-1109), was born in Italy, became abbot of a Norman monastery, and was then appointed archbishop in England. English adolescent boys were sent to Paris and Chartres for schooling. The kings of England often spent more time on the Continent than they did on the island. When, on the death of William's son, King Henry I (r.1100-1135), no male descendent survived to take the throne, two counts from the Continent — Geoffrey of Anjou and Stephen of Blois — disputed it as their right through two rival females of the royal line. (See Genealogy 6.1 again.)

Christian Spain

While initially the product of defeat, Christian Spain in the eleventh and twelfth centuries turned the tables and became, in effect, the successful western counterpart of the Crusader States. The disintegration of al-Andalus into *taifas* opened immense opportunities to the Spanish princes of the north. Wealth flowed into their coffers not only from plundering raids and the confiscation of lands and cities but also (until the Almoravids put an end to it) from tribute, paid in gold by *taifa* rulers to stave off attacks.

Not just the rulers were enriched. When Rodrigo Díaz de Vivar, the Cid (from the Arabic *sidi*, lord), fell out of favor with his lord, King Alfonso VI (r.1065-1109) of León-Castile, he and a band of followers found employment with al-Mutamin, ruler of Zaragoza. There the Cid defended the city against Christian and Muslim invaders alike. In 1090, he struck out on his own, taking his chances in Valencia:

My Cid knew well   that God was his strength.
There was great fear   in the city of Valencia
It grieves those of Valencia.   Know, they are not pleased
They took counsel   and came to besiege him.[10]

Thus were the two sides depicted in the *Poem of the Cid*, written perhaps a century later: beleaguered inhabitants versus an army of God, even though the Cid had just come from serving a Muslim ruler. In the end, the Cid took Valencia in 1094 and ruled there until his death in 1099. He was a Spaniard, but other opportunistic armies sometimes came from elsewhere. The one that Pope Alexander II authorized to besiege Barbastro in 1064 was made up of Frenchmen.

The French connection was symptomatic of a wider process: the Europeanization of Spain. Initially the Christian kingdoms had been isolated islands of Visigothic culture. But already in the tenth century, pilgrims from France, England, Germany, and Italy were clogging the roads to the shrine of Saint James (Santiago de Compostela); in the eleventh century, monks from Cluny and other reformed monasteries arrived to colonize Spanish cloisters. Alfonso VI actively reached out beyond the Pyrenees, to Cluny — where he doubled the annual gift of 1000 gold pieces that his father, Fernando I, had given in exchange for prayers for his soul — and to the papacy. He sought recognition from Pope Gregory VII as "king of Spain," and in return he imposed the Roman liturgy throughout his kingdom, stamping out the traditional Visigothic music and texts.

In 1085 Alfonso made good his claim to be more than the king of León-Castile by conquering Toledo. (See Map 5.5.) After his death, his daughter Queen Urraca (r.1109–1126) ruled in her own right a realm larger than England. Her strength came from many of the usual sources: control over land, which, though granted out to counts and others, was at least in theory revocable; church appointments; an army—everyone was liable to be called up once a year, even arms-bearing slaves—and a court of great men to offer advice and give their consent.

Praising the King of France

Map 5.5: Spain at the Death of Alfonso VI (1109)

Not all rulers had opportunities for grand conquest. How did they maintain themselves? The example of the kings of France reveals the possibilities. Reduced to bat-

tling a few castles in the vicinity of the Ile-de-France, the Capetian kings nevertheless wielded many of the same instruments of power as their conquering contemporaries: vassals, taxes, commercial revenues, military and religious reputations. Louis VI the Fat (r.1108-1137), so heavy that he had to be hoisted onto his horse by a crane, was nevertheless a tireless defender of royal power. (See Genealogy 5.4: The Capetian Kings of France.)

Louis's virtues were amplified and broadcast by his biographer, Suger (1081-1152), the abbot of Saint-Denis, a monastery just outside Paris. A close associate of the king, Suger was his chronicler and propagandist. When Louis set himself the task of consolidating his rule in the Ile-de-France, Suger portrayed the king as a righteous hero. He was more than a lord with rights over the French nobles as his vassals; he was a peacekeeper with the God-given duty to fight unruly strongmen. Careful not to claim that Louis was head of the church, which would have scandalized the papacy and its supporters, Suger nevertheless emphasized Louis's role as protector of the church and the poor and insisted on the sacred importance of the royal dignity. When a pope happened to arrive in France, Louis, not yet king, and his father, Philip I (r.1060-1108), bowed low, but (wrote Suger) "the lord pope lifted them up and made them sit before him like devout sons of the apostles. In the manner of a wise man acting wisely, he conferred with them privately on the present condition of the church."[11] Here the pope was shown needing royal advice. Meanwhile, Suger stressed Louis's piety and active defense of the faith:

> Helped by his powerful band of armed men, or rather by the hand of God, he abruptly seized the castle [of Crécy] and captured its very strong tower as if it were simply the hut of a peasant. Having startled those criminals [Thomas of Marle, a regional castellan, and his retinue], he piously slaughtered the impious, cutting them down without mercy because he found them to be merciless.[12]

When Louis VI died in 1137, Suger's notion of the might and right of the king of France reflected reality in an extremely small area. Nevertheless, Louis laid the groundwork for the gradual extension of royal power. As the lord of vassals, the king could call upon his men to aid him in times of war (though the great ones could defy him). As king and landlord, he collected dues and taxes with the help of his officials, called *prévôts*. Revenues came from Paris as well, a thriving commercial and cultural center. With money and land, Louis could employ civil servants while dispensing the favors and giving the gifts that added to his prestige and power.

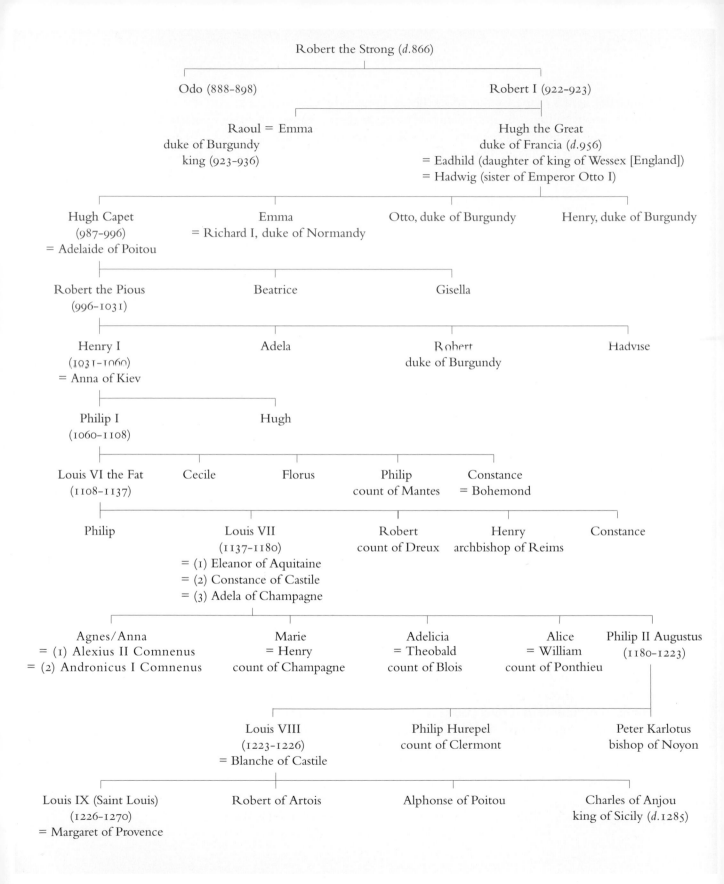

Robert the Strong (*d.866*)

Odo (888–898)　　　　　　　　　　　Robert I (922–923)

Raoul = Emma　　　　　　　　　　Hugh the Great
duke of Burgundy　　　　　　　　duke of Francia (*d.956*)
king (923–936)　　　　　　　= Eadhild (daughter of king of Wessex [England])
　　　　　　　　　　　　　= Hadwig (sister of Emperor Otto I)

Hugh Capet　　　　　　　Emma　　　　　　Otto, duke of Burgundy　　　Henry, duke of Burgundy
(987–996)　　　= Richard I, duke of Normandy
= Adelaide of Poitou

Robert the Pious　　　　　　Beatrice　　　　　　Gisella
(996–1031)

Henry I　　　　　　　Adela　　　　　　Robert　　　　　　Hadvise
(1031–1060)　　　　　　　　　　　　duke of Burgundy
= Anna of Kiev

Philip I　　　　　　Hugh
(1060–1108)

Louis VI the Fat　　Cecile　　　　Florus　　　　Philip　　　　　Constance
(1108–1137)　　　　　　　　　　　　count of Mantes　= Bohemond

Philip　　　　　Louis VII　　　　Robert　　　　Henry　　　　Constance
　　　　　　　(1137–1180)　　count of Dreux　archbishop of Reims
　　　　　　= (1) Eleanor of Aquitaine
　　　　　　= (2) Constance of Castile
　　　　　　= (3) Adela of Champagne

Agnes/Anna　　　　　　　Marie　　　　　Adelicia　　　　　Alice　　　Philip II Augustus
= (1) Alexius II Comnenus　　= Henry　　　= Theobald　　　= William　　(1180–1223)
= (2) Andronicus I Comnenus　count of Champagne　count of Blois　count of Ponthieu

Louis VIII　　　　　Philip Hurepel　　　　Peter Karlotus
(1223–1226)　　　　count of Clermont　　　bishop of Noyon
= Blanche of Castile

Louis IX (Saint Louis)　　Robert of Artois　　Alphonse of Poitou　　Charles of Anjou
(1226–1270)　　　　　　　　　　　　　　　　　　　　　　king of Sicily (*d.1285*)
= Margaret of Provence

NEW FORMS OF LEARNING AND RELIGIOUS EXPRESSION

The commercial revolution, the newly reorganized church, close contact with the Islamic world, and the revived polities of the early twelfth century paved the way for the growth of schools and new forms of scholarship. Money, learning, and career opportunities attracted many to the new centers. On the other hand, the cities and the schools repelled others, who retreated from the world to seek poverty and solitude. Yet the new learning and the new money had a way of seeping into the cracks and crannies of even the most resolutely separate institutions.

Schools and the Liberal Arts

Genealogy 5.4 (facing page): The Capetian Kings of France

Connected to monasteries and cathedrals since the Carolingian period, schools had traditionally trained young men to become monks or priests. Some schools were better endowed than others with books and masters (teachers); a few developed reputations for particular expertise. By the end of the eleventh century, the best schools were those connected to cathedrals in the larger cities. Reims, Paris, Bologna, Montpellier.

Eager students sampled nearly all of them. The young monk Gilbert of Liège was typical: "Instilled with an insatiable thirst for learning, whenever he heard of somebody excelling in the arts, he rushed immediately to that place and drank whatever delightful potion he could draw from the master there."[13] For Gilbert and other students, a good lecture had the excitement of the theater. Teachers at some schools were sometimes forced to find larger halls to accommodate the crush of students. Other teachers simply declared themselves "masters" and set up shop by renting a room. If they could prove their mettle as lecturers, they had no trouble finding paying students.

What the students sought, above all, was knowledge of the seven liberal arts. Grammar, rhetoric, and logic (or dialectic) belonged to the "beginning" arts, the so-called trivium. Logic, involving the technical analysis of texts as well as the application and manipulation of arguments, was a transitional subject leading to the second, higher part of the liberal arts, the quadrivium. This comprised four areas of study that might today be called theoretical math and science: arithmetic (number theory), geometry, music (theory rather than practice), and astronomy. Of these arts, logic had pride of place in the schools, while masters and students who studied the quadrivium generally did so outside of the classroom.

The goal of twelfth-century scholars was to gather, order, systematize, and clarify all knowledge. That God existed, nearly everyone believed. But scholars like Anselm of Bec were not satisfied by belief alone. Anselm's faith, as he put it, "sought understanding." He emptied his mind of all concepts except that of God and then, using the tools of logic, proved God's very existence in his *Monologion*. Gilbert of Poitiers (*c.*1075-1154) systematized Bible commentaries, helping to create the *Glossa Ordinaria*, the standard compendium of all teachings on the Bible. Peter Abelard (1079-1142), who declared that "nothing can be believed unless it is first understood," drew together conflicting authoritative texts on 156 key subjects in his *Sic et Non* (*Yes and No*), including "That God is one and the contrary" and "That it is permitted to kill men and the contrary." Leaving the propositions unresolved, Abelard urged his students to discover the reasons behind the disagreements. Soon Peter Lombard (*c.*1100-1160) adopted Abelard's method of juxtaposing opposing positions, but he supplied his own reasoned resolutions as well. His *Sententiae* was perhaps the most successful theology textbook of the entire Middle Ages.

One key logical issue for twelfth-century scholars involved the question of "universals": whether a universal—something that can be said of many—is real or simply a linguistic or mental entity. Abelard argued that "things either individually or collectively cannot be called universal, i.e., said to be predicated of many." He was maintaining a position later called "nominalist."[14] The other view was the "realist" position that claimed that things "predicated of many" were universal and real. For example, when we look at diverse individuals of one kind, say Fluffy and Mittens, we say of each of them that they are members of the same species: cat. Realists argued that "cat" was real. Nominalists thought it a mere word.

Later in the twelfth century, scholars found precise tools for this and other logical questions in the works of Aristotle. During Abelard's lifetime, very little of Aristotle's work was available in Europe because it had not been translated from Greek into Latin. By the end of the century, however, that lack had been filled by translators who traveled to Islamic or formerly Islamic cities—Toledo in Spain, Palermo in Sicily—where Aristotle had already been translated into Arabic and carefully commented on by Islamic scholars like Ibn Sina (Avicenna; see p. 150 above) (980-1037) and Ibn Rushd (Averroes) (1126-1198). By the thirteenth century, Aristotle had become the primary philosopher for the scholastics (the scholars of the European medieval universities).

The lofty subjects of the schools had down-to-earth, practical consequences in books for preachers, advice for rulers, manuals for priests, textbooks for students, and guides for living addressed to laypeople. Nor was mastery of the liberal arts the end of everyone's education. Many students went on to study medicine (the great schools for that were at Salerno and Montpellier) or theology (for which Paris was the center). Others studied law; at Bologna, for example, where Gratian worked on canon law, other jurists—such as the so-called Four Doctors—achieved fame by teaching and writing about Roman law. By the mid-twelfth century, scholars had made real progress toward a systematic understanding of Justinian's law codes (see pp. 54–56). The lawyers who emerged from the school at Bologna went on to serve popes, bishops, kings, princes, or communes. Thus the learning of the schools was preached in the churches, consulted in the law courts, and used on the operating tables. It came to unify European culture.

Robert Pullen's life may serve to illustrate the career of a moderately successful schoolman while suggesting some of the practical benefits of the new learning. Born in England, Pullen was sent to school at Laon, in France. Good at his studies, he became a master in turn. Back in England, he was (in the 1130s) the first lecturer in theology at Oxford. But Paris beckoned as the center of theological studies, and as soon as he got a church position in England (and the revenues attached to it), he went off to France. From there, he went to Rome, where his academic training helped him get appointed papal chancellor. He served perfectly capably in this post, meanwhile finding good jobs at the papal curia for some of his students, helping his nephew get a church post (the very one that Pullen had abandoned in England), and obtaining papal privileges for the monastery of yet another of his relatives.

Monastic Splendor and Poverty

That monastery, Sherborne Abbey, was an old-fashioned Benedictine house. There were many others. One that has been excavated particularly fully is Saint-Germain at Auxerre. In the twelfth century (see Fig. 5.1), it boasted a very large church with an elaborate narthex that served as a grand entranceway for liturgical processions. Toward the east of the church, where the altar stood and the monks sang the Offices, stairs led down to a crypt constructed during the Carolingian period. To the north and south were the conventual buildings — the sacristy (which stored liturgical vessels and vestments), the "chapter house" (where *The Benedictine Rule* was read), the common room, refectory (dining hall), kitchens, and cellar. At the center of all was the cloister, entirely enclosed by graceful arcades. Beyond these buildings were undoubtedly others — not yet excavated — for the craftsmen and servants of the monastery, for the ill, for pilgrims and other guests.

The whole purpose of this complex was to allow the monks to carry out a life of arduous and nearly continuous prayer. Every detail of their lives was ordered, every object splendid, every space adorned to render due honor to the Lord of heaven.

The chant mirrored this development. It had expanded enormously since the time of Charlemagne. By the twelfth century, a large repertoire of melodies had

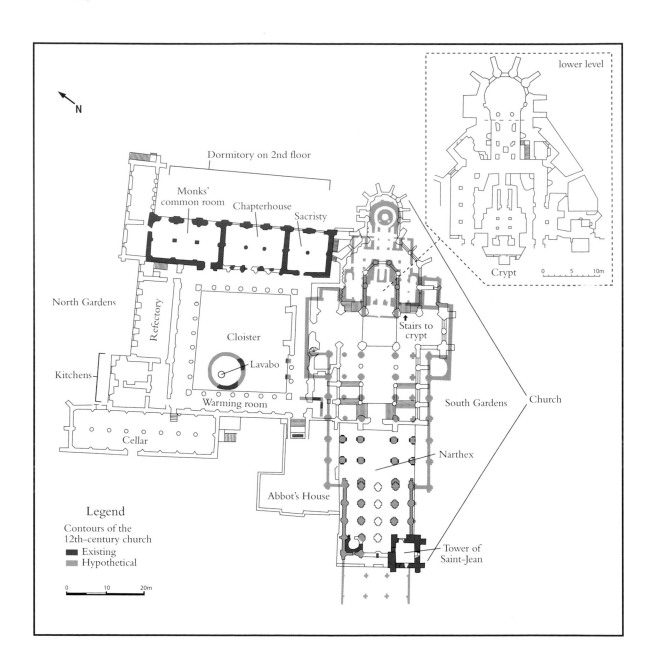

lower level

Crypt

0   5   10m

Dormitory on 2nd floor

Monks' common room

Chapterhouse

Sacristy

North Gardens

Refectory

Cloister

Lavabo

Stairs to crypt

South Gardens

Church

Kitchens

Warming room

Cellar

Narthex

Abbot's House

Tower of Saint-Jean

Legend

Contours of the 12th-century church

■ Existing

■ Hypothetical

0   10   20m

N

grown up, and new methods of musical notation had been elaborated to convey them. Scribes drew staves, sometimes multicolored, to show pitch. In Plate 5.3, a manuscript from the monastery of Saint-Evroult in Normandy, the scribe used a four-line staff (one red, one green, and two others lightly sketched) to indicate the locations of the pitches a-c-e-f.

The architecture and sculpture of twelfth-century churches like Saint-Germain were suited both to showcasing the chant and the honor due to God. The style, called Romanesque, represents the first wave of European monumental architecture. Built of stone, Romanesque churches are echo chambers for the sounds of the chant. Massive, weighty, and dignified, they nevertheless are often enlivened by sculpture, wall paintings, or patterned textures. At Durham Cathedral (built between 1093 and 1133 in the north of England), the stone itself is a warm yellow/pink color, given added zest by piers incised with diamond or zig-zag patterns. (See Plate 5.4.) By contrast, the

Figure 5.1 (facing page): Saint-Germain of Auxerre (12th cent.)

Plate 5.3: Gloria with Musical Notation, Saint-Evroult (12th cent.). The "Gloria," for which this manuscript page gives both text and music, was a chant of the Mass. Here the usual text of the Gloria has additional tropes (new words and music).

entire length of the vault of Sant Tomàs de Fluvià, a tiny monastic church in the County of Barcelona, was covered with paintings, a few of which remain today; Plate 5.5 shows the Last Supper. At the pilgrimage church of Vézelay, you see a forest of pillars enlivened by piers whose sculpted capitals are both beautiful and strange (see Plate 5.6). Pisa's famous leaning tower is in fact a Romanesque bell tower; here (Plate 5.7) the decoration is on the exterior, where the bright Italian sun heightens the play of light and shadow.

Santiago de Compostela (built between 1078 and 1124) may serve as an example of a "typical" Romanesque church, though in fact the most typical aspect of that style is its extreme variety. Most of Santiago's exterior was rebuilt in the Baroque period, but the interior is still much as it must have been when twelfth-century pilgrims entered the shrine of Saint James. (See Plate 5.8.) Striking is the "barrel" or "tunnel" vault whose ribs, springing from thin columns attached to the piers, mark the long church

Plate 5.4 (facing page): Durham Cathedral, Interior (1093–1133). Huge and imposing, Durham Cathedral is also inviting and welcoming, with its lively piers, warm colors, and harmonious spaces. Built by Norman bishops, it housed the relics of the Anglo-Saxon Saint Cuthbert; in just such ways did the Normans appropriate the power and prestige of English saints' cults.

Plate 5.5: Sant Tomàs de Fluvià, The Last Supper, Painted Vault (early 12th cent.). Sant Tomàs was one of many monastic and parish churches in the county of Barcelona richly decorated with paintings in the twelfth century. Here Christ is at the Last Supper with his apostles. The depiction closely follows John 13:23 when Jesus announces that one of his disciples will betray him: "Now there was leaning on Jesus's bosom one of his disciples [John] .... [John asked], 'Lord, who is it?' Jesus answered, 'He it is to whom I shall reach bread dipped.' And when he had dipped the bread, he gave it to Judas."

into sections called bays. There are only two levels: the first is formed by the arches that open onto the side aisles of the church; the second is the gallery (or triforium). (Many other Romanesque churches have a third story—a clerestory—of windows.) The plan of Santiago (see Figure 5.2) shows its typical basilica shape with a transept crossing and, at the east end, an aisle (called an "ambulatory") that allows pilgrims to visit the relics housed in the chapels.

Not all medieval people agreed that such opulence pleased or praised God, however. At the end of the eleventh century, the new commercial economy and the profit motive that fueled it led many to reject wealth and to embrace poverty as a key element of religious life. The Carthusian order, founded by Bruno, one-time bishop of Cologne, was such a group. La Grande Chartreuse, the chief house of the order, was built in an Alpine valley, lonely and inaccessible. Each monk took a vow of silence and lived as a hermit in his own small hut. Only occasionally would the monks join the others for prayer in a common oratory. When not engaged in prayer or meditation, the Carthusians copied manuscripts: for them, scribal work was a way to preach God's

word with the hands rather than the mouth. Slowly the Carthusian order grew, but each monastery was limited to only twelve monks, the number of Christ's Apostles.

By contrast, the Cistercians, another new monastic order, expanded rapidly, often by reforming and incorporating existing monasteries. The first Cistercian house was Cîteaux (in Latin, *Cistercium*), founded in 1098 by Robert of Molesme (*c.*1027-1110) and a few other monks seeking a more austere way of life. Austerity they found—and also success. With the arrival of Saint Bernard (*c.*1090-1153), who came to Cîteaux in 1112 along with about thirty friends and relatives, the original center sprouted a small congregation of houses in Burgundy. (Bernard became abbot of one of them, Clairvaux.) By the mid-twelfth century there were more than 300 monasteries—many in France, but also in Italy, Germany, England, Austria, and Spain—following what they took to be the customs of Cîteaux. By the end of the twelfth century, the Cistercians were an order: their member houses adhered to the decisions of a General Chapter; their liturgical practices and internal organization were

Plate 5.7: Leaning Tower (Bell Tower) of Pisa (late 12th cent.). The tower is part of a large cathedral and baptistery complex which, in its layout and design, was meant to imitate—and outshine—the Temple Mount complex at Jerusalem.

standardized. Many nuns, too, as eager as monks to live the life of simplicity and poverty that the Apostles had endured and enjoyed, adopted Cîteaux's customs; some convents later became members of the order.

Although the Cistercians claimed *The Benedictine Rule* as the foundation of their customs, they elaborated a style of life and an aesthetic all their own, largely governed by the goal of simplicity. They even rejected the conceit of dyeing their robes—hence their nickname, the "white monks." White, too, were their houses. Despite regional variations and considerable latitude in interpreting the meaning of "simplicity," Cistercian buildings had a different feel than the great Romanesque churches and Benedictine monasteries of black monks. Foursquare and regular, Cistercian churches and other buildings conformed to a fairly standard plan. (See Figure 5.3.) The churches tended to be small, made of smooth-cut, undecorated stone. Wall and vault

paintings were eschewed, any sculpture was modest at best. Indeed, Saint Bernard wrote a scathing attack on Romanesque sculpture in which, ironically, he admitted its sensuous allure:

> But what can justify that array of grotesques in the cloister where the brothers do their reading? .... What place have obscene monkeys, savage lions, unnatural centaurs, manticores, striped tigers, battling knights or hunters sounding their horns? You can see a head with many bodies and a multi-bodied head.... With such a bewildering array of shapes and forms on show, one would sooner read the sculptures than the books.[15]

The Cistercians had few such diversions, but the simplicity of their buildings and of their clothing also had its beauty. Illuminated by the pure white light that came through clear glass windows, Cistercian churches were luminous, cool, and serene. Plate 5.9 shows the nave of Fontenay Abbey, begun in 1139. There are no wall paintings, no sculpture, no incised pillars. Yet the subtle play of thick piers and thin columns along with the alternation of curved and linear capitals lends the church a sober charm.

True to their emphasis on purity, the Cistercians simplified their communal liturgy, pruning the many additions that had been tacked on in the houses of the black monks. Only the liturgy as prescribed in the *The Benedictine Rule* and one daily Mass were allowed. Even the music for the chant was modified: the Cistercians rigorously suppressed the B flat, even though doing so made the melody discordant, because of their insistence on strict simplicity.

On the other hand, *The Benedictine Rule* did not prevent the Cistercians from creating a new class of monks—the lay brothers—who were illiterate and unable to participate in the liturgy. These men did the necessary labor—field work, stock raising—to support the community at large. Compare Figure 5.3 with Figure 5.1: the Cistercian monastery was in fact a house divided. The eastern half was for the "choir" monks, the western half for the lay brethren. Each half had its own dining room, latrines, and dormitories. The monks were strictly segregated, even in the church, where a screen kept them apart.

Plate 5.8 (facing page): Santiago de Compostela, Interior (1078-1124). Santiago (in the far northwest corner of Spain) was known for its relics of Saint James the Great (*d.*44), apostle and martyr. From the twelfth through fifteenth centuries a major pilgrimage center, the cathedral was built to hold crowds and to usher them, via aisles, from chapel to chapel.

Figure 5.2: A Model Romanesque Church: Santiago de Compostela

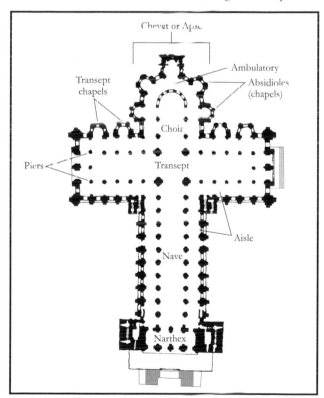

Plate 5.9 (facing page): Fontenay Abbey Church, Interior (1139-1147). Compare the bare walls of this Cistercian church with the frescoes of Sant Tomàs de Fluvià (Plate 5.5). How do these different artistic choices reflect different religious sensibilities?

Figure 5.3: Schematic Plan of a Cistercian Monastery

The choir monks dedicated themselves to private prayer and contemplation and to monastic administration. The Cistercian *Charter of Charity* (c.1165), in effect a constitution of the order, provided for a closely monitored network of houses, and each year the Cistercian abbots met to hammer out legislation for all of them. All the houses had large and highly organized farms and grazing lands called "granges," and the monks spent much of their time managing their estates and flocks of sheep, both of which yielded handsome profits by the end of the twelfth century. Clearly part of the agricultural and commercial revolutions of the Middle Ages, the Cistercian order made managerial expertise a part of the monastic life.

Yet the Cistercians also elaborated a spirituality of intense personal emotion. Their writings were filled with talk of love. When we pray, wrote Saint Bernard, "our breast expands .... our interior is filled with an overflowing love."[16] The Cistercians were devoted to the humanity of Christ and to his mother, Mary. While pilgrims continued to stream to the tombs and reliquaries of saints, the Cistercians dedicated all their churches to the Virgin Mary (for whom they had no relics) because for them she signified the model of a loving mother. Indeed, the Cistercians regularly used maternal

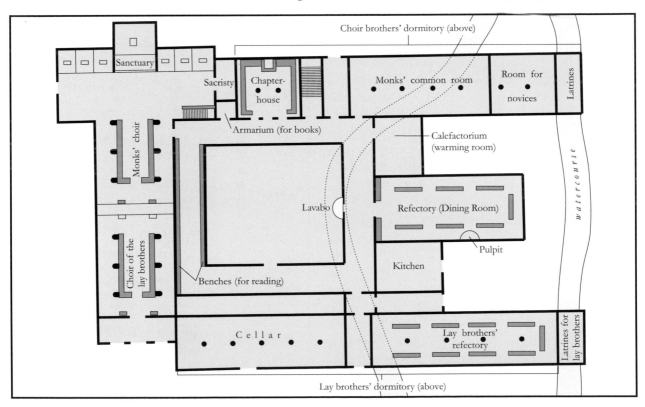

imagery to describe the nurturing care provided to humans by Jesus himself. The Cistercian God was approachable, human, protective, even mothering.

★ ★ ★ ★

In the twelfth century, Europe was coming into its own. Growing population and the profitable organization of the countryside promoted cities, trade, and wealth. Townspeople created new institutions of self-regulation and self-government. Kings and popes found new ways to exert their authority and test its limits. Scholars mastered the knowledge of the past and put it to use in classrooms, royal courts, and papal offices. Monks who fled the world ended up in positions of leadership; the great entrepreneurs of the twelfth century were the Cistercians; and Saint Bernard was the most effective preacher of the Second Crusade.

The power of communities was recognized in the twelfth century: the guilds and communes depended on this recognition. So too did the new theology of the time. In his theological treatise, *Why God Became Man*, Saint Anselm put new emphasis on Christ's humanity: Christ's sacrifice was that of one human being for another. The Cistercians spoke of God's mothering. Historians are in this sense right to speak of the importance of "humanism" — with its emphasis on the dignity of human beings, the splendor of the natural world, and the nobility of reason — in the twelfth century. Yet the stress on the loving bonds that tied Christians together also led to the persecution of others, like Jews and Muslims, who lived outside the Christian community. In the next century European communities would become more ordered, regulated, and incorporated. By the same token, they became even more exclusive.

NOTES

1. *Frederick of Hamburg's Agreement with Colonists from Holland*, in *Reading the Middle Ages. Sources from Europe, Byzantium, and the Islamic World*, ed. Barbara H. Rosenwein (Peterborough, ON, 2006), p.277.

2. *Chronicle of Saint-Bertin*, quoted in *Histoire de la France urbaine*, Vol. 2: *La ville médiévale* (Paris, 1980), p.71, here translated from the French.

3. Henry I, *Privileges for the Citizens of London*, in *Reading the Middle Ages*, p.279.

4. Pope Gregory VII, *Admonition to Henry* in *Power and the Holy in the Age of the Investiture Conflict: A Brief History with Documents*, ed. and trans. Maureen C. Miller (Boston, 2005), p.85.

5. *Roman Lenten Synod* in *The Correspondence of Pope Gregory VII: Selected Letters from the Registrum*, ed. and trans. Ephraim Emerton (New York, 1969), p.91.

6. Donald White, ed., *Medieval History. A Source Book* (Homewood, IL, 1965), pp.351-52.

7. Rabbi Eliezer b. Nathan, *O God, Insolent Men*, in *Reading the Middle Ages*, p.287.

8. Ibn al-Athir, *The First Crusade*, in *Reading the Middle Ages*, p.299.

9. *Anglo-Saxon Chronicle "E,"* quoted in David C. Douglas, *William the Conqueror: The Norman Impact upon England* (Berkeley, 1967), p.348.

10. *Poem of the Cid*, trans. W.S. Merwin (New York, 1959), pp.119-20.

11. Suger, *The Deeds of Louis the Fat*, ed. and trans. Richard C. Cusimano and John Moorhead (Washington, DC, 1992), p.48.

12. Suger, p.107.

13. Helene Wieruszowski, *The Medieval University* (Princeton, 1966), pp.123-24.

14. Abelard, *Glosses on Porphyry*, in *Reading the Middle Ages*, p.314.

15. St. Bernard, *Apologia*, in *Reading the Middle Ages*, p.331.

16. Bernard of Clairvaux, *On the Song of Songs*, Vol. 1, trans. Kilian Walsh, Cistercian Fathers Series, 4 (Kalamazoo, 1977), p.58.

FURTHER READING

Asbridge, Thomas. *The First Crusade: A New History*. Oxford, 2004.

Benson, Robert L., and Giles Constable, eds. *Renaissance and Renewal in the Twelfth Century*. Cambridge, 1982.

Berman, Constance Hoffman. *The Cistercian Evolution: The Invention of a Religious Order in Twelfth-Century Europe*. Philadelphia, 2000.

Blumenthal, Uta-Renate. *The Investiture Controversy: Church and Monarchy from the Ninth to the Twelfth Century*. Philadelphia, 1988.

Harris, Jonathan. *Byzantium and the Crusades*. London, 2003.

Iogna-Prat, Dominique. *Order and Exclusion: Cluny and Christendom Face Heresy, Judaism, and Islam (1000-1150)*. Translated by Graham Robert Edwards. Ithaca, NY, 2002.

Lawson, M.K. *Cnut: The Danes in England in the Early Eleventh Century*. London, 1993.

Little, Lester K. *Religious Poverty and the Profit Economy in Medieval Europe*. Ithaca, NY, 1978.

Mews, Constant J. *Abelard and Heloise*. Oxford, 2005.

Miller, Maureen C. *The Formation of a Medieval Church: Ecclesiastical Change in Verona, 950-1150*. Ithaca, NY, 1993.

Reilly, Bernard F. *The Kingdom of León-Castilla under Queen Urraca, 1109-1126*. Princeton, 1982.

Riley-Smith, Jonathan, ed. *The Oxford History of the Crusades*. Oxford, 1999.

Robinson, Ian S. *Henry IV of Germany*. Cambridge, 2000.

Southern, R.W. *Scholastic Humanism and the Unification of Europe*. Vol. 1: *Foundations*. Oxford, 1995.

Tyerman, Christopher. *God's War: A New History of the Crusades*. Cambridge, MA, 2006.

Weinfurter, Stefan. *The Salian Century: Main Currents in an Age of Transition*. Trans. Barbara M. Bowlus. Philadelphia, 1999.

Winroth, Anders. *The Making of Gratian's Decretum*. Cambridge, 2000.

To test your knowledge of this chapter, please go to
www.rosenweinshorthistory.com
and click "Study Questions."

SIX

INSTITUTIONALIZING ASPIRATIONS (c.1150-c.1250)

The lively developments of early twelfth-century Europe were institutionalized in the next decades. Fluid associations became corporations. Rulers hired salaried officials to staff their administrations. Churchmen defined the nature and limits of religious practice. While the Islamic world largely went its own way, only minimally affected by European developments, Byzantium was carved up by its Christian neighbors.

TWO NON-EUROPEAN HEIRS OF THE ROMAN EMPIRE: THE SEQUEL

Nothing could be more different than the fates of the Islamic world and of Byzantium at the beginning of the thirteenth century. The Muslims remained strong; the Byzantine Empire nearly came to an end.

Islam on the Move

Like grains of sand in an oyster's shell—irritating but also generative—the Christian states of the Levant and Spain helped spark new Islamic principalities, one based in the Maghreb, the other in Syria and Egypt. In the Maghreb, the Almohads (1147-1266), a

Berber group espousing a militant Sunni Islam, combined conquest with a program to "purify" the morals of their fellow Muslims. In al-Andalus their appearance induced some Islamic rulers to seek alliances with the Christian rulers to the north. But other Andalusian rulers joined forces with the Almohads, who replaced the Almoravids as rulers of the whole Islamic far west by 1172. (See Map 6.1.) At war continuously with Christian Spanish rulers, in 1212 they suffered a terrible defeat. For the Christian victors, the battle was known simply by its place name, Las Navas de Tolosa; but for the Almohads, it was known as "The Punishment." It was the beginning of the end of al-Andalus.

Meanwhile, however, in the shadow of the Crusader States, Nur al-Din (*r.*1146-1174), son of Zengi (see p. 197), forged a united Syria. Soon, in the 1150s, he conquered the county of Edessa and cut the principality of Antioch in half. In 1168 he sent his general Shirkuh to Egypt to aid the Fatimid vizier there. But Shirkuh turned against the vizier and took his place. Two months later, when Shirkuh died, his nephew Saladin (*r.*1171-1193) succeeded him, and when the Fatimid caliph died, Saladin simply took over Egypt, ostensibly in the name of Nur al-Din.

Map 6.1: The Almohads before the Battle of Las Navas de Tolosa (1212)

Three years later, when Nur al-Din died, Saladin was ready to take over Syria. By 1183 he was master of Egypt, most of Syria, and part of Iraq. Like the Almohads, Saladin was determined to reform the faith along the Sunni model and to wage *jihad* against the Christian states in his backyard:

> [Saladin] perceived that his gratitude for God's favor towards him, evidenced by his strong grasp on sovereignty, his God-given control over the lands, and the people's willing obedience, could only be demonstrated by his endeavoring to exert himself to the utmost and to strive to fulfill the precept of Jihad.[1]

Thus did ibn Shaddad, a close associate of Saladin's, describe the motivations behind the battle of Hattin in 1187, in which the Kingdom of Jerusalem was taken by Saladin's forces. The Christian army was badly defeated, the Crusader States reduced to a few port cities. For about a half-century thereafter, Saladin's descendants (the Ayyubids) held on to the lands he had conquered. Then the dynasty gave way (as we have often seen happen) to new military leaders. The chief difference this time was that these leaders were uniformly of Turkic slave and ex-slave origins—they were *mamluks*. The Mamluk Sultanate was exceptionally stable, holding on to Egypt and most of Syria until 1517.

The Undoing of Byzantium

In 1204 the leaders of the Fourth Crusade made a "detour" and conquered Constantinople instead. We shall later explore some of the reasons why they did so. But in the context of Byzantine history, the question is not why the Europeans attacked but rather why the Byzantines lost the fight.

Certainly the Byzantines themselves had no idea they were "in decline." Prior to 1204, they had reconquered some of Anatolia. In the capital, the imperial court continued to function; its bureaucracy and machinery of taxation were still in place; and powerful men continued to vie to be emperors—as if there were still power and glory in the position. Yet much had changed from the heyday of the Comneni.

While the economy, largely based on peasant labor, boomed in the twelfth century, this ironically brought the peasants to their knees. Every landowner needed cultivators, but peasants had no way to bargain to improve their lot. Peasants worked for the state on imperial lands. They worked for military men when the emperors took to giving out *pronoiai*— grants of land to soldiers rather than wages in return for military service. Finally, peasants worked for the *dynatoi*, the great landowners who dominated

N O R W A Y

S W E D E N

North Sea

Baltic Sea

D E N M A R K

Lithuania *(1263)*

Lithuania

Lithuania *(1263)*

Dvina

Teutonic Knights

Mecklenburg

Pomerania

Brandenburg

Saxony

Cologne

Meissen

P o l a n d

R u s

Kiev

Elbe

Oder

Vistula

G E R M A N Y

Rhine

T h e

Prague

Bohemia

Dniester

Swabia

Danube

Bavaria

Austria

Vienna

Danube

Carpathian Mountains

G o l d e n   H o r d e

France

Besançon

E m p i r e

Burgundy

H u n g a r y

Legnano

Milan

Venice

Croatia

Pavia

Po

Roncaglia

I t a l y

Zara

Split

Bosnia

Danube

Black Sea

Genoa

Bologna

Florence

Pisa

Adriatic Sea

S e r b i a

B u l g a r i a

Marseille

Assisi

Papal States

Ragusa (Đubrovnik)

Latin Empire

Constantinople

Corsica
(Pisan c. 1020)

Rome

Venice Route of the Fourth Crusade

Epirus

Nicaea

Sardinia
(Pisan c. 1050)

Apulia

Corfu

Aegean Sea

Empire of Nicaea

Naples

Salerno

Kingdom of Sicily

Calabria

Latin Empire

Athens

Rhodes

Palermo

Mediterranean

Crete

Sea

Legend

━━━ Borders of the Empire

░░░ Byzantine successor states

▓▓▓ Latin Empire of Constantinople

▒▒▒ Held by Venice

Scale

0 ———— 300 km

0 ———— 200 mi

whole regions. To all they paid taxes and rents. But there were only so many peasants, certainly not enough to cultivate all the land that the elites wanted to bring into production.

Manpower was scarce in every area of the economy. Skilled craftsmen, savvy merchants, and seasoned warriors were needed, but where were they to be found? Sometimes Jews were called upon; more often foreigners took up the work. Whole army contingents were made up of foreigners: Cumans, "Franks" (the Byzantine name for all Europeans), Turks. Forced to fight on numerous fronts, the army was not very effective; by the end of the twelfth century the Byzantines had lost much of the Balkans to what historians call the Second Bulgarian Empire.

Foreigners, mainly Italians, dominated Byzantium's long-distance trade. Italian neighborhoods (complete with homes, factories, churches, and monasteries) crowded the major cities of the empire. At the capital city itself, stretched along the Golden Horn like pearls on a string, were the Venetian Quarter, the Amalfitan Quarter, the Pisan Quarter, and the Genoese Quarter: these were the neighborhoods of the Italian merchants, exempt from imperial taxes and uniformly wealthy. (See Map 4.1 on p. 140.) They were heartily resented by the rest of Constantinople's restive and impoverished population, which needed little prodding to attack and loot the Italian quarters in 1182 and again in 1203, when they could see the crusaders camped right outside their city.

None of this meant that Europeans had to take over, of course. Yet in 1204, crusader armies breached the walls of Constantinople, encountered relatively little opposition, plundered the city for three days, and finally declared one of their leaders, Baldwin of Flanders, the new emperor. The Venetians gained the city harbor, Crete, and key Greek cities; other crusaders carved out other states. (See Map 6.2.) So did some Byzantines, however, and eventually, in 1261, their successors managed to recapture Constantinople and re-establish their empire until it fell for good in 1453 to the Ottoman Turks.

Map 6.2 (facing page): Central Europe, *c.*1250

THE INSTITUTIONALIZATION OF GOVERNMENT IN THE WEST

Some Byzantines thought that the West bested them in 1204 because it had a better "sense of decorum," a better sense of order, than they had.[2] Given the meticulous court protocol and well-oiled bureaucracy at Constantinople, it is hard to see how people there could have viewed the Europeans as better organized. But the Byzantine critics had a point. While their emperors were favoring family members and their *dynatoi* were creating regional dynasties, some Western governments were becoming more impersonal. They were, in effect, in the midst of a new phase of self-definition, codification, and institutionalization.

Law, Authority, and the Written Word in England

One good example is England. The king hardly needed to be present: the government functioned by itself, with its own officials to handle administrative matters and record keeping. The very circumstances of the English king favored the growth of an administrative staff: his frequent travels to and from the Continent meant that officials needed to work in his absence, and his enormous wealth meant that he could afford them.

True, a long period of civil war (1135-1154) between the forces of two female heirs

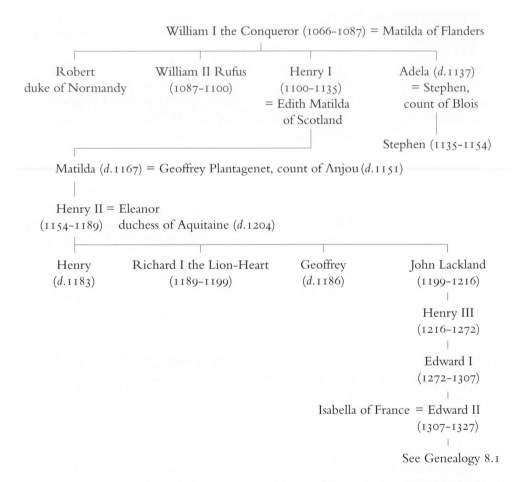

Genealogy 6.1: The Norman and Angevin Kings of England

to the Norman throne (Matilda, daughter of Henry I, and Adela, Henry's sister) threatened royal power. As in Germany during the Investiture Conflict, so in England the barons and high churchmen consolidated their own local lordships during the war; private castles, symbols of their independence, peppered the countryside. But the war ended when Matilda's son, Henry of Anjou, ascended the throne as the first "Angevin" king of England.[3] (See Genealogy 6.1: The Norman and Angevin Kings of England.) Under Henry II (r.1154-1189), the institutions of royal government in England were extended and strengthened.

THE REFORMS OF HENRY II

Henry was count of Anjou, duke of Normandy, and overlord of about half the other counties of northern France. He was also duke of Aquitaine by his marriage to Eleanor, heiress of that vast southern French duchy. As for his power in the British Isles: the princes of Wales swore him homage and fealty; the rulers of Ireland were forced to submit to him; and the king of Scotland was his vassal. Thus Henry exercised sometimes more, sometimes less power over a realm stretching from northern England to the Pyrenees. (See Map 6.3.) For his Continental possessions, he was vassal of the king of France.

Once on the English throne, Henry destroyed or confiscated the private castles built during the civil war and regained the lands that had belonged to the crown. Then he proceeded to extend his power, above all by imposing royal justice. Already the Anglo-Saxon kings had claimed rights in local courts, particularly in capital cases, even though those courts were dominated by powerful men largely independent of royal authority. The Norman kings added to Anglo-Saxon law in the area of land holding. Henry built on these institutions, regularizing, expanding, and systematizing them. The Assize of Clarendon in 1166 recorded that the king

> decreed that inquiry shall be made throughout the several counties and
> throughout the several hundreds ... whether there be ... any man accused
> or notoriously suspect of being a robber or murderer or thief.... And let the
> justices inquire into this among themselves and sheriffs among themselves.[4]

"Throughout the several counties and throughout the several hundreds": these were the districts into which England had long been divided. Henry aimed to apply a *common* law regarding chief crimes—a law applicable throughout England—to all men and women in the land. Moreover, he meant his new system to be habitual and routine. There had always been justices to enforce the law, but under Henry, there were many more of them; they were trained in the law and required to make regular

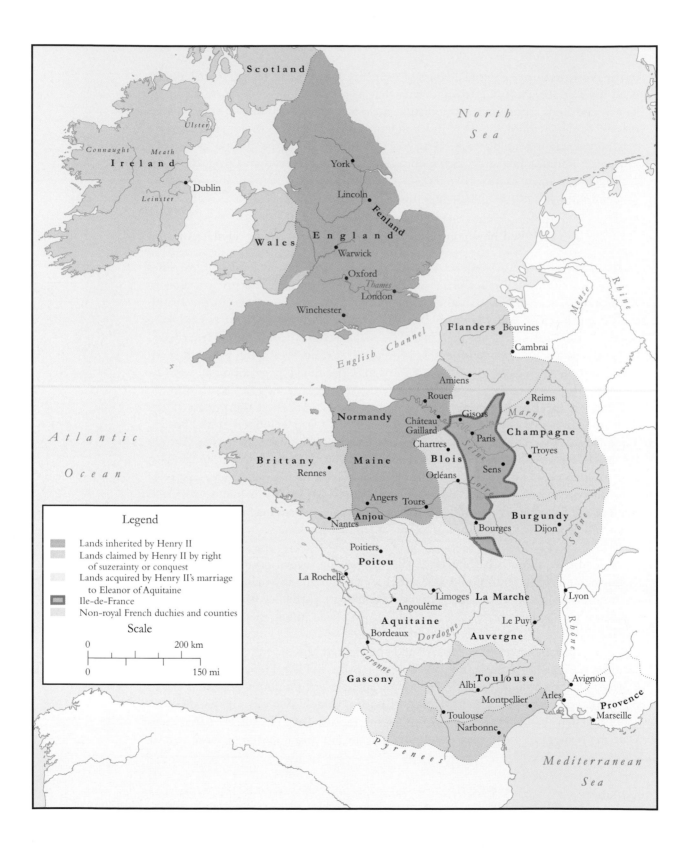

Scotland

Ireland

Connaught
Ulster
Meath
Leinster

Dublin

North Sea

York
Lincoln
Fenland

Wales

England

Warwick
Oxford *Thames*
London
Winchester

English Channel

Flanders Bouvines
Cambrai

Amiens
Rouen
Normandy Château Gisors
Gaillard Paris
Chartres
Blois Sens
Orléans
Seine
Loire
Bourges

Marne Reims

Champagne
Troyes

Atlantic Ocean

Brittany **Maine**
Rennes

Angers Tours
Anjou
Nantes

Poitiers
Poitou

La Rochelle

Burgundy
Dijon
Saône

Limoges **La Marche**
Angoulême
Lyon

Aquitaine
Bordeaux *Dordogne*

Le Puy
Auvergne

Rhône

Gascony

Albi **Toulouse**
Montpellier
Toulouse
Narbonne

Pyrenees

Avignon
Arles
Provence
Marseille

Mediterranean Sea

Meuse *Rhine*

Legend

Lands inherited by Henry II
Lands claimed by Henry II by right of suzerainty or conquest
Lands acquired by Henry II's marriage to Eleanor of Aquitaine
Ile-de-France
Non-royal French duchies and counties

Scale

0   200 km
0   150 mi

visitations to each locality, inquiring about crimes and suspected crimes. (They were therefore called "itinerant justices"—from *iter*, Latin for journey. The local hearing that they held was called an eyre, also from *iter*.) The king required twelve representatives of the local knightly class—the middling aristocracy, later on known as the "gentry"— to meet during each eyre and either give the sheriff the names of those suspected of committing crimes in the vicinity or arrest the suspects themselves and hand them over to the royal justices. While convicted members of the knightly class often got off with only a fine, hanging or mutilation were the normal penalties for criminals. Even if acquitted, people "of ill repute" were to "cross the sea," exiled from England.[5]

Henry also exercised new control over cases that we would call "civil," requiring all cases of property ownership to be authorized by a royal writ. Unlike the Angevin reforms of criminal law, this requirement affected only the class of free men and women—a minority. While often glad to have the king's protection, they grumbled at the expense and time required to obtain writs. Consider Richard of Anstey's suit to gain his uncle's property: over the course of five years, he paid out a great deal of money for royal writs; for journeys to line up witnesses and to visit various courts; for the expenses of his clerical staff; and for gifts to numerous officials. Yet it was all worthwhile in the end, for "*at length* by grace of the lord king and by the judgment of his court my uncle's land was adjudged to me."[6]

The whole system was no doubt originally designed to put things right after the civil war. Although these law-and-order measures were initially expensive for the king—he had to build many new jails, for example—they ultimately served to increase royal income and power. Fines came from condemned criminals and also from any knightly representative who might shirk his duties before the eyre; revenues poured in from the purchase of writs. The exchequer, as the financial bureau of England was called, recorded all the fines paid for judgments and the sums collected for writs. The amounts, entered on parchment leaves sewn together and stored as rolls, became the Receipt Rolls and Pipe Rolls, the first of many such records of the English monarchy and an indication that writing had become a tool to institutionalize royal rule in England.

Perhaps the most important outcome of this expanded legal system was the enhancement of royal power and prestige. The king of England touched (not personally but through men acting in his name) nearly every man and woman in the realm. However, the extent of royal jurisdiction should not be exaggerated. Most petty crimes did not end up in royal courts but rather in more local ones under the jurisdiction of a lord. Thus the case of Hugh Tree came before a manorial court run by officials of the monastery of Bec. They held that he was "in mercy [liable to a fine] for his beasts caught in the lord's garden."[7] He had to pay 6 pence to his lord (in this case the monastery); no money went to the king. This helps explain why manorial

Map 6.3 (facing page): The Angevin and Capetian Realms in the Late Twelfth Century

lords—barons, knights, bishops, and monasteries like Bec—held on tenaciously to their local prerogatives.

In addition to local courts were those run by and for the clergy. Had Hugh Tree committed murder, he would have come before a royal court. Had he been a homicidal cleric, however, he would have come before a church court, which could be counted on to give him a mild punishment. No wonder that churchmen objected to submitting to the jurisdiction of Henry II's courts. But Henry insisted, and the ensuing contest between the king and his appointed archbishop, Thomas Becket (1118-1170), became the greatest battle between the church and the state in the twelfth century. The conflict over whose courts should have jurisdiction over "criminous clerks"—clerics accused of crimes— simmered for six years, until Henry's henchmen murdered Thomas, unintentionally turning him into a martyr. Although Henry's role in the murder remained ambiguous, public outcry forced him to do public penance for the deed. In the end, the struggle made both institutions stronger, as church and royal courts expanded side-by-side to address the concerns of an increasingly litigious society.

DEFINING THE ROLE OF THE ENGLISH KING

Henry II and his sons Richard I the Lion-Heart (r.1189-1199) and John (r.1199-1216) were English kings with an imperial reach. Richard was rarely in England, since half of France was his to subdue (see Map 6.3, paying attention to the areas in various shades of peach). Responding to Saladin's conquest of Jerusalem, Richard went on the abortive Third Crusade (1189-1192), capturing Cyprus on the way and arranging a three-year truce with Saladin before rushing home to reclaim his territory from his brother, John, and the French king, Philip II (r.1180-1223). (His haste did him no good; he was captured by the duke of Austria and released only upon payment of a huge ransom, painfully squeezed out of the English people.)

When Richard died in battle in 1199, John took over. But if he began with an imperial reach, John must have felt a bit like the Byzantine emperor in 1204, for in that very year the king of France, Philip II, confiscated his northern French territories for defying his overlordship. It was a purely military victory, and John set out to win the territories back by gathering money wherever and however he could in order to pay for an abler military force. He forced his barons and many members of the gentry to pay him "scutage"—a tax—in lieu of army service. He extorted money in the form of "aids"—the fees that his barons and other vassals ordinarily paid on rare occasions, such as the knighting of the king's eldest son. He compelled the widows of his barons and other vassals to marry men of his choosing or pay him a hefty fee to remain single. With the wealth pouring in from these effective but unpopular measures, John was able to pay for a navy and hire mercenary troops.

All was to no avail. Philip's forces soundly defeated John's in 1214 at the battle of Bouvines. It was a defining moment, not so much for the Continent (English rule would continue there until the fifteenth century) as for England, where the barons—supported by many members of the gentry and the towns—organized, rebelled, and called the king to account. At Runnymede, just south of London, in June 1215, John was forced to agree to the charter of baronial liberties called Magna Carta, or "Great Charter," so named to distinguish it from a smaller charter issued around the same time concerning royal forests.

Magna Carta was intended to be a conservative document defining the "customary" obligations and rights of the nobility and forbidding the king to break from these without consulting his barons. Beyond this, it maintained that all free men in England had certain customs and rights in common that the king was obliged to uphold. "To no one will we sell, to no one will we refuse or delay right or justice."[8] In this way, Magna Carta documented the subordination of the king to written provisions; it implied that the king was not above the law. Copies of the charter were sent to sheriffs and other officials, to be read aloud in public places. Everyone knew what it said, and later kings continued to issue it—and have it read out—in one form or another. Though not a "constitution," nevertheless Magna Carta was an important step in the institutionalization of the English government.

Spain and France in the Making

Two states—Spain and France—started small and beleaguered but slowly grew to embrace the territory we associate with them today. In Spain, the *reconquista* was the engine driving expansion. Like the king of England, the kings from northern Spain came as conquerors. But unlike England, Christian Spain had numerous kings who competed with one another. By the mid-thirteenth century, Spain had the three-fold political configuration that would last for centuries (compare Map 6.1 on p. 220 with Map 7.5 on p. 276 and Map 8.5 on p. 320): to the east was the kingdom of Aragon-Catalonia; in the middle was Castile; and in the southwest was Portugal.

All of the Spanish kings appointed military religious orders similar to the Templars to form permanent garrisons along their ever-moving frontier with al-Andalus. But how were the kings to deal with formerly Muslim-controlled lands? When he conquered Cuenca in 1177, King Alfonso VIII of Castile (r.1158-1214) established a bishopric and gave the city a detailed set of laws (*fueros*) that became the model for other conquests. Confiding enforcement to local officials, the king issued the *fueros* to codify, as its preface puts it, "judicial institutions in behalf of safeguarding peace and the rights of justice between clergy and laity, between townsmen and peasants, among the needy and the poor."[9] The preface might have added that the laws also regulated relations between local Christians, Muslims, and Jews.

The kingdom of France was smaller and more fragile than Spain; it was lucky that it did not confront an Islamic frontier or competing royal neighbors (though a glance at Map 6.3 shows that it was surrounded by plenty of independent counts and dukes). When Philip II (r.1180-1223) came to the throne at the age of fourteen, his kingdom consisted largely of the Ile-de-France, a dwarf surrounded by giants. Philip seemed an easy target for the ambitions of English King Henry II and the counts of Flanders and Champagne. Philip, however, played them off against one another. Through inheritance he gained a fair portion of the county of Flanders in 1191. Soon his military skills came to the fore as he wrenched Normandy from the king of England in 1204. This was the major conquest of his career, and in its wake he soon forced the lords of Maine, Anjou, and Poitou, once vassals of the king of England, to submit to him. A contemporary chronicler dubbed him Philip Augustus — after the expansionist first Roman emperor — and Philip's seal, used to authenticate his documents, boasted an eagle, the symbol of imperial power.

Philip did more than expand; he integrated his Norman conquest into his kingdom. Norman nobles promised him homage and fealty, while Philip's royal officers went about their business in Normandy — taxing, hearing cases, careful not to tread on local customs, but equally careful to enhance the flow of income into the French king's treasury. Gradually the Normans were brought into a new "French" orbit just beginning to take shape, constructed partly out of the common language of French and partly out of a new notion of the king as ruler of all the people in his territory.

Although there was never a French "common law" to supersede local ones, the French king, like the Spanish and English, succeeded in extending royal power through governmental bureaucracy. After 1194, Philip had all his decrees written down, establishing permanent repositories in which to keep them. Like the Angevin kings of England, Philip relied on members of the lesser nobility — knights and clerics, most of them educated in the city schools — to do the work of government. They served as officers of his court; as *prévôts*, officials who oversaw the king's estates and collected his taxes; and as *baillis* (or, in some places, seneschals) who not only supervised the *prévôts* but also functioned as judges, presiding over courts that met monthly, making the king's power felt locally as never before.

Of Empires and City-States

The empire ruled by the German king was an oddity. Elsewhere, smaller states were the norm. But the German king's empire spanned both Germany and Italy. In its embrace of peoples of contrasting traditions, it was more like Byzantium than like England. The location of the papacy made the empire different as well. Every other state was a safe distance away from the pope; but the empire had the pope in its throat. Tradition, prestige, and political self-respect demanded that the German king also be the emperor: Conrad III (r.1138-1152), though never actually crowned at Rome, nevertheless delighted in calling himself "August Emperor of the Romans" (while demeaning the Byzantine emperor as "King of the Greeks"). But being emperor meant controlling Italy and Rome. The difficulty was not only the papacy, defiantly opposed to another major power in Italy, but also the northern Italian communes, independent city-states in their own right.

THE REVIVAL AND DETERIORATION OF THE EMPIRE

Like the Angevin Henry II of England, Frederick I Barbarossa (r.1152-1190) came to the throne after a long period of bitter civil war between families—the Staufen and the Welfs—spawned in the wake of the Investiture Conflict. Contemporaries hailed him as a reconciler of enemies: he was Staufen on his father's side and Welf on his mother's. (See Genealogy 6.2: Rulers of Germany and Sicily.) Like the English king, Frederick held a kingdom and more. But he lacked Henry's wealth. As a result he was forced to rely on personal loyalties, not salaried civil servants. He could not tear down princely castles as Henry had done. Instead, he conceded the German princes their powers, requiring them in turn to recognize him as the source of those powers, and committing them to certain obligations, such as attending him at court and providing him with troops.

Frederick had to deal with more than the princes; he had to confront the papacy. In 1157, at the Diet of Besançon, Pope Adrian IV sent Frederick a letter that coyly referred to the imperial crown as the pope's *beneficium*— "benefit" or, more ominously, "fief." "A great tumult and uproar arose from the princes of the realm at so insolent a message," wrote Rahewin, a cleric who had access to many of the documents and people involved at the time. "It is said that one of the [papal] ambassadors, as though adding sword to flame, inquired: 'From whom then does he have the empire, if not from our lord the pope?' Because of this remark, anger reached such a pitch that one of [the princes] ... threatened the ambassador with his sword."[10]

Frederick calmed his supporters, but in the wake of this incident, he countered the "holy church" by coining an equally charged term for his empire: *sacrum imperium*— the "sacred empire." In 1165 he exhumed the body of Charlemagne, enclosing the

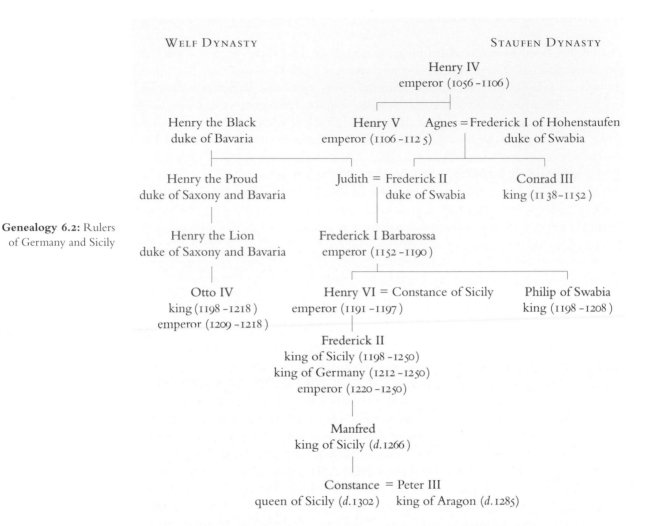

WELF DYNASTY   STAUFEN DYNASTY

Henry IV
emperor (1056–1106)

Henry the Black   Henry V   Agnes = Frederick I of Hohenstaufen
duke of Bavaria   emperor (1106–1125)   duke of Swabia

Henry the Proud   Judith = Frederick II   Conrad III
duke of Saxony and Bavaria   duke of Swabia   king (1138–1152)

Henry the Lion   Frederick I Barbarossa
duke of Saxony and Bavaria   emperor (1152–1190)

Otto IV   Henry VI = Constance of Sicily   Philip of Swabia
king (1198–1218)   emperor (1191–1197)   king (1198–1208)
emperor (1209–1218)
                        Frederick II
                   king of Sicily (1198–1250)
                   king of Germany (1212–1250)
                     emperor (1220–1250)

                         Manfred
                   king of Sicily (d.1266)

                Constance = Peter III
          queen of Sicily (d.1302)   king of Aragon (d.1285)

Genealogy 6.2: Rulers of Germany and Sicily

dead emperor's arm in an ornate reliquary casket (Plate 6.1) and setting the wheels of canonization in motion. (Charlemagne was named a saint by Frederick's anti-pope, Pascal III. See the list of Popes and Antipopes to 1500 on p. 359 to see the many competing popes of Barbarossa's reign.)

Finally, Frederick had to deal with Italy. As emperor, he had claims on the whole peninsula, but he had no hope—or even interest—in controlling the south. By contrast, northern Italy beckoned: added to his own inheritance in Swabia (in southwestern Germany), its rich cities promised to provide him with both a compact power base and the revenues that he needed. (See Map 6.2.)

Taking northern Italy was, however, nothing like, say, conquering Normandy, which was used to ducal rule. The communes of Italy were themselves states (autonomous cities, yes, but each also with a good deal of surrounding land, their *contado*), jealous of their liberties, rivalrous, and fiercely patriotic. Frederick made no concessions to their sensibilities. Emboldened by theories of sovereignty that had been elaborated by the revival of Roman law, he marched into Italy and, at the Diet of Roncaglia (1158), demanded all

> dukedoms, marches, counties, consulates, mints, market tolls, forage taxes, wagon tolls, gate tolls, transit tolls, mills, fisheries, bridges, all the use accruing from running water, and the payment of an annual tax, not only on the land, but also on their own persons.[11]

Meanwhile, Frederick brought the Four Doctors (see p. 204) from Bologna to Roncaglia to hear court cases. He insisted that the conquered cities be governed by his own men, sending in *podestà* (city managers) who were often German-speaking and heavy-handed. No sooner had the *podestà* at Milan taken up his post, for example, than he immediately ordered an inventory of all taxes due the emperor and levied new and demeaning labor duties. He even demanded that the Milanese carry the wood and stones of their plundered city to Pavia, to build new houses there. This was a double humiliation: Milan had been at war with Pavia.

By 1167, most of the cities of northern Italy had joined with Pope Alexander III (1159-1181) to form the Lombard League against Frederick. Defeated at the battle of Legnano in 1176, Frederick agreed to the Peace of Venice the next year and withdrew most of his forces from the region. But his failure in the north led him to try a southern strategy. By marrying his son Henry VI (r.1190-1197) to Constance, heiress of the Kingdom of Sicily, Frederick Barbarossa linked the fate of his dynasty to a well-organized monarchy that commanded dazzling wealth.

As we have seen (p. 181), the Kingdom of Sicily had been created by Normans. In theory, it was held as a fief from the pope, who recognized its boundaries (lapping at the southern edge of the papal states) in 1156 in the treaty of Benevento. Both multilingual and multi-religious, the Kingdom of Sicily embraced Jews, Muslims, Greeks, and Italians. Indeed, the Normans saw themselves as heirs to the Byzantines and Muslims and frequently came close to conquering Byzantium and North Africa. Taking over the Byzantine and Islamic administrative apparatuses already in place in their kingdom, they crafted a highly centralized government, with royal justices circuiting the kingdom and salaried civil servants drawn from the level of knights and townsmen.

Henry and Constance's son Frederick II (1194-1250) tried to unite Sicily, Italy, and

Germany into an imperial unit. He failed: the popes, eager to carve out their own well-ordered state in the center of Italy, could not allow a strong monarch to encircle them. Declaring war on Frederick, the papacy not only excommunicated him several times but also declared him deposed and accused him of heresy, a charge that led to declaring a crusade against him in the 1240s. These were fearsome actions. The king of France urged negotiation and reconciliation, but others saw in Frederick the devil himself. In the words of one chronicler, Frederick was "an evil and accursed man, a schismatic, a heretic, and an epicurean, who 'defiled the whole earth' (Jer.51:25)" because he sowed the seeds of division and discord in the cities of Italy.[12]

This was one potent point of view. There were others, more admiring. Frederick was a poet, a patron of the arts, and the founder of the first state-supported university, which he built at Naples. His administrative reforms in Sicily were comparable to Henry II's in England: he took what he found and made it routine. In the *Constitutions of Melfi* (1231) he made sure that his salaried officials worked according to uniform procedures, required nearly all litigation to be heard by royal courts, regularized commercial privileges, and set up a system of royal taxation. In 1232 he began minting gold coins, a turning point in European currency.

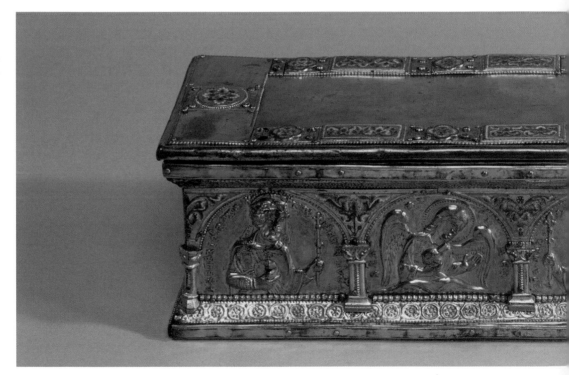

Plate 6.1: Reliquary Casket for Charlemagne's Arm (*c.*1166-1170). Pairing the cult of Charlemagne with that of the Madonna, this reliquary casket, made to hold Charlemagne's arm, depicts Mary and the Child in the center of an arcade. Mother and child are flanked on either side by archangels. Frederick Barbarossa is depicted within the arch on the far left, while his wife, Beatrice, is on the far right, thus associating the reigning rulers with the sainted emperor.

The struggle with the papacy obliged Frederick to grant enormous concessions to the German princes to give himself a free hand. In effect, he allowed the princes to turn their territories into independent states. Until the nineteenth century, Germany was a mosaic, not of city-states like Italy but of principalities. Between 1254 and 1273 the princes, split into factions, kept the German throne empty by electing two different foreigners who spent their time fighting each other. Oddly enough, it was during this low point of the German monarchy that the term "Holy Roman Empire" was coined. In 1273, the princes at last united and elected a German, Rudolf I (*r*.1273-1291), whose family, the Habsburg, was new to imperial power. Rudolf used the imperial title to help him gain Austria for his family. But he did not try to assert his power in Italy. For the first time, the word "emperor" was freed from its association with Rome.

The Kingdom of Sicily was similarly parceled out. The papacy tried to ensure that the Staufen dynasty would never again rule by calling upon Charles of Anjou, brother of the king of France, to take it over in 1263. Undeterred, Frederick's granddaughter, Constance, married to the King of Aragon (Spain), took the proud title "Queen of Sicily." In 1282, the Sicilian communes revolted against the Angevins in the uprising

known as the "Sicilian Vespers," begging the Aragonese for aid. Bitter war ensued, ending only in 1302, when the Kingdom of Sicily was split: the island became a Spanish outpost, while its mainland portion (southern Italy) remained under Angevin control.

A Hungarian Mini-Empire

Unlike the Kingdom of Sicily, the Kingdom of Hungary reaped the fruits of a period of expansion. In the eleventh century, having solidified their hold along the Danube River (the center of their power), the kings of Hungary moved north and east. In an arc ending at the Carpathian Mountains, they established control over a multi-ethnic population of Germans and Slavs. In the course of the twelfth century, the Hungarian kings turned southward, taking over Croatia and fighting for control over the coastline with the powerful Republic of Venice. They might have dominated the whole eastern Adriatic had not the Kingdom of Serbia re-established itself west of its original site, eager for its own share of seaborne commerce.

The Triumph of the City-States

That Venice was strong enough to rival Hungary in the eastern Adriatic was in part due to the confrontations between popes and emperors in Italy, which weakened both sides. The winners of those bitter wars were not the papacy, not the Angevins, not even the Aragonese, and certainly not the emperors. The winners were the Italian city-states. Republics in the sense that a high percentage of their adult male population participated in their government, they were also highly controlling. For example, to feed themselves, the communes prohibited the export of grain while commanding the peasants in the *contado* to bring a certain amount of grain to the cities by a certain date each year. City governments told the peasants which crops to grow and how many times per year they should plow the land. The state controlled commerce as well. At Venice, exceptional in lacking a *contado* but controlling a vast maritime empire instead, merchant enterprises were state run, using state ships. When Venetians went off to buy cotton in the Levant, they all had to offer the same price, determined by their government back home.

Italian city-state governments outdid England, Sicily, and France in their bureaucracy and efficiency. While other governments were still taxing by "hearths," the communes devised taxes based on a census (*catasto*) of property. Already at Pisa in 1162 taxes were being raised in this way; by the middle of the thirteenth century, almost all the communes had such a system in place. But even efficient methods of taxation did not bring in enough money to support the two main needs of the commune: paying their officials and, above all, waging war. To meet their high military expenses, the communes created state loans, some voluntary, others forced. They were the first in Europe to do so.

CULTURE AND INSTITUTIONS IN TOWN AND COUNTRYSIDE

Organization and accounting were the concerns of lords outside of Italy as well. But no one adopted the persona of the business tycoon; the prevailing ideal was the chivalrous knight. Courts were aristocratic centers, organized not only to enhance but also to highlight the power of lord and lady. Meanwhile, in the cities, guilds constituted a different kind of enclave, shutting out some laborers and women but giving high status to masters. Universities too were a sort of guild. Artistic creativity, urban pride, and episcopal power were together embodied in Gothic cathedrals.

Inventorying the Countryside

Not only kings and communes but great lords everywhere hired literate agents to administer their estates, calculate their profits, draw up accounts, and make marketing decisions. Money financed luxuries, to be sure, but even more importantly it enhanced aristocratic honor, so dependent on personal generosity, patronage, and displays of wealth. In the late twelfth century, when some townsmen could boast fortunes that rivaled the riches of the landed nobility, noble extravagance tended to exceed income. Most aristocrats went into debt.

The nobles' need for money coincided with the interests of the peasantry, whose numbers were expanding. The solution was the extension of farmland. By the middle of the century, isolated and sporadic attempts to bring new land into cultivation had become regular and coordinated. Great lords offered special privileges to peasants who would do the backbreaking work of plowing marginal land. In 1154, for example, the bishop of Meissen (in Germany) proclaimed a new village and called for peasants from Flanders to settle there. Experts in drainage, the colonists received rights to the swampland they reclaimed. They owed only light monetary obligations to the bishop, who nevertheless expected to reap a profit from their tolls and tithes. Similar encouragement came from lords throughout Europe, especially in northern Italy, England, Flanders, and Germany. In Flanders, where land was regularly inundated by seawater, the great monasteries sponsored drainage projects, and canals linking the cities to the agricultural regions let boats ply the waters to virtually every nook and cranny of the region.

Sometimes free peasants acted on their own to clear land and relieve the pressure of overpopulation, as when the small freeholders in England's Fenland region cooperated to build banks and dikes to reclaim the land that led out to the North Sea. Villages were founded on the drained land, and villagers shared responsibility for repairing and maintaining the dikes even as each peasant family farmed its new holding individually.

On old estates, the rise in population strained to its breaking point the manse organization that had developed in Carolingian Europe, where each household was settled on the land that supported it. Now, in the twelfth century, many peasant families might live on what had been, in the ninth century, the manse of one family. Labor services and dues had to be recalculated, and peasants and their lords often turned services and dues into money rents, payable once a year. With this change, peasant men gained more control over their plots—they could sell them, will them to their sons, or even designate a small portion for their daughters. However, for these privileges they had either to pay extra taxes or, like communes, join together to buy their collective liberty for a high price, paid out over many years to their lord. Peasants, like town citizens, gained a new sense of identity and solidarity as they bargained with a lord keen to increase his income at their expense.

The Culture of the Courts

When Henry II and his wife Eleanor came to Aquitaine, they were never alone. Accompanying them were relatives, vassals, officials, priests, knights, probably a doctor or two, and certainly troubadours. These were poets, musicians, and entertainers all in one. They sang love poems in Occitan, the vernacular of southern France. Eleanor's grandfather, Duke William IX of Aquitaine (1071-1126), is counted the first of the troubadours. But there were certainly people singing his kind of poetry in both Arabic and Hebrew in al-Andalus, which, as we have seen, was just at this time regularly coming into contact (mainly violently, to be sure) with the cultures of the north. By Eleanor's day, there were many troubadours, welcomed at major courts as essential personnel. Bernart de Ventadorn (*fl.*1150-1180) was among them. Here is one of his verses:

Ai Deus! car no sui ironda,   Ah, God! couldn't I be a swallow
que voles per l'aire   and fly through the air
e vengues de noih prionda   and come in the depths of the night
lai dins so repaire?   into her dwelling there?[13]

The rhyme scheme *seems* simple: *ironda* goes with *prionda*, *aire* with *repaire*. But consider that the verse before it (not printed here) has the *-onda* rhyme in the second and fourth lines (rather than the first and third), while the verse after it has *-aire* in the first and third lines (rather than the second and fourth). In fact the scheme is extremely complex and subtle, an essential skill for a poet whose goal was to dazzle his audience with brilliant originality.

In rhyme and meter, troubadour songs resembled Latin liturgical chants of the same region and period. Clearly, lay and religious cultures overlapped. They overlapped in musical terms as well, in the use, for example, of plucking and percussive instruments. Above all, they overlapped in themes: they spoke of love. The monks (as we have seen with the Cistercians, on p. 216) thought about the love between God and mankind; the troubadours thought about erotic love. Yet the two were deliciously entangled. The verse in which Bernart wishes he could be a swallow continues:

> I fear the heart will melt within me
> if this lasts a little longer.
> Lady, for your love
> I join my hands and worship.
> Beautiful body of the colors of youth,
> what suffering you make me bear.[14]

This is playing with religious imagery. Bernart is ready to pray; he is thinking of a youthful body; he is suffering: he could be a worshiper identifying with Christ on the Cross. At the same time, he subverts the religious: he is thinking of his mistress as (he says) he tosses and turns "on the edge of the bed."[15]

Female troubadours (called *trobairitz*) flirted with the same themes. La Comtessa de Dia (*fl.c.*1200?) sang,

> I've been in great anguish
> over a noble soldier I once had,
> and I want everyone to know, for all time,
> that I loved him—too much!
> Now I see I'm betrayed
> because I didn't yield my love to him.
> For that I've suffered greatly,
> both in my bed and fully clad.[16]

As with the *adab* literature of the Islamic world (see p. 114), the ideals of such courtly poetry emphasized refinement, beauty, and wit, all summed up in the word *cortezia*, "courtliness" or "courtesy."

Historians and literary critics used to use the term "courtly love" to emphasize one of the themes of this literature: the poet expressing overwhelming love for a beautiful married noblewoman who is far above him and utterly unattainable. But this was only one of the many aspects of love that the troubadours sang about: some boasted of sexual conquests; others played with the notion of equality between lovers; still others preached that love was the source of virtue. The real theme of these poems was not courtly love; it was the power of women. No wonder Eleanor of Aquitaine and other aristocratic women patronized the troubadours: they enjoyed the image that it gave them of themselves. Nor was this image a delusion. There were many powerful female lords in southern France. They owned property, commanded vassals, led battles, decided disputes, and entered into and broke political alliances as their advantage dictated. Both men and women appreciated troubadour poetry, which recognized and praised women's power even as it eroticized it.

From southern France the lyric love song spread to Italy, northern France, England, and Germany. Here Occitan was a foreign language, so other vernaculars were used: the *minnesinger* (literally, "love singer") sang in German; the *trouvère* sang in the Old French of northern France. In northern France another genre of poetry grew up as well, poking fun at courtliness and its pretensions. This was the *fabliau* (pl. *fabliaux*), which boasted humbler folk as its protagonists.

Some troubadours wrote about war, not love. "I feel a great joy," wrote the poet Bertran de Born (*fl.* 2nd half of 12th c.), "when I see ranged along the field/ knights and horses armed for war."[17] But warfare was more often the subject of another kind of poem, the *chanson de geste*, "song of heroic deeds." Long recited orally, these vernacular poems appeared in written form at about the same time as troubadour poetry and, like them, the *chansons de geste* played with aristocratic codes of behavior, in this case on the battlefield rather than at court.

The *chansons de geste* were responding to social and military transformations. By the end of the twelfth century, nobles and knights had begun to merge into one class, threatened from below by newly rich merchants and from above by newly powerful kings. At the same time, the knights' importance in battle—unhorsing one another with lances and long swords and taking prisoners rather than killing their opponents—was waning in the face of mercenary infantrymen who wielded long hooks and knives that ripped easily through chain mail, killing their enemies outright. A knightly ethos and sense of group solidarity emerged within this changed landscape. Like Bertran de Born, the *chansons de geste* celebrated "knights and horses armed for war." But they also examined the moral issues that confronted knights, taking up the often contradictory values of their society. Should the fealty of a vassal trump loyalty to his family? In *Raoul de Cambrai*, the answer is no, with tragic results. Bernier, faithful vassal of Raoul de Cambrai, discovers that Raoul has burned the town of Origny and Bernier's mother within it. Renouncing his fidelity to Raoul, Bernier cries out, "Raoul, you scoundrel, may God bring disaster on you! I no longer want to be your vassal, and if I can't avenge this outrage, I shan't think myself worth a penny."[18]

The *chansons de geste*, later also called "epics," focused on battle; other long poems, later called "romances," explored relationships between men and women. Enormously popular in the late twelfth and early thirteenth centuries, romances took up such themes as the tragic love between Tristan and Isolde and the virtuous knight's search for the Holy Grail. Above all, romances were woven around the many fictional stories of King Arthur and his court. In one of the earliest, Chrétien de Troyes (*c.*1150–1190) wrote about the noble and valiant Lancelot, in love with Queen Guinevere, wife of Arthur. Finding a comb bearing some strands of her radiant hair, Lancelot is overcome:

> Never will the eye of man see anything receive such honor as when he begins to adore these tresses. A hundred thousand times he raises them to his eyes and mouth, to his forehead and face… . Even for Saint Martin and Saint James he has no need.[19]

By making Guinevere's hair an object of adoration, a sort of secular relic, Chrétien here not only conveys the depths of Lancelot's feeling but also pokes a bit of fun at his hero. When Guinevere tests Lancelot in the middle of a tournament by sending him a message to do his "worst," the poet evokes a similar mix of humor and loftiness:

> When he heard this, he replied: "Very willingly," like one who is altogether hers. Then he rides at another knight as hard as his horse can carry him, and misses his thrust which should have struck him. From that time till evening he continued to do as badly as possible in accordance with the Queen's desire.[20]

It is an odd, funny, and pitiful episode: the greatest of all knights bested at the whim of a lady. Yet this is part of the premise of "chivalry." The word, deriving from the French *cheval* ("horse"), emphasizes above all that the knight was a horseman, a warrior of the most prestigious sort. Perched high in the saddle, his heavy lance couched in his right arm, the knight was an imposing and menacing figure. Chivalry made him gentle, gave his battles a higher meaning, whether for love of a lady or of God. The chivalric hero was constrained by courtesy, fair play, piety, and devotion to an ideal. Did real knights live up to these ideals? They knew perfectly well that they could not and that it would be absurd if they tried to do so in every particular. But they loved playing with the idea. They were the poets' audience, and they liked to think of themselves as fitting into the tales. When William the Marshal, advisor of English kings, died, his biographer wrote of him as a model knight, courteous with the ladies, brave on the battlefield.

Urban Guilds Incorporated

Courtly "codes" were poetic and playful. City codes were drier but no less compelling. In the early thirteenth century, guilds drew up statutes to determine dues, regulate working hours, fix wages, and set standards for materials and products. Sometimes they came into conflict with town government; this happened to some bread-bakers' guilds in Italy, where communes considered bread too important a commodity to be left to its producers. At other times, the communes supported guild efforts to control wages, reinforcing guild regulations with statutes of their own. When great lords rather than communes governed a city, they too tried to control and protect the guilds. King Henry II of England, for example, eagerly gave some guilds in his Norman duchy special privileges so that they would depend on him.

There was nothing democratic about guilds. In the cloth-making business, the merchant guild that imported the raw wool was generally the overseer of the other related guilds—the shearers, weavers, fullers (the workers who beat the cloth to shrink it and make it heavier), and dyers. In Florence, professional guilds of notaries and judges ranked in prestige and power above craft guilds. Within each guild was another kind of hierarchy. Apprentices were at the bottom, journeymen and -women in the middle, and masters at the top. Young boys and occasionally girls were the apprentices; they worked for a master for room and board, learning a trade. An apprenticeship in the felt-hat trade in Paris, for example, lasted seven years. After their apprenticeship, men and women often worked many years as day laborers, hired by a master when he needed extra help. Some men, but almost never women, worked their way up to master status. They were the ones who dominated the offices and set guild policies.

The codification of guild practices and membership tended to work against women, who were slowly being ousted from the world of workers during the late twelfth century. In Flanders, for example, as the manufacture of woolen cloth shifted from rural areas to cities, and from light to heavy looms, women were less involved in cloth production than they had been on traditional manors. Similarly, water- and animal-powered mills took the place of female hand labor grinding grain into flour—and most millers were male. Nevertheless, at Paris guild regulations for the silk fabric makers assumed that the artisans would be women:

No journeywoman maker of silk fabric may be a mistress [the female equivalent of "master"] of the craft until she has practiced it for a year and a day.... No mistress of the craft may weave thread with silk, or foil with silk.... No mistress or journeywoman of the craft may make a false hem or border.[21]

By contrast, universities were all-male guilds. (The word *universitas* is Latin for "guild.") Beginning as organizations of masters and students, the term eventually came to apply to the school itself. At the beginning of the thirteenth century, the universities regulated student discipline, scholastic proficiency, and housing while determining the masters' behavior in equal detail. At the University of Paris, for example, the masters were required to wear long black gowns, follow a particular order in their lectures, and set the standards by which students could become masters themselves. The University of Bologna was unique in having two guilds, one of students and one of masters. At Bologna, the students participated in the appointment, payment, and discipline of the masters.

The University of Bologna was unusual because it was principally a school of law, where the students were often older men, well along in their careers (often in imperial service) and used to wielding power. At the University of Paris, young students predominated, drawn by its renown in the liberal arts and theology. The universities of Salerno (near Naples) and Montpellier (in southern France) specialized in medicine. Oxford, once a sleepy town where students clustered around one or two masters, became a center of royal administration; its university soon developed a reputation for teaching the liberal arts, theology, science, and mathematics.

The curriculum of each university depended on its speciality and its traditions. At Paris in the early thirteenth century, students spent at least six years studying the liberal arts before gaining the right to teach. If they wanted to specialize in theology, they attended lectures on the subject for at least another five years. With books both expensive and hard to find, lectures were the chief method of communication. These were centered on important texts: the master read an excerpt aloud, delivered his commentary on it, and disputed any contrary commentaries that rival masters might have proposed. Students committed the lectures to memory.

Within the larger association of the university, students found more intimate groups with which to live: "nations," linked to the students' place of origin. At Bologna, for example, students belonged to one of two nations, the Italians and the non-Italians. Each nation protected its members, wrote statutes, and elected officers.

Masters and students both were considered part of another group: clerics. This was an outgrowth of the original, church-related, purposes of the schools, and it had two important consequences. First, there were no university women. And second, university men were subject to church courts rather than the secular jurisdiction of towns or lords. Many universities could also boast generous privileges from popes and kings, who valued the services of scholars. The combination of clerical status and special privileges made universities virtually self-governing corporations within the towns. This sometimes led to friction. When the townsmen of Oxford tried to punish a student suspected of killing his mistress, the masters protested by refusing to teach and leaving the city. Such disputes are called "town against gown" struggles because students and masters wore gowns (the distant ancestors of American graduation gowns). But since university towns depended on scholars to patronize local taverns, shops, and hostels, town and gown normally learned to negotiate with one another to their mutual advantage.

Gothic Style

Certainly town and gown agreed on building style: by *c.*1200, "Gothic" (the term itself comes from the sixteenth century) was the architecture of choice. Beginning as a variant of Romanesque in the Ile-de-France, Gothic style quickly took on an identity of its own. Gothic architects tried to eliminate heavy walls by enlivening them with sculpture or piercing them with glass, creating a soaring feel by using pointed arches. Suger, abbot of Saint-Denis and the promoter of Capetian royal power (see p. 201), was the style's first sponsor. When he rebuilt portions of his church around 1135, he tried to meld royal and ecclesiastical interests and ideals in stone and glass. At the west end of his church, the point where the faithful entered, Suger decorated the portals with figures of Old Testament kings, queens, and patriarchs, signaling the links between the present king and his illustrious predecessors. Rebuilding the interior of the east end of his church as well, Suger used pointed arches and stained glass to let in light, which Suger believed to be God's own "illumination," capable of transporting the worshiper from the "slime of earth" to the "purity of Heaven."

Gothic was an urban architecture, reflecting—in its grand size, jewel-like windows, and bright ornaments—the aspirations, pride, and confidence of rich and powerful merchants, artisans, and bishops. The Gothic cathedral, which could take centuries to complete, was often the religious, social, and commercial focal point of a city. Funds for these buildings might come from the bishop himself, from the canons (priests) who served his cathedral, or from townsmen. Notre Dame of Paris (Plate 6.2) was begun in 1163 by Bishop Maurice de Sully, whose episcopal income from estates, forests, taxes, and Parisian properties gave him plenty of money to finance the tallest church of its day. Under his successors, the edifice took shape with three stories, the upper one filled with stained glass. Bristling on the outside with flying buttresses—the characteristic "look" of a French Gothic church—it gave no hint of the light and calm within. (See Plate 6.3.) But at Mantes-la-Jolie (about 25 miles west of Paris), it was the merchant guild and the Capetian king together—rather than a bishop—who sponsored the building of the new collegiate church.

However financed, Gothic cathedrals were community projects, enlisting the labor and support of a small army of quarrymen, builders, carpenters, and glass cutters. Houses of relics, they attracted pilgrims as well. At Chartres Cathedral, proud home of the Virgin's tunic, crowds thronged the streets, the poor buying small lead figures of the Virgin, the rich purchasing wearable replicas of her tunic.

The technologies that made Gothic churches possible were all known before the twelfth century. The key elements included ribbed vaulting, which could give a sense of precision and order (as at Notre Dame; consider Plate 6.3 again, concentrating on the orderly rhythm of piers and ribs) or of richness and playful inventiveness (as at Lincoln Cathedral in England: see Plate 6.4). Flying buttresses took the weight of the vault off the walls, allowing most of the wall to be cut away and the open spaces filled by glass. (See Figure 6.1.) Pointed arches made the church appear to surge heavenward.

By the mid-thirteenth century, Gothic architecture had spread to most of Europe. Yet the style varied by region, most dramatically in Italy. San Francesco in Assisi is an example of what *Italian* architects meant by a Gothic church. It has high stained glass windows and a pointed, ribbed vault. (See Plate 6.5.) But the focus is not on light and height but on walls, painted decoration, and well-proportioned space. With flying buttresses rare and portal sculpture unobtrusive, Italian Gothic churches convey a spirit of spare and quiet beauty.

Gothic art, both painting and sculpture, echoed and decorated the Gothic church. While Romanesque sculpture played upon a flat surface, Gothic figures were liberated from their background, turning, bending, interacting. At Reims Cathedral the figure of Saint Joseph on the west portal, elegant and graceful, reveals a gentle smile. (See Plate 6.6.) Above his head is carved foliage of striking naturalness. Portals like this were meant to be "read" for their meaning. Joseph is not smiling for nothing; in the original arrangement of the portal he was looking at the figure of a servant while, further to his left, his wife, Mary, presented the baby Jesus in the temple. This was the New Testament story brought to life.

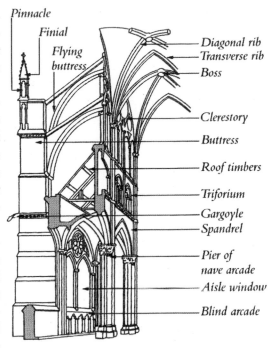

Pinnacle
Finial
Flying buttress
Diagonal rib
Transverse rib
Boss
Clerestory
Buttress
Roof timbers
Triforium
Gargoyle
Spandrel
Pier of nave arcade
Aisle window
Blind arcade

Figure 6.1: Elements of a Gothic Church. This drawing of a section through the nave at Amiens shows the most important features of a Gothic church.

Plate 6.2: Notre Dame of Paris, Exterior (begun 1163). To take the weight of the vault off the walls and open them to glass and light, the architects of Gothic churches such as Notre Dame used flying buttresses, which sprang from the top of the exterior wall. In this photograph they look rather like oars jutting out from the church; see, in particular, the apse (on the viewer's right).

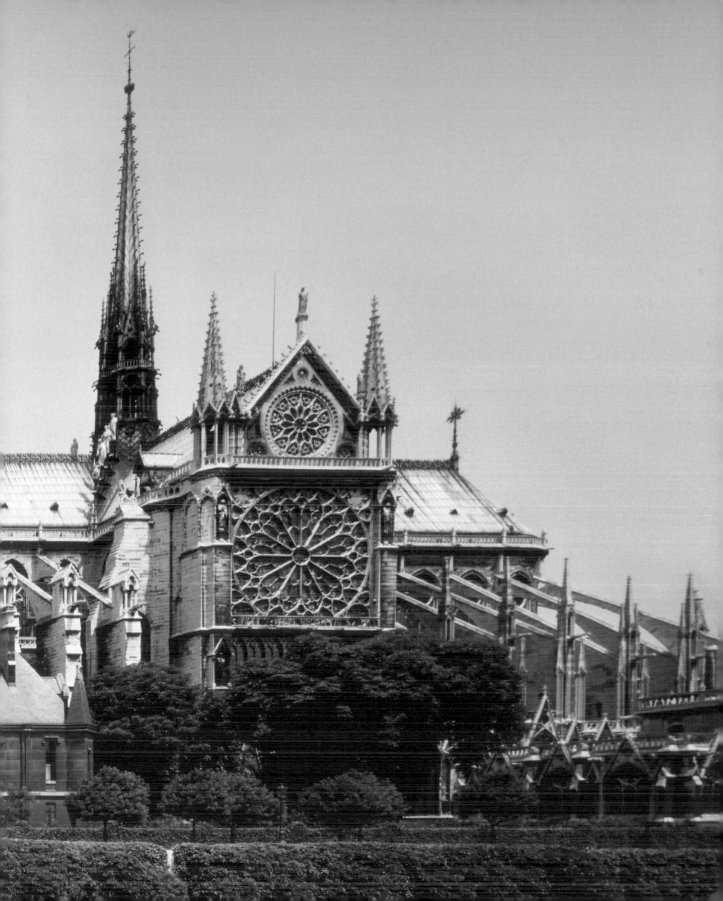

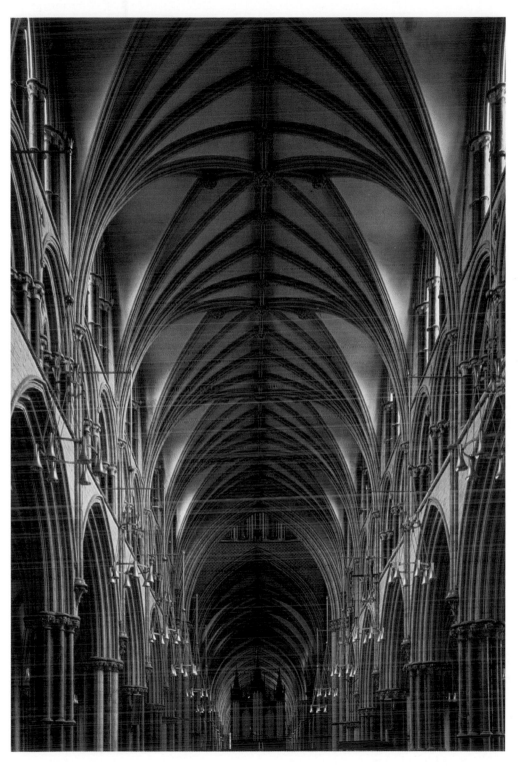

Plate 6.3 (facing page): Notre Dame of Paris, Interior (begun 1163). Compare this interior with that of Santiago in Plate 5.8 (p. 212). Santiago is a typical Romanesque church, with a barrel vault, two stories, and little natural light. By contrast, the Gothic cathedral of Notre Dame (shown here) has an arched vault that soars three stories high, while light from large stained-glass windows suffuses the entire nave.

Plate 6.4: Lincoln Cathedral, Interior (begun c.1225). Many English Gothic cathedrals emphasized surface ornament. Here the ribs, which spring from carved moldings on the walls of the nave, are splayed into fans on the vault. Can you find other decorative elements?

THE CHURCH IN THE WORLD

Just as the church was taking new interest in the human dimension of Joseph and his wife, so it concerned itself as never before in the lives of ordinary Christians. Under Innocent III (1198-1216)—the first pope to be trained at the city schools and to study both theology and law—the papacy gained a newly grand sense of itself. Innocent thought of himself as ruling in the place of Christ the King; secular kings and emperors existed simply to help the pope, who was the real lawmaker—the maker of laws that would lead to moral reformation. In the thirteenth century, the church sought to define Christianity, embracing some doctrines, rejecting others, and turning against Jews and Muslims with new vigor.

The Fourth Lateran Council (1215)

A council was the traditional method of declaring church law, and this is what Innocent intended when he convened one at his Lateran Palace at Rome in 1215. Presided over by the pope himself, the Fourth Lateran Council produced a comprehensive set of canons—most of them prepared by the pope's committees beforehand—to reform both clergy and laity. In effect it produced a code, in this case one for Christian society as a whole.

For laymen and -women perhaps the most important canons concerned the sacraments. The Fourth Lateran Council required Christians to attend Mass and to confess their sins to a priest at least once a year. Marriage was declared a sacrament, and bishops were assigned jurisdiction over marital disputes. Forbidding secret marriages, the council expected priests to uncover evidence that might impede a marriage. There were many impediments: people were not allowed to marry their cousins, nor anyone related to them by godparentage, nor anyone related to them through a former marriage. Children conceived within clandestine or forbidden marriages were to be considered illegitimate; they could not inherit property from their parents, nor could they become priests.

Like the code of chivalry, the rules of the Fourth Lateran Council about marriage worked better on parchment than in life. Well-to-do London fathers included their bastard children in their wills. On English manors, sons conceived out of wedlock regularly took over their parents' land. The prohibition against secret marriages was only partially successful. Even churchmen had to admit that the consent of both parties made a marriage valid.

The most important sacrament was the Mass, the ritual in which the bread and wine of the Eucharist was transformed into the flesh and blood of Christ. In the twelfth century a newly rigorous explanation of this transformation was promulgated according to which Christ's body and blood were truly present in the bread and wine on the altar. The Fourth Lateran Council not only declared this as church doctrine but also explained it by using a technical term coined by twelfth-century scholars. The bread and wine were "transubstantiated": though the Eucharist continued to *look* like bread and wine, after the consecration during the Mass the bread became the actual body and the wine the real blood of Christ. The council's emphasis on this potent event strengthened the role of the priest, for only he could celebrate this mystery (the transformation of ordinary bread and wine into the flesh of Christ) through which God's grace was transmitted to the faithful.

The Ins and the Outs

As the Fourth Lateran Council provided rules for good Christians, it turned against all others. Some canons singled out Jews and heretics for special punitive treatment; others were directed against Byzantines and Muslims. These laws were of a piece with wider movements. With the development of a papal monarchy that confidently declared a single doctrine and the laws pertaining to it, dissidence was perceived as heresy, non-Christians seen as treacherous.

New Groups within the Fold

The Fourth Lateran Council prohibited the formation of new monastic orders. It recognized that the trickle of new religious groups — the Carthusians is one example — of the early twelfth century had become a torrent by 1215. Only a very few of the more recent movements were accepted into the church, among them the Franciscans, the Beguines, and the Dominicans.

Saint Francis (*c.*1182-1226) had begun a promising career as a cloth merchant at Assisi when he experienced a complete conversion. Clinging to poverty as if, in his words, "she" were his "lady" (thus borrowing the vocabulary of chivalry), he accepted no money, walked without shoes, wore only one coarse tunic, and refused to be confined even in a monastery. He and his followers (called "friars," from the Latin term for "brothers") spent their time preaching, ministering to lepers, and doing manual labor. In time they dispersed, setting up fraternal groups throughout Italy, France, Spain, the Crusader States, and later Germany, England, Scotland, Poland, and elsewhere. Always they were drawn to the cities. Sleeping in "convents" on the outskirts of the towns, the Franciscans became a regular part of urban community life as they preached to crowds and begged their daily bread. Early converts included women: in

1212 the young noblewoman Clare determined to become a Franciscan herself, founding a community of women at San Damiano, a church near Assisi. She meant for the Damianites to follow the rule and lifestyle of the friars. But the church disapproved of the women's worldly activities, and the many sisters following Francis — by 1228 there were at least 24 female communities inspired by him in central and northern Italy — were confined to cloisters under the *Rule* of Saint Benedict. In the course of the thirteenth century the Order of the Sisters of St Francis was joined by a third order, the "Tertiaries," which was made up of laypeople, many of them married. They dedicated themselves to works of charity and to daily church attendance.

The Beguines were still more integral to town life. In the cities of northern France, the Low Countries, and Germany, these women plied the trades of launderers, weavers, and spinners. (Their male counterparts, the "Beghards," were far less numerous). Choosing to live together in informal communities, taking no vows, free to marry if they wished, they dedicated themselves to simplicity and piety. If outwardly ordinary, however, inwardly their religious lives were often emotional and ecstatic, infused with the imagery of love. Mary of Oignies (1177-1213), for example, felt herself to be a pious mother entrusted with the Christ-child, who "nestled between her breasts like a baby.... Sometimes she kissed him as though He were a little child and sometimes she held Him on her lap as if He were a gentle lamb."[22]

Saint Dominic (1170-1221), founder of the Dominican order, was more hardheaded. Reckoning that most preachers failed to counter the sway of heretics in southern France because they came richly clad, on horseback, and followed by a retinue, he and his followers rejected material riches and instead went about on foot, preaching and begging. They soon came to resemble the Franciscans, both organizationally and spiritually; they too were called friars.

Defining the Other

The heretics that Dominic confronted were the Albigensians (also called Cathars), one of a number of dualist groups that sprang up in the twelfth century in Italy, the Rhineland, and Languedoc (southern France). Calling themselves Christ's Poor, they preached a world torn between two great forces, one good and the other evil. As the material world was the creation of the devil, they renounced it, rejecting wealth, sex, and meat, and denying the efficacy of the sacraments. Attracting both men and women, these "friends of God" (as they called themselves) believed they were followers of Christ's original message. But the church called them heretics.

The church condemned other, non-dualist movements as heretical not on doctrinal grounds but because these groups allowed their lay members to preach, assuming for themselves the privilege of bishops. At Lyon (in southeastern France) in the 1170s, for example, a rich merchant named Waldo decided to take literally the Gospel message, "If you wish to be perfect, then go and sell everything you have, and give to the poor" (Matt. 19:21). The same message had inspired countless monks and would worry the church far less several decades later, when Saint Francis established his new order. But when Waldo went into the street and gave away his belongings, announcing, "I am not out of my mind, as you think,"[23] he scandalized not only the bystanders but the church as well. Refusing to retire to a monastery, Waldo and his followers, men and women called Waldensians, lived in poverty and went about preaching, quoting the Gospel in the vernacular so that everyone would understand them. But the papacy rejected Waldo's bid to preach freely; and the Waldensians—denounced, excommunicated, and expelled from Lyon—wandered to Languedoc, Italy, northern Spain, and the Mosel valley, just east of France.

EUROPEAN AGGRESSION WITHIN AND WITHOUT

Jews, heretics, Muslims, Byzantines, and pagans: all felt the heavy hand of Christian Europeans newly organized, powerful, and zealous. Meanwhile, even the undeniable Catholicism of Ireland did not prevent its takeover by England.

The Jews

Prohibited from joining guilds, Jews increasingly were forced to take the one job Christians could not have: lending on credit. Even with Christian moneylenders available (for some existed despite official prohibitions), lords borrowed from Jews. Then, relying on dormant anti-Jewish feeling, they sometimes "righteously" attacked their creditors. This happened in 1190 at York, for example, where local nobles orchestrated a brutal attack on the Jews of the city to rid themselves of their debts and the men to whom they owed money. Kings claimed the Jews as their serfs and Jewish property as their own. In England a special royal exchequer of the Jews was created in 1194 to collect unpaid debts due after the death of Jewish creditors. In France, Philip Augustus expelled the Jews from the Ile-de-France in 1182, confiscating their houses, fields, and vineyards for himself. He allowed them to return—minus their property—in 1198.

Attacks against Jews were inspired by more than resentment against Jewish money or desire for power and control. They grew out of the codification of Christian religious doctrine. The newly rigorous definition of the Eucharist as the true body and blood of Christ meant to some that Christ, wounded and bleeding, lay upon the altar. Miracle tales sometimes reported that the Eucharist bled. Reflecting Christian anxieties about real flesh upon the altar, sensational stories, originating in clerical circles but soon widely circulated, told of Jews who secretly sacrificed Christian children in a morbid revisiting of the crucifixion of Jesus. This charge, called "blood libel" by historians, led to massacres of Jews in cities in England, France, Spain, and Germany. In this way, Jews became convenient and vulnerable scapegoats for Christian guilt and anxiety about eating Christ's flesh.

After the Fourth Lateran Council, Jews were easy to spot as well. The council required all Jews to advertise their religion by some outward sign, some special dress. Local rulers enforced this canon with zeal, not so much because they were anxious to humiliate Jews as because they saw the chance to sell exemptions to Jews eager to escape the requirement. Nonetheless, sooner or later Jews almost everywhere had to wear a badge as a sign of their second-class status: in southern France and Spain they had to wear a round badge; in Vienna they were forced to wear pointed hats.

Crusades

Attacks against Jews coincided with newly vigorous crusades. A new kind of crusade was launched against the heretics in southern France; along the Baltic, rulers and crusaders redrew Germany's eastern border; and the Fourth Crusade was rerouted and took Constantinople.

Against the Albigensians in southern France, Innocent III demanded that northern princes take up the sword, invade Languedoc, wrest the land from the heretics, and populate it with orthodox Christians. This Albigensian Crusade (1209-1229) marked the first time the pope offered warriors fighting an enemy within Christian Europe all the spiritual and temporal benefits of a crusade to the Holy Land. In the event, the political ramifications were more notable than the religious results. After twenty years of fighting, leadership of the crusade was taken over in 1229 by the Capetian kings. Southern resistance was broken and Languedoc was brought under the control of the French crown. (On Map 6.3, the area taken over by the French crown corresponds more or less with the region of Toulouse.)

Like Spain's southern boundary, so too Europe's northeast was a moving frontier, driven ever further eastward by crusaders and settlers. By the twelfth century, the peoples living along the Baltic coast—partly pagan, mostly Slavic- or Baltic-speaking—had learned to make a living and even a profit from the inhospitable soil and climate. Through fishing and trading, they supplied the rest of Europe and Russia with slaves, furs, amber, wax, and dried fish. Like the earlier Vikings, they combined commercial competition with outright raiding, so that the Danes and the Saxons (that is, the Germans in Saxony) both benefited and suffered from their presence. It was Saint Bernard (see p. 211) who, preaching the Second Crusade in Germany, urged one to the north as well. Thus began the Northern Crusades, which continued intermittently until the early fifteenth century.

In key raids in the 1160s and 1170s, the king of Denmark and Henry the Lion, the duke of Saxony, worked together to bring much of the region between the Elbe and Oder rivers under their control. They took some of the land outright, leaving the rest in the hands of the Baltic princes, who surrendered, converted, and became their vassals. Churchmen arrived: the Cistercians built their monasteries right up to the banks of the Vistula River, while bishops took over newly declared dioceses. In 1204 the "bishop of Riga"—in fact he had to bring his own Christians with him to his lonely outpost amidst the Livs—founded a military/monastic order called the Sword-Brothers. The monks soon became a branch of the Teutonic Knights, a group originally founded in the Crusader States. They organized crusades, defended newly conquered regions, and launched their own holy wars against the "Northern Saracens." By the end of the thirteenth century, they had brought the lands between Estonia and the Vistula under their sway. (See Map 6.4.) Meanwhile knights, peasants, and townspeople streamed in, colonists of the new frontier. Although less well-known than the crusades to the Levant, the Northern Crusades had more lasting effects, settling the Baltic region with a German-speaking population that brought its western institutions—cities, laws, guilds, universities, castles, manors, vassalage—with it.

Colonization was the unanticipated consequence of the Fourth Crusade as well. Called by Innocent III, who intended it to re-establish the Christian presence in the Holy Land, the crusade was diverted when the organizers overestimated the numbers joining the expedition. The small army mustered was unable to pay for the large fleet of ships that had been fitted out for it by the Venetians. Making the best of adversity, the Venetians convinced the crusaders to "pay" for the ships by attacking Zara (today Zadar), one of the coastal cities that Venice disputed with Hungary. Then, taking up the cause of one claimant to the Byzantine throne, the crusaders turned their sights on Constantinople. We already know the political results. The religious results are more subtle. Europeans disdained the Greeks for their independence from the pope; on the other hand, they considered Constantinople a treasure trove of the most precious of relics, including the True Cross. When, in the course of looting the city, one crusader, the abbot of a German Cistercian monastery, came upon a chest of relics, he "hurriedly and greedily thrust in both hands."[24] There was a long tradition of relic theft in the West; it was considered pious, a sort of holy sacrilege. Thus, when the abbot returned to his ship to show off his booty, the crusaders shouted, "Thanks be to God." In this sense Constantinople was taken so that the saints could get better homes.

Ireland

In 1169 the Irish king of Leinster, Diarmait Mac Murchada (Dermot MacMurrough), enlisted some lords and knights from England to help him first keep, then expand, his kingdom. The English fighters succeeded all too well; when Diarmait died (1171), some of the English decided to stay, claiming Leinster for themselves. The king of England, Henry II, reacted swiftly. Gathering an army, he invaded Ireland in 1171. The lords of the 1169 expedition recognized his overlordship almost immediately, keeping their new territories, but now redefined as fiefs from the king. Most of the native Irish kings submitted in similar manner. The whole of one kingdom, Meath, was given to one of Henry's barons.

The English came to stay, and more—they came to put their stamp on the Irish world. It became "English Ireland": England's laws were instituted; its system of counties and courts was put in place; its notions of lordship (in which the great lords parceled out some of their vast lands to lesser lords and knights) prevailed. Small wonder that Gerald of Wales (*d.*1223) could see nothing good in native Irish culture:

Map 6.4: The German Push to the East, Twelfth to Fourteenth Centuries

"they are uncultivated," he wrote, "not only in the external appearance of their dress, but also in their flowing hair and beards. All their habits are the habits of barbarians."[25]

★ ★ ★ ★

In the fifty years before and after 1200, Europe, aggressive and determined, pushed against its borders. Whether gaining territory from the Muslims in Spain and Sicily, colonizing the Baltic region and Ireland, or creating a Latin empire at Constantinople, Europeans accommodated the natives only minimally. For the most part, they imposed their institutions and their religion, each defined, formalized, and self-confident.

Self-confidence also led lords and ladies to pay poets to celebrate their achievements and bishops and townspeople to commission architects to erect towering Gothic churches in their midst. Similar certainties lay behind guild statutes, the incorporation of universities, the development of common law, and the Fourth Lateran Council's written definitions of Christian behavior and belief.

An orderly society would require institutions so fearlessly constructed as to be responsive to numerous individual and collective goals. But in the next century, while harmony was the ideal and sometimes the reality, discord was an ever-present threat.

CHAPTER SIX KEY EVENTS

1152–1190	Frederick Barbarossa (king of Germany and emperor)
1154–1189	King Henry II of England
1170	Murder of Thomas Becket
1171	Henry II conquers Ireland
1171–1193	Saladin's rule
1176	Battle of Legnano
1182	Jews expelled from the Ile-de-France
1187	Battle of Hattin
1189–1192	Third Crusade
1192–1250	Frederick II
1198–1216	Pope Innocent III
1204	Fall of Constantinople to Crusaders
1204	Philip II of France takes King John of England's northern French possessions
1212	Battle of Las Navas de Tolosa
1214	Battle of Bouvines
1215	Magna Carta
1215	Fourth Lateran Council
1226	Death of Saint Francis
1273	Election of Rudolf of Habsburg as Holy Roman Emperor

NOTES

1. Ibn Shaddad, *The Rare and Excellent History of Saladin*, in *Reading the Middle Ages: Sources from Europe, Byzantium, and the Islamic World*, ed. Barbara H. Rosenwein (Peterborough, ON, 2006), p.334.

2. *Michael Akominatou tou Choniatou ta sozomena*, ed. Spiro P. Lampros (Athens, 1879-80), 1:183, as quoted in Michael Angold, *The Byzantine Empire: A Political History, 1025-1204*, 2nd ed. (London, 1997), p.314.

3. Henry's father, Geoffrey of Anjou, was nicknamed Plantagenet from the *genêt*, the name of a shrub ("broom" in English) that he liked. Historians sometimes use the sobriquet to refer to the entire dynasty, so Henry II was the first "Plantagenet" as well as the first "Angevin" king of England.

4. *The Assize of Clarendon*, in *Reading the Middle Ages*, p.350.

5. Ibid., p.352.

6. *The Costs of Richard of Anstey's Law Suit*, in *Reading the Middle Ages*, p.354.

7. *Proceedings for the Abbey of Bec*, in *Reading the Middle Ages*, p.361.

8. *Magna Carta*, in *Reading the Middle Ages*, p.381.

9. *The Laws of Cuenca*, in *Reading the Middle Ages*, p.355.

10. *Diet of Besançon*, in *Reading the Middle Ages*, p.376.

11. Otto of Freising and his continuator, Rahewin, *The Deeds of Frederick Barbarossa*, trans. Charles Christopher Mierow with the collaboration of Richard Emery (New York, 1966), p.238, slightly modified.

12. *The Chronicle of Salimbene de Adam*, ed. and trans. Joseph L. Baird, Giuseppe Baglivi and John Robert Kane, Medieval & Renaissance Texts & Studies 40 (Binghamton, NY, 1986), p.5.

13. *Lyrics of the Troubadours and Trouvères: An Anthology and a History*, ed. and trans. Frederick Goldin (New York, 1973), pp.132-33.

14. Ibid., p.133.

15. Ibid.

16. Comtessa de Dia, *I've Been in Great Anguish*, in *Reading the Middle Ages*, p.391.

17. Bertran de Born, *I Love the Joyful Time*, in *Reading the Middle Ages*, p.390.

18. *Raoul de Cambrai*, in *Reading the Middle Ages*, p.388.

19. Chrétien de Troyes, *Arthurian Romances*, trans. W.W. Comfort (New York, 1975), pp.288-89.

20. Ibid., p.341.

21. *Guild Regulations of the Parisian Silk Fabric Makers*, in *Reading the Middle Ages*, pp.362-63.

22. Jacques de Vitry, *The Life of Mary of Oignies*, in *Reading the Middle Ages*, p.408.

23. *Peter Waldo in the Chronicle of Laon*, in *Reading the Middle Ages*, p.404.

24. Gunther of Pairis, *Hystoria Constantinopolitana*, in *The Capture of Constantinople*, ed. and trans. Alfred J. Andrea (Philadelphia, 2007), p.111.

25. Gerald of Wales, *The History and Topography of Ireland* (Harmondsworth, 1982), p.102.

FURTHER READING

Abulafia, David. *Frederick II: A Medieval Emperor*. London, 1988.

Angold, Michael. *The Byzantine Empire, 1025-1204*. 2nd. ed. London, 1997.

Baldwin, John. *The Government of Philip Augustus: Foundations of French Royal Power in the Middle Ages*. Berkeley, 1986.

Bartlett, Robert. *England under the Norman and Angevin Kings, 1075-1225*. Oxford, 2000.

—. *The Making of Europe: Conquest, Colonization and Cultural Change, 950-1350*. Princeton, 1993.

Binski, Paul. *Becket's Crown: Art and Imagination in Gothic England, 1170-1300*. New Haven, 2004.

Bouchard, Constance Brittain. *Strong of Body, Brave and Noble: Chivalry and Society in Medieval France*. Ithaca, NY, 1998.

Cheyette, Fredric L. *Ermengard of Narbonne and the World of the Troubadours*. Ithaca, NY, 2001.

Christiansen, Eric. *The Northern Crusades*. 2nd ed. London, 1997.

Clanchy, Michael T. *England and Its Rulers, 1066-1307*. 3rd ed. 2006.

Cobb, Paul M. *Usama ibn Munqidh: Warrior-Poet of the Ages of Crusades*. Oxford, 2005.

Duggan, Anne. *Thomas Becket*. Oxford, 2005

Frame, Robin. *The Political Development of the British Isles, 1100-1400*. Oxford, 1990.

Gaunt, Simon, and Sarah Kay, eds. *The Troubadours: An Introduction*. Cambridge, 1999.

Geary, Patrick J. *Furta Sacra: Thefts of Relics in the Central Middle Ages*. Princeton, 1990.

Haverkamp, Alfred. *Medieval Germany, 1056-1273*. Trans. Helga Braun and Richard Mortimer. Oxford, 1988.

Lawrence, C.H. *The Friars: The Impact of the Early Mendicant Movement on Western Society*. London, 1994.

Menocal, Maria Rosa. *The Arabic Role in Medieval Literary History: A Forgotten Heritage*. Philadelphia, 1987

Möhring, Hannes. *Saladin: The Sultan and His Times, 1138-1193*. Trans. David S. Bachrach. Baltimore, 2008.

Moore, R.I. *The First European Revolution, c. 970-1215*. Oxford, 2000.

—. *The Formation of a Persecuting Society: Power and Deviance in Western Europe, 950-1250*. Oxford, 1987.

Pegg, Mark Gregory. *The Corruption of Angels: The Great Inquisition of 1245-1246*. Princeton, 2001.

Simons, Walter. *Cities of Ladies: Beguine Communities in the Medieval Low Countries, 1200-1565*. Philadelphia, 2001.

Tyerman, Christopher. *God's War: A New History of the Crusades*. Cambridge, MA, 2006.

To test your knowledge of this chapter, please go to
www.rosenweinshorthistory.com
and click "Study Questions."

SEVEN

DISCORDANT HARMONIES
(c.1250-c.1350)

In the shadow of a great Mongol empire that, for about a century, stretched from the East China Sea to the Black Sea and from Moscow to the Himalayas, Europeans were bit players in a great Eurasian system tied together by a combination of sheer force and open trade routes. Taking advantage of the new opportunities for commerce and evangelization offered by the mammoth new empire, Europeans ventured with equal verve into experiments in their own backyards: in government, thought, and expression. Above all, they sought to harmonize disparate groups, ideas, and artistic modes. At the same time, unable to force everything into unified and harmonious wholes and often confronted instead with discord and strife, they tried to purge their society of deviants of every sort.

THE MONGOL HEGEMONY

The Mongols, like the Huns and Seljuks before them, were pastoralists. Occupying the eastern edge of the great steppes that stretch west to the Hungarian plains, they herded horses and sheep while honing their skills as hunters and warriors. Believing in both high deities and slightly lower spirits, the Mongols were also open to other religious ideas, easily assimilating Buddhism, Islam, and even some forms of Christianity. Their empire, in its heyday stretching about 4000 miles from east to west, was the last to be created by the nomads from the steppes.

The Contours of the Mongol Empire

The Mongols formed under the leadership of Chingiz (or Genghis) Khan (*c.*1162-1227). Fusing together various tribes of mixed ethnic origins and traditions, Chingiz created a highly disciplined, orderly, and sophisticated army. Impelled out of Mongolia in part by new climatic conditions that threatened their grasslands, the Mongols were equally inspired by Chingiz's vision of world conquest. All of China came under their rule by 1279; meanwhile, the Mongols were making forays to the west as well. They took Rus in the 1230s, Poland and Hungary in 1241, and might well have continued into the rest of Europe, had not unexpected dynastic disputes and insufficient pasturage for their horses drawn them back east. In the end, the borders of their European dominion rolled back east of the Carpathian Mountains.

Something rather similar happened in the Islamic world, where the Mongols took Seljuk Rum, the major power in the region, by 1243. They then moved on to Baghdad (putting an end to the caliphate there in 1258) and Syria (1259-1260), threatening the fragile Crusader States a few miles away. Yet a few months later the Mongols with-

Map 7.1: The Mongol Empire, *c.*1260-1350

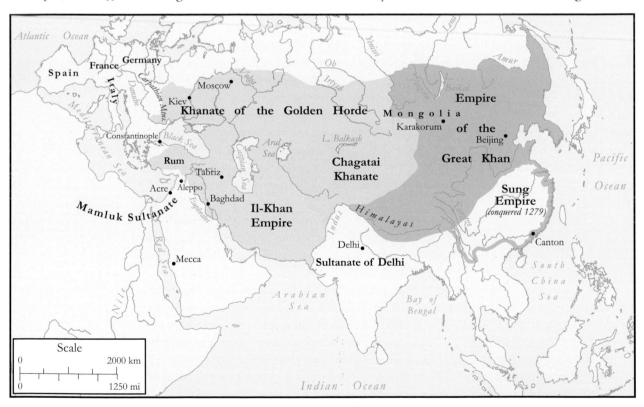

drew their troops from Syria, probably (again) because of inadequate grasslands and dynastic problems. The Mamluks of Egypt took advantage of the moment to conquer Syria themselves. This effectively ended the Mongol push across the Islamic world. It was the Mamluks, not the Mongols, who took Acre in 1291, snuffing out the last bit of the original Crusader States.

By the middle of the thirteenth century, the Mongol empire had taken on the contours of a settled state. (See Map 7.1.) It was divided into four regions, each under the rule of various progeny of Chingiz. The western-most quadrant was dominated by the rulers of Rus, the so-called Golden Horde ("horde" derived from the Turkic word for "court"). Settled along the lower Volga River valley, the Mongols of the Golden Horde combined traditional pastoralism with more settled activities. They founded cities, fostered trade, and gradually gave up their polytheism in favor of Islam. While demanding regular and exactly calculated tribute, troops, and recognition of their overlordship from the indigenous Rus rulers, they nevertheless allowed the Rus princes considerable autonomy. Their policy of religious toleration allowed the Orthodox church to flourish, untaxed, and willing in turn to offer up prayers for the soul of the Mongol khan (ruler). Kiev-based Rus, largely displaced by the Mongols, gave way to the hegemony of northern Rus princes, such as those centered in Lithuania (on the Baltic) and Muscovy, the area around Moscow. As Mongol rule fragmented, in the course of the fifteenth century, Moscow-based Russia emerged.

Mongols and Europeans

Once settled, the Mongols wooed Europe. They sent embassies west, welcomed Christian missionaries, and encouraged European trade. For their part, Europeans initially thought that the Mongols must be Christians; news of Mongol onslaughts in the Islamic world gave ballast to the myth of a lost Christian tribe led by a "Prester John" and his son "King David." Even though Europeans soon learned that the Mongols were not Christians, they dreamed of new triumphs: they imagined, for example, that Orthodox Christians under the Golden Horde would now accept papal protection (and primacy); they flirted with the idea of a Mongol-Christian alliance against the Muslims; and they saw the advent of the "new" pagans as an opportunity to evangelize. Thus in the 1250s the Franciscan William of Rubruck traveled across Asia to convert the Mongols in China; on his way back he met some Dominicans determined to do the same. European missions to the east became a regular feature of the West's contact with the Mongol world.

Such contact was further facilitated by trade. European caravans and ships crisscrossed the Mongol world, bringing silks, spices, ceramics, and copper back from

China, while exporting slaves, furs, and other commodities. (See Map 7.2.) The Genoese, who allied with the Byzantines to overthrow the Latin Empire of Constantinople in 1261, received special trading privileges from both the newly installed Byzantine emperor, Michael VIII Paleologus, and the khans of the Golden Horde. Genoa, which set up a permanent trading post at Caffa (today Feodosiya), on the Black Sea, was followed by Venice, which established its own trade-stations at Tana and Tabriz. These were sites well poised to exploit overland routes. Other European traders and missionaries traveled arduous sea routes, setting sail from the Persian Gulf (controlled by the Mongols) and rounding India before arriving in China. Marco Polo (1254-1324) was the most famous of the travelers to the east only because he left a fascinating travel book:

Map 7.2: Mongol-European Trade Routes, *c.*1350

[At Kinsai, today Hangzhou] there are ten principal market-places, not to speak of innumerable local ones.... Other streets are occupied by women of the town, ... [who] are to be found throughout the city, attired with great magnificence, heavily perfumed, attended by many handmaids, and

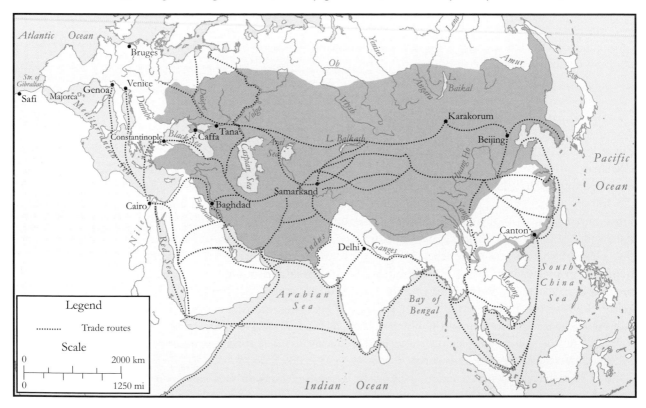

lodged in richly ornamented apartments.... In other streets are established the doctors and astrologers, who also teach reading and writing; and countless other crafts have their allotted places round the squares.[1]

Descriptions such as this fired up new adventurers, eager to seek out the fabulous wealth of the orient. In a sense, the Mongols initiated the search for exotic goods and missionary opportunities that culminated in the European "discovery" of a new world, the Americas.

THE MATURATION OF THE EUROPEAN ECONOMY

The pull of the East on the trade of the great Italian maritime cities was part of a series of shifts in Europe's commercial patterns. Another one, even more important, was towards the Atlantic. At the same time, new roads and bridges within Europe made land trade both possible and profitable. The linkages gave Europeans access to material goods of every sort, but they also heightened social tensions, especially within the cities.

New Routes

The first ships to ply the Atlantic's waters in regular trips were the galleys of Genoese entrepreneurs. By the 1270s they were leaving the Mediterranean via the Strait of Gibraltar, stopping to trade at various ports along the Spanish coast, and then making their way north to England and northern France. (See Map 7.3.) In the western Mediterranean, Majorca, recently conquered by the king of Aragon, sent its own ships to join the Atlantic trade at about the same time. Soon the Venetians began state-sponsored Atlantic expeditions using new-style "great galleys" that held more cargo yet required fewer oarsmen. Eventually, as sailing ships—far more efficient than any sort of galley—were developed by the Genoese and others, the Atlantic passage replaced older overland and river routes between the Mediterranean and Europe's north.

Equally important for commerce were new initiatives in North Africa. As the Almohad Empire collapsed, weak successor states allowed Europeans new elbow room. Genoa had outposts in the major Mediterranean ports of the Maghreb and new ones down the Atlantic coast, as far south as Safi (today in Morocco). Pisa, Genoa's traditional trade rival, was entrenched at Tunis. Catalonia and Majorca, by

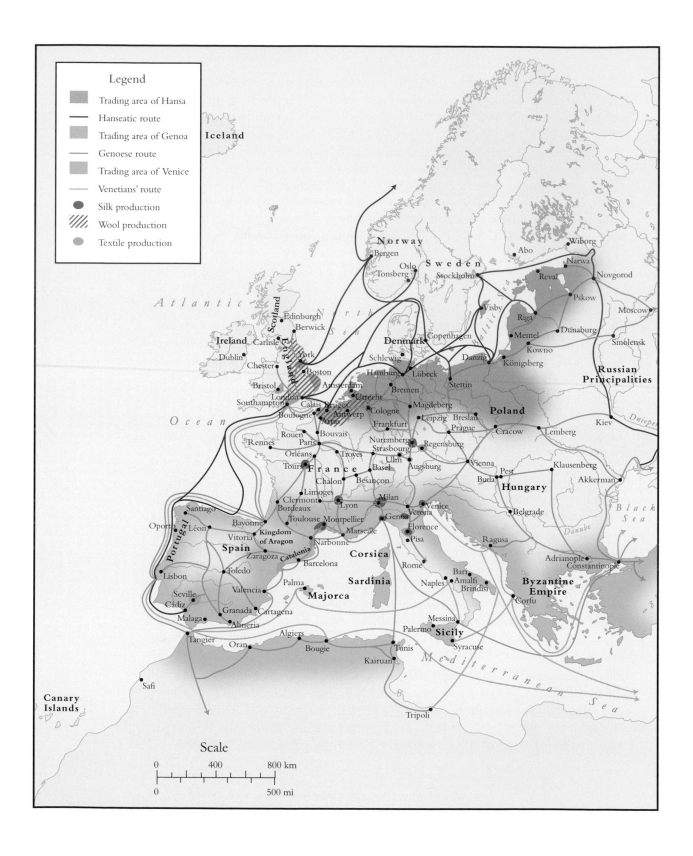

Legend

Trading area of Hansa

Hanseatic route

Trading area of Genoa

Genoese route

Trading area of Venice

Venetians' route

Silk production

Wool production

Textile production

Iceland

Norway
Bergen
Oslo
Tonsberg

Sweden
Abo
Stockholm
Wiborg
Narwa
Reval
Novgorod
Visby
Pskow
Moscow
Riga
Memel
Dunaburg
Smolensk
Kowno
Danzig
Königsberg

Russian Principalities

Atlantic
North Sea
Baltic Sea

Scotland
Edinburgh
Berwick

Ireland
Dublin
Carlisle
Chester
York
Bristol
Boston
Southampton
London
Calais
Bruges
Boulogne
Antwerp
Arras

Ocean

Denmark
Schlewig
Hamburg
Lübeck
Copenhagen
Stettin
Bremen
Magdeberg
Amsterdam
Utrecht
Cologne
Frankfurt
Leipzig
Breslau
Prague
Poland
Cracow
Lemberg
Kiev

Dnieper

Rouen
Bouvais
Paris
Rennes
Orléans
Troyes
Tours
France
Chàlon
Limoges
Clermont
Bordeaux
Lyon
Nuremberg
Strasbourg
Ulm
Basel
Besançon
Augsburg
Regensburg
Vienna
Buda
Pest
Hungary
Klausenberg
Akkerman

Black Sea

Milan
Verona
Venice
Genoa
Florence
Pisa
Rome
Ragusa
Belgrade

Danube

Adrianople
Constantinople

Santiago
Oporto
Léon
Bayonne
Vitoria
Portugal
Zaragoza
Toledo
Lisbon
Seville
Cádiz
Malaga
Tangier
Spain
Kingdom of Aragon
Narbonne
Catalonia
Barcelona
Palma
Valencia
Granada
Almeria
Cartagena
Oran
Algiers
Bougie
Montpellier
Marseille
Toulouse

Corsica
Sardinia
Majorca
Naples
Bari
Amalfi
Brindisi
Tunis
Kairuan
Palermo
Messina
Sicily
Syracuse
Corfu

Byzantine Empire

Mediterranean Sea

Tripoli

Canary Islands
Safi

Scale

0   400   800 km

0   500 mi

now ruled by the king of Aragon, found their commercial stars rising fast. Catalonia established its own settlements in the port cities of the Maghreb; Majorcans went off to the Canary Islands. Profits were enormous. Besides acting as middlemen, trading goods or commodities from northern Europe, the Italian cities had their own products to sell (Venice had salt and glass products, Pisa had iron) in exchange for African cotton, linen, spices, and, above all, gold. In the mid-thirteenth century, Genoa and Florence were minting coins from gold panned on the upper Niger River, while Venice began minting gold ducats in 1284. The silver standard, which most of Europe had adhered to since the Carolingian age, was giving way to the gold.

At the same time as Genoa, Pisa, Venice, Majorca, and Catalonia were forging trade networks in the south, some cities in the north of Europe were creating their own marketplace in the Baltic Sea region. Built on the back of the Northern Crusades, the Hanseatic League was created by German merchants following in the wake of Christian knights to prosper in cities like Danzig (today Gdansk, in Poland), Riga, and Reval (today Tallinn, in Estonia). Lübeck, founded by the duke of Saxony, formed the Hansa's center. Formalized through legislation, the association of cities agreed that

Map 7.3 (facing page): European Trade Routes, c.1300

> Each city shall ... keep the sea clear of pirates.... Whoever is expelled from one city because of a crime shall not be received in another ... If a lord besieges a city, no one shall aid him in any way to the detriment of the besieged city.[2]

There were no mercantile rivalries here, unlike the competition between Genoa and Pisa in the south. But there was also little glamor. Pitch, tar, lumber, furs, herring: these were the stuff of northern commerce.

The opening of the Atlantic and the commercial uniting of the Baltic were dramatic developments. Elsewhere the pace of commercial life quickened more subtly. By 1200 almost all the cities of pre-industrial Europe were in existence. By 1300 they were connected by a spider's web of roads that brought even small towns of a few thousand inhabitants into wider networks of trade. To be sure, some old trading centers declined: the towns of Champagne, for example, had been centers of major fairs— periodic but intense commercial activity. By the mid-thirteenth century the fairs' chief functions were as financial markets and clearing houses. On the whole, however, urban centers grew and prospered. As the burgeoning population of the countryside fed the cities with immigrants, the population of many cities reached their medieval maximum: in 1300 Venice and London each had perhaps 100,000 inhabitants, Paris an extraordinary 200,000. Many of these people became part of the urban labor force, working as apprentices or servants; but others could not find jobs or became disabled and could not keep them. The indigent and sick posed new challenges for

hands of the Sienese painter Pietro Lorenzetti (*c.*1280/90-1348), for example, Mary's life took on lively detail. In Plate 7.1, an altarpiece depicting the Birth of the Virgin, two servants—one probably the midwife—tenderly wash the infant Mary. Her mother, clearly modeled on the mistress of a well-to-do Italian household, sits up in bed, gazing at the child with dreamy eyes, while, in another room, a little serving boy whispers news of the birth to the expectant father. Both publicly, in feasts dedicated to the major events in Mary's life, and privately, in small and concentrated images made to be contemplated by individual viewers, the Virgin was the focus of intense religious feeling. The ivory carving in Plate 7.2, tiny enough to be held in one hand, was meant to be an aid to private devotion. Books of Hours—small prayer books for laymen and (especially) women—almost always included images of the Virgin for worshippers to contemplate. In Plate 7.3, on the right-hand side, Jeanne d'Evreux, queen of France and the original owner of this Book of Hours, is shown kneeling in prayer within the initial D. This is the first letter of "Domine," "Lord," the opening word of the first prayer of the Office of the Virgin Mary. Above Jeanne is the Annunciation, when Gabriel tells Mary that she will bear the Savior.

That worship could be a private matter was part of wider changes in the ways that people negotiated the afterlife while here on earth. The doctrine of Purgatory, informally believed long before it was declared dogma in 1274, held that the Masses and prayers of the living could shorten the purgative torments that had to be suffered by the souls of the dead. Soon families were endowing special chapels for themselves, private spaces for offering private Masses on behalf of their own members. High churchmen and wealthy laymen insisted that they be buried within the walls of the church rather than outside of it, reminding the living—via their grand tombs and effigies—to pray for them. The effigy of English King Edward II (1307-1327) lies alert: his eyes are open, and an angel guards him at his head

Plate 7.1 (facing page): Pietro Lorenzetti, *Birth of the Virgin* (1342). This painted altarpiece creates an architectural space of real depth in which figures of convincing solidity act and interact; compare them with Saint Joseph in Plate 6.6, p. 251. Note how the ribs and arches of a Gothic church are used here as both decorative and unifying elements.

Plate 7.2: Virgin and Child (1330-1350). Carved in France, this ivory was once painted in color and gilded with gold. Flanked by wings on both sides (each probably containing scenes from the Virgin's life) that could close over the central portion, this portable "box" was a devotional aid suitable for a lay person.

Plate 7.3: Jean Pucelle, *Hours of Jeanne d'Evreux* (c.1325–1328). Meant for private devotion, this Book of Hours was lavishly illustrated. Scenes from the life of Christ, the Virgin, and King Louis IX (Jeanne's great-grandfather) contrast with delicate illustrations at the foot of each page. On the left-hand side of the two pages illustrated here is Christ's Betrayal, the moment when Judas brings soldiers and priests to capture Jesus, while Peter cuts off the ear of Malchus, the high priest's slave. This horrific moment is juxtaposed on the right with the promise of the Annunciation. Below, in delicate line-drawings, the frivolity of the world is highlighted: on the left a man on a ram and another on a goat practice jousting with a barrel; on the right, young people play a game of "frog in the middle."

Plate 7.4 (facing page): Tomb and Effigy of Edward II (1330s). From the end of the twelfth century, great laymen and ecclesiastics were remembered with more and more elaborate tombs and effigies. This alabaster effigy of Edward II in the north ambulatory of Gloucester Cathedral was enclosed by a delicate envelope of pinnacles and arches, a shrine fit for a relic.

Plate 7.8: Nicola Pisano, Pulpit (1265-1268). *The Adoration of the Magi*, the scene on this panel of the Siena pulpit, was a very traditional Christian theme (see an early representation on the Franks Casket, Plate 2.7, pp. 94-95), but here the sculptor, Nicola Pisano, has imagined it as a crowd scene and filled it with little details — like the camels — to make it "come to life."

Plate 7.9 (facing page): Giotto, Arena Chapel, Padua (1304-1313). Giotto brought to painting the sensibilities of a sculptor. Just as Nicola Pisano's figures (see Plate 7.8) had depth and roundness, so did Giotto's painted ones. And just as Nicola used telling details to humanize scenes from the Bible, so Giotto's paintings, which covered the walls of the Arena Chapel with the narrative of humanity's redemption through Christ and the Final Judgment, were filled with homey particulars.

left) against the moral authority of the church (on the right) represented by pleading mothers, innocent babes, and a baptistery looming above them all.

Just as Italian art was influenced by northern Gothic style, so in turn the new Italian currents went north. In France, for example, illuminators for the royal court made miniature spaces for figures in the round, creating illusions of depth. Have another look at Jean Pucelle's *Hours of Jeanne d'Evreux* (Plate 7.3 on p. 284). In the picture of Christ's Betrayal on the left-hand side, the old S-shape figures are still favored, but the soldiers who crowd around Christ are as dense and dramatic as Herod's minions in Giotto. On the right-hand page, Mary, surprised by the angel of the Annunciation, sits in a space as deep as Herod's tower in Plate 7.10. Influenced perhaps by the look of sculpted figures such as those on Nicola's Siena pulpit, Pucelle painted in *grisaille*, a bare gray highlighted by light tints of color.

292 SEVEN: DISCORDANT HARMONIES (*c*.1250–*c*.1350)

CRISIS

The artistic interest in crowd scenes may have been inspired not only by ancient art but by current living conditions. The cities were swollen with immigrants from the overcrowded countryside. By 1300, the only land left uncleared in France and England was marginal or unworkable with the tools of the day. It is true that farms were producing more than ever before, but families also had more hungry mouths to feed. One plot that had originally supported a single family in England was, by the end of the thirteenth century, divided into twenty tiny parcels for the progeny of the original peasant holder. The last known French *villeneuve* ("new town") was founded in 1246; after that, new settlements ceased.

Consider the village of Toury, about 45 miles south of Paris (Map 7.6). It originally consisted of a few peasant habitations (their houses and gardens) clustered around a central enclosure belonging to the lord, in this case the monastery of Saint-Denis (see p. 201). Nearby, across the main route that led from Paris to Orléans, was a parish church. In 1110 Abbot Suger constructed a well-fortified castle on the site of the enclosure. In the course of the thirteenth century, encouraged both by Saint-Denis's policy of giving out lots in return for rents and by a market granted by the king, the village grew rapidly, expanding to the east, then to the west, and finally (by the fourteenth century) to the north. Meanwhile the lands cultivated by the villagers—once called upon to support only a small number of householders—were divided into more than 5000 parcels, which appear as tiny rectangles on Map 7.7.

In general, population growth seems to have leveled off by the mid-thirteenth century, but the static supply of farmland meant that from that time onward France and England would face sudden and severe grain shortages. Climatic changes

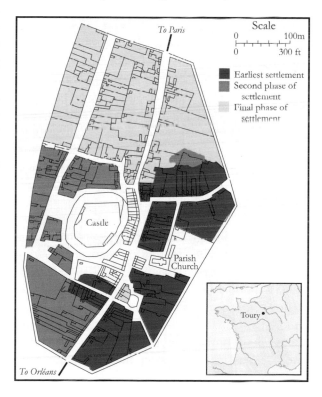

Map 7.6: The Village of Toury, Fourteenth and Fifteenth Centuries

Plate 7.10 (facing page): Giotto, *Massacre of the Innocents*, Arena Chapel (1304–1313). Giotto organized the Arena Chapel paintings like scenes in a comic book, to be read from left to right. The Massacre of the Innocents—illustrating Matt. 2:16–18, where Herod orders the execution of all male children two years old and younger—is at the far right on the south wall; the next scene, in the band underneath, is on the far left. Viewers must make a sort of pilgrimage around the church as they follow the scenes from start to finish.

The Black Death

The Black Death (1346-1353), so named by later historians looking back on the disease, was likely caused by *Yersinia pestis*, the bacterium of the plague. (Some historians dispute this.) Its symptoms, as an eye witness reported, included "tumorous outgrowths at the roots of thighs and arms and simultaneously bleeding ulcerations, which, sometimes the same day, carried the infected rapidly out of this present life."[1]

The disease probably spread from China, arriving in the West along well-worn trade routes with the Mongols. Caffa, the Genoese trading post on the northern shore of the Black Sea, was hit in 1347. From there the plague traveled to Europe and the Middle East, quickly striking Constantinople and Cairo and soon leaving the port cities for the hinterlands. In early 1348 the citizens of Pisa and Genoa, fierce rivals on the seas, were being felled without distinction by disease. Early spring of the same year saw the Black Death at Florence; two months later it had hit Dorset in England. Dormant during the winter, it revived the next spring to infect French ports and countryside, moving on swiftly to Germany. By 1351 it was at Moscow, where it stopped for a time, only to recur in ten- to twelve-year cycles throughout the fourteenth century. (Only the attack of 1346-1353 is called the Black Death.) The disease continued to strike, though at longer intervals, until the eighteenth century.

The effect on Europe's population was immediate and devastating. Famines had already weakened many people's resistance to disease. At Paris, by no means the city hardest hit, about half the population died, mainly children and poor people. In eastern Normandy, perhaps 70 to 80 per cent of the population succumbed. At Bologna, even the most robust—men able to bear arms—were reduced by 35 per cent in the course of 1348. Demographic recovery across Europe began only in the second half of the fifteenth century.

Deaths, especially of the poor, led to acute labor shortages in both town and country. Already in 1351, King Edward III of England issued the Statute of Laborers, forbidding workers to take pay higher than pre-plague wages and fining employers who offered more. Similar laws were promulgated—and flouted—elsewhere. In the countryside, landlords needed to keep their profits up even as their workforce was decimated. They were forced to strike bargains with enterprising peasants, furnishing them, for example, with oxen and seed; or they turned their land to new uses, such as pasturage. In the cities, the guilds and other professions recruited new men, survivors of the plague. Able to marry and set up households at younger ages, these *nouveaux riches* helped reconstitute the population. Although many widows were now potentially the heads of households, deeply rooted customs tended to push them either into new marriages (in northern Europe) or (in southern Europe) into the house of some male relative, whether brother, son, or son-in-law.

Plate 8.1 (facing page): Woodcut from *Der Ackermann aus Böhmen* (*c*.1462). In this book, Death and a plowman (the "Ackermann") argue before God, the plowman accusing Death of injustice. (Death wins in the end.) The dialogue was published with a series of woodcuts by the first printer of illustrated books, Albrecht Pfister (*d.c.*1470). Color tints were then added by hand.

went into the library [of the monastery there], we found *Jason's Argonauticon*, written by C. Valerius Flaccus in verse that is both splendid and dignified and not far removed from poetic majesty. Then we found some discussions in prose of a number of Cicero's orations.... In fact we have copies of all these books. But when we carefully inspected the nearby tower of the church of St. Gall in which countless books were kept like captives and the library neglected and infested with dust, worms, soot, and all the things associated with the destruction of books, we all burst into tears.[9]

Plate 8.2 (facing page): Donatello, *David Standing on the Head of Goliath* (*c.*1430-1440). David is here portrayed neither as an Old Testament king nor as the author of the psalms, but rather as a beautiful boy.

Cicero, Varro, Livy: these provided the models of Latin and the rules of expression that Cincius and his friends admired. To them the monks of St. Gall were "barbarians" for not wholeheartedly valuing ancient Latin rhetoric, prose, and poetry over all other writings. In the course of the fourteenth century Italian intellectuals turned away from the evolved Latin of their contemporaries to find models in the ancients. Already in 1333 the young Francis Petrarch (1304-1374) traveled through the Low Countries looking for manuscripts of the ancient authors; he discovered Cicero's *Pro Archia*, a paean to poetry, and carefully copied it out.

Petrarch's taste for ancient eloquence and his ability to write in a new, elegant, "classical" style (whether in Latin or in the vernacular) made him a star. But he was not alone, as Cincius' letter proves; he was simply one of the more famous exemplars of a new group calling themselves "humanists." There had been humanists before: we have seen Saint Anselm's emphasis on Christ's saving humanity, Saint Bernard's evocation of human religious emotion, and Thomas Aquinas's confidence in human reason to scale the heights of truth (see pp. 216 and 286). But the new humanists were more self-conscious about their calling, and they tied it to the cultivation of classical literature.

As Cincius' case also shows, if the humanists' passion was antiquity, their services were demanded with equal ardor by ecclesiastical and secular princes. Cincius served Pope John XXIII. Petrarch was similarly employed by princes: for several years, for example, he worked for the Visconti family, the rulers of Milan. As Italian artists associated themselves with humanists, working in tandem with them, they too became part of the movement.

Historians have come to give the name Renaissance to this era of artists and humanists. But the Renaissance was not so much a period as a program. It made the language and art of the ancient past the model for the present; it privileged classical books as "must" reading for an eager and literate elite; and it promoted old, sometimes crumbling, and formerly little-appreciated classical art, sculpture, and architecture as inspiring models for Italian artists and builders. Meanwhile, it downgraded the immediate past — the last thousand years! — as a barbarous "Middle" Age. Above all, the Renaissance gave city communes and wealthy princes alike a new repertory of symbols and styles, drawn from a resonant and heroic past, with which to associate their present power.

At Florence, for example, where the Medici family held sway in the fifteenth century behind a facade of communal republicanism, the sculptor Donatello (c.1386-1466) cast a bronze figure of David (see Plate 8.2) to stand in the courtyard of the Medici palace. It was accompanied by a Latin inscription, "Behold, a boy overcame the great tyrant. Conquer, O citizens."[10] The appeal to the Florentines to overcome the enemy (very likely Milan) subtly associated the Medici family with the liberty of the citizenry while disparaging the dukes of Milan as tyrants. Donatello's *David* is strikingly young, self-absorbed—and utterly nude apart from his hat and boots. The first bronze nude cast since antiquity, it combines Christian iconography (David here evokes Christ trampling the serpent) with classical grace (compare David's easy pose with that of the equally triumphant Theseus the Minotaur-slayer in Plate 1.2 on p. 34).

Corporate sponsors also patronized the new-style artists and architects. The Florentine Silk Guild paid the architect Filippo Brunelleschi (1377-1446) to build a Foundling Hospital, a home for abandoned children. The building broke radically from the soaring Gothic style to emphasize calm regularity and low horizontal steadiness (see Plate 8.3). Soon the Opera del Duomo, which was responsible for the upkeep of Florence's cathedral, called on Brunelleschi to provide a dome for Florence's unfinished Gothic cathedral, "vast enough to cover the entire Tuscan population with its shadow," as his admirer Alberti put it.[11]

The Renaissance flourished in many Italian cities besides Florence, among them Rome, Urbino, Mantua, Venice, Milan, and Perugia. At Perugia, for example, the artist Raphael (1483-1520) was commissioned by a noblewoman, Atalanta Baglioni, to paint an altarpiece for her private chapel to commemorate the death of her son. In the *Entombment of Christ* (see Plate 8.4), Raphael joined religious with family feeling, portraying (as the artist's biographer Vasari [d.1574] put it) "the grief as they lay him [Christ] to rest felt by the nearest and dearest relations of some much loved person, who had sustained the happiness, dignity and well-being of a whole family."[12]

At Milan, Duke Ludovico il Moro (r.1480-1499) gave Leonardo da Vinci (1452-1519) a number of commissions, including painting the *Last Supper* (see Plate 8.5) on one of the walls of the dining hall of a Dominican convent c.1497. Here Leonardo demonstrated his mastery of the

Plate 8.8: Rogier van der Weyden, *Columba Altarpiece* (1450s). Depicting three standard scenes from Christ's childhood—the Annunciation, the Adoration of the Magi, and the Presentation in the Temple—the *Columba Altarpiece* subtly introduces new themes alongside the old. For example, Christ's death is suggested by the crucifix above Mary in the central panel, while the present time (the fifteenth century) is suggested by the cityscape in the background, which probably represents Cologne, the native city of the man who commissioned the altar and the proud home of the relics of the Magi.

kings to Italian *signori* (and on to Ottoman sultans)—all wanted tapestries from Burgundy for *their* palaces.

At the same time, dukes and other northern European patrons favored a new style of art that emphasized devotion, sentiment, and immediacy. (This style would later be one of the inspirations for Raphael's *Entombment* in Plate 8.4.) Painted in oil-based pigments, capable of showing the finest details and the subtlest shading, Netherlandish art was valued above all for its true-to-life expressivity. In the *Columba Altarpiece* by Rogier van der Weyden—likely commissioned by Johann Dasse, a wealthy merchant from Cologne (Germany)—the donor himself is depicted, hat in hand (to the left), humbly witnessing the visit of the Magi. (See the central panel of Plate 8.8.) Time itself is compressed in this picture, as the immediacy of the painting—its here-and-now presence—belies the historical reality: no merchant of the fifteenth century could possibly have been at the scene.

The emphasis on the natural details of the moment was equally striking in secular paintings from the Netherlands. In *Man in a Red Turban* (see Plate 8.9) by Jan van Eyck (*c.*1390-1441), we even see the stubble of the man's beard. Yet this entirely secular theme—a man in stylish red headgear (evidence of the Turkish allure)—is infused with a quiet inner light that endows its subject with a kind of otherworldliness.

Both the Italian and Northern Renaissances cultivated music and musicians, above all for the aura that they gave rulers, princes, and great churchmen. In Italy, Isabella d'Este (1474-1539), marchesa of Mantua, employed her own musicians—singers, woodwind and string players, percussionists, and keyboard players—while her husband had his own band. In Burgundy the duke had a fine private chapel and musicians, singers, and composers to staff it. In England wealthy patrons founded colleges—Eton (founded by King Henry VI in 1440-1441) was one—where choirs offered up prayers in honor of the Virgin. Motets continued to be composed and sung, but now polyphonic music for larger groups became common as well. In the hands of a composer like John Dunstable (*c.*1385-1453), who probably worked for the duke of Bedford, regent for Henry VI in France during the Hundred Years' War, dissonance was smoothed out. In the compositions of Dunstable and his followers, old juxtapositions of independent lines were replaced by harmonious chords that moved together even as they changed. As Martin le Franc put it in *Le Champion des dames* (1441-1442), "marvelous pleasantness makes their song joyous and notable."[15] Working within the old modal categories, composers made their mark with music newly sonorous and smooth.

Plate 8.9 (facing page): Jan van Eyck, *Man in a Red Turban* (1433). Compare this head with that of the idealized Theseus (Plate 1.2 on p. 34), the somber Saint Mark (Plate 3.8 on p. 132), the jovial Saint Joseph, (Plate 6.6 on p. 251) and the insouciant David (Plate 8.2 on p. 329). Only van Eyck paints his anonymous subject without idealizing or beautifying him; the man's worth and dignity derive only (but importantly) from his individuality.

NEW HORIZONS

Experiment and play within old traditions were thus the major trends of the period. They can be seen in explorations of interiority, in creative inventions, even in the conquest of the globe. Yet their consequences may fairly be said to have ushered in a new era.

Interiority

Donatello's David, dependent on no one for his quiet satisfaction, and van Eyck's red-turbaned man, glowing from within, are similar in their self-involved interiority. David's self-centeredness is that of the hero; van Eyck's man's is that of any ordinary creature of God, the artist's statement about the holiness of nature.

These two styles of interiority were mirrored in religious life and expression. Saint Catherine of Siena (1347-1380) was a woman in the heroic mold. A reformer with a message, she was one of the first in a long line of women (Jeanne d'Arc is another example) to intervene on the public stage because of her private agonies. Chosen by God in distinct words to be his intermediary in the Great Schism, she wrote (or rather dictated) nearly 400 letters to the great leaders of the day, working ceaselessly to bring the pope back to Rome and urging crusade as the best way to purge and revivify the church.

In the Low Countries, northern Germany, and the Rhineland, the *devotio moderna* (the "new devotion") movement, to the contrary, found purgation and renewal in individual reading and contemplation rather than on the public stage. Founded *c.*1380 by Gerhard Groote (1340-1384), the Brethren of the Common Life lived in male or female communities that focused on education, the copying of manuscripts, material simplicity, and individual faith. The Brethren were not quite humanists and not quite mystics, but they drew from both for a religious program that depended very little on the hierarchy or ceremonies of the church. Their style of piety would later be associated with Protestant groups.

Inventions

The enormous demand for books—whether by ordinary lay people, adherents of the *devotio moderna*, or humanists eager for the classics—made printed books a welcome addition to the repertory of available texts, though manuscripts were neither quickly nor easily displaced. The printing press, however obvious in thought, marked a great practical breakthrough: it depended on a new technique to mold metal type. This was first achieved by Johann Gutenberg at Mainz (in Germany) around 1450. The next trick was to get the raw materials that were needed to ensure ongoing production. Paper required water mills and a steady supply of rag (pulp made of cloth); the metal for the type had to be mined and shaped; an ink had to be found that would adhere to metal letters as well as spread evenly on paper.

By 1500 many European cities had publishing houses, with access to the materials that they needed and sufficient clientele to earn a profit. Highly competitive, the presses advertised their wares. They turned out not only religious and classical books but whatever the public demanded. Martin Luther (c.1483-1546) may not in fact have nailed his 95 Theses to the door of the church at Wittenberg in 1517, but he certainly allowed them to be printed and distributed in both Latin and German. Challenging prevailing church teachings and practice, the Theses ushered in the Protestant Reformation. The printing press was a powerful instrument of mass communication.

More specialized yet no less decisive for the future were new developments in navigation. Portolan maps, which charted the shape of the Mediterranean coast through accurate measurements from point to point, were used as practical tools by sailors plying the waters. When, at the end of the fifteenth century, Portuguese adventurers made their way down the coast of Africa, they used the same system. But navigating the Atlantic depended on more than maps; it required methods for exploiting the powerful ocean wind systems. New ship designs—the light caravel, the heavy galleon—featured the rigging and sails needed to harness the wind.

Voyages

As we have seen (p. 267), already in the thirteenth century merchants and missionaries from Genoa and Majorca were making forays into the Atlantic. In the fifteenth century the initiative that would eventually take Europeans around the Cape of Good Hope in one direction and to the Americas in the other came from the Portuguese royal house. The enticements were gold and slaves as well as honor and glory. Under King João I (r.1385-1433) and his successors, Portugal extended its rule to the Muslim port of Ceuta and a few other nearby cities. (See Map 8.6.) More importantly, João's son Prince Henry "the Navigator" (1394-1460) sponsored expeditions—mainly by Genoese sailors—to explore the African coast: in the mid-1450s they reached the Cape Verde Islands and penetrated inland via the Senegal and Gambia rivers. A generation later, Portuguese explorers were working their way far past the equator; in 1487 Bartholomeu Dias (c.1450-1500) sighted the Cape of Good Hope, and at the end of the century Vasco da Gama (c.1460-1524) went around Africa and sailed all the way to Calicut (today Kozhikode) in India. In his account of the voyage he made no secret of his methods: when he needed water, he landed on an island and bombarded the inhabitants, taking "as much water as we wanted."[16]

Da Gama's cavalier treatment of the natives was symptomatic of a more profound development: European colonialism. Already in the 1440s, Henry was portioning out the uninhabited islands of Madeira and the Azores to those of his followers who promised to find peasants to settle them. The Azores remained a grain producer, but, with financing by the Genoese, Madeira began to grow cane sugar. The product took Europe by storm. Demand was so high that a few decades later, when few European settlers could be found to work sugar plantations on the Cape Verde Islands, the Genoese Antonio da Noli, discoverer and governor of the islands, brought in African slaves instead. Cape Verde was a microcosm of later European colonialism, which depended on just such slave labor.

Map 8.6: Long-distance Sea Voyages of the Fifteenth Century

Portugal's successes and pretensions roused the hostility and rivalry of Castile. Ferdinand and Isabella's determination to conquer the Canary Islands was in part their "answer" to Portugal's Cape Verde. When, in 1492, they half-heartedly sponsored the

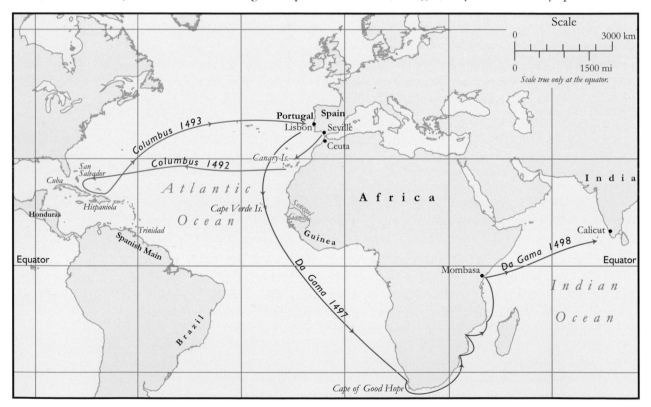

Genoese Christopher Columbus (1451-1506) on a westward voyage across the Atlantic, they knew that they were playing Portugal's game.

Although the conquistadores confronted a New World, they did so with the expectations and categories of the Old. When the Spaniard Hernán Cortés (1485-1547) began his conquest of Mexico, he boasted in a letter home that he had reprimanded one of the native chiefs for thinking that Mutezuma, the Aztec emperor who ruled much of Mexico at the time, was worthy of allegiance:

> I replied by telling him of the great power of Your Majesty [Emperor Charles V, who was also king of Spain] and of the many other princes, greater than Mutezuma, who were Your Highness's vassals and considered it no small favor to be so; Mutezuma also would become one, as would all the natives of these lands. I therefore asked him to become one, for if he did it would be greatly to his honor and advantage, but if, on the other hand, he refused to obey, he would be punished.[17]

The old values lived on.

★　　★　　★　　★

Between the years 1350 and 1500, a series of catastrophes struck Europe. The Black Death felled at least a fifth of the population of Europe. The Hundred Years' War wreaked havoc when archers shot and cannons roared; it loosed armies of freebooters in both town and country during its interstices of peace. The Ottomans conquered Byzantium, took over the Balkans, and threatened Austria and Hungary. The church splintered as first the Great Schism and then national churches tore at the loyalties of churchmen and laity alike.

Yet these catastrophes were confronted, if not always overcome, with both energy and inventiveness. In England, peasants loosed the bonds of serfdom; in Portugal and Spain, adventurers discovered gold and land via the high seas; and everywhere bibliophiles and artists discovered wisdom and beauty in the classical past while princes flexed the muscles of sovereignty. History books normally divide this period into two parts, the crises going into a chapter on the Middle Ages, the creativity saved for a chapter on the Renaissance. But the two happened together, witness to Europe's aggressive resilience. Indeed, in the next century it would parcel out the globe.

*c.*1299-1324	Rule of Osman, founder of Ottomans
1304-1374	Francis Petrarch
*c.*1330-1384	John Wyclif
1337-1453	Hundred Years' War
*c.*1340-1400	Geoffrey Chaucer
1346-1353	Black Death
1351	Statute of Laborers in England
1358	Jacquerie in France
1364-*c.*1430	Christine de Pisan
*c.*1370-1415	Jan Hus
1378	Ciompi revolt in Florence
1378-1417	Great Schism of the papacy
1381	Wat Tyler's Rebellion
*c.*1390-1441	Jan van Eyck
1414-1418	Council of Constance
1429	Jeanne d'Arc leads French army to victory at Orléans
1438	Pragmatic Sanction of Bourges
1444-1446, 1451-1481	Rule of Mehmed II the Conqueror, Ottoman sultan
*c.*1450	Gutenberg invents the printing press
1452-1519	Leonardo da Vinci
1453	Ottoman conquest of Constantinople; end of Byzantine Empire
1454	Peace of Lodi in Northern Italy
1455-1487	Wars of the Roses
1477	Battle of Nancy; end of the Burgundian state
1492	Conquest of Granada; expulsion of Jews from Spain; first trans-Atlantic voyage of Columbus

NOTES

1. Nicephorus Gregoras, *Roman History*, in *Reading the Middle Ages: Sources from Europe, Byzantium, and the Islamic World* (Peterborough, ON, 2006), p.484.

2. Geoffrey Chaucer, *The Canterbury Tales*, trans. Nevill Coghill (Harmondsworth, 1977), p.88.

3. Ashikpashazade, *Osman Comes to Power*, in *Reading the Middle Ages*, p.494.

4. Froissart, *Chronicles*, in *Reading the Middle Ages*, p.512.

5. Jeanne d'Arc, *Letter to the English*, in *Reading the Middle Ages*, p.518.

6. Christine de Pisan, *The Tale of Joan of Arc*, quoted in Nadia Margolis, "The Mission of Joan of Arc," in *Medieval Hagiography: An Anthology*, ed. Thomas Head (New York, 2000), p.822.

7. Froissart, *Chronicles*, ed. and trans. Geoffrey Brereton (Harmondsworth, 1968), p.151.

8. *Wat Tyler's Rebellion*, in *Reading the Middle Ages*, p.523.

9. Cincius Romanus, *Letter to His Most Learned Teacher Franciscus de Fiana*, in *Reading the Middle Ages*, pp.536-37.

10. Quoted in Evelyn Welch, *Art and Society in Italy, 1350-1500* (Oxford, 1997), p.211.

11. Leon Battista Alberti, *On Painting and On Sculpture*, ed. and trans. Cecil Grayson (London: Phaidon Press, 1972), p.32.

12. Giorgio Vasari, *The Lives of the Artists*, ed. and trans. George Bull (Baltimore, 1965), p.290.

13. "A Sforza Banquet Menu (1491)," in *The Renaissance in Europe: An Anthology*, ed. Peter Elmer, Nick Webb, and Roberta Wood (New Haven, 2000), pp.172-75.

14. "A Sforza Banquet Menu," p.173.

15. Quoted in Gustave Reese, *Music in the Renaissance*, rev. ed. (New York, 1959), p.13; translated by Charles Brauner.

16. *A Journal of the First Voyage of Vasco da Gama, 1497-1499*, ed. and trans. E.G. Ravenstein (rpt. New York, 1963), p.30.

17. Hernán Cortés, *The Second Letter*, in *Reading the Middle Ages*, p.558.

FURTHER READING

Aberth, John. *From the Brink of the Apocalypse: Confronting Famine, War, Plague, and Death in the Later Middle Ages*. New York, 2001.

Belozerskaya, Marina. *Rethinking the Renaissance: Burgundian Arts across Europe*. Cambridge, 2002.

Benedictow, Ole J. *The Black Death, 1346-1353: The Complete History*. Woodbridge, Suffolk, 2004.

Blockmans, Wim, and Walter Prevenier. *The Promised Lands: The Low Countries under Burgundian Rule, 1369-1530*. Trans. Elizabeth Fackelman. Ed. Edward Peters. Philadelphia, 1999.

Blumenfeld-Kosinski, Renate. *Poets, Saints, and Visionaries of the Great Schism, 1378-1417*. University Park, 2006.

Cohn, Samuel K., Jr., *The Black Death Transformed: Disease and Culture in Early Renaissance Europe*. London, 2002.

——. *Lust for Liberty: The Politics of Social Revolt in Medieval Europe, 1200-1425*. Cambridge, MA, 2006.

Curry, Ann. *The Hundred Years' War, 1337-1453*. Oxford, 2002.

Fernández-Armesto, Felipe. *Pathfinders: A Global History of Exploration*. New York, 2006.

Goffman, Daniel. *The Ottoman Empire and Early Modern Europe*. Cambridge, 2002.

Hudson, Anne. *The Premature Reformation: Wycliffite Texts and Lollard History*. Oxford, 1988.

Imber, Colin. *The Ottoman Empire, 1300-1650: The Structure of Power*. New York, 2002.

Jardine, Lisa, and Jerry Brotton. *Global Interests: Renaissance Art between East and West*. Ithaca, NY, 2000.

Keen, Maurice. *Chivalry*. New Haven, 1984.

Johnson, Geraldine A. *Renaissance Art: A Very Short Introduction*. Oxford, 2005.

Klassen, John Martin. *The Nobility and the Making of the Hussite Revolution*. New York, 1978.

McKitterick, David. *Print, Manuscript and the Search for Order, 1450-1830*. Cambridge, 2003.

Parker, Geoffrey. *The Cambridge History of Warfare*. Cambridge, 2005.

Wheeler, Bonnie, and Charles Wood, eds. *Fresh Verdicts on Joan of Arc*. New York, 1996.

**To test your knowledge of this chapter, please go to
www.rosenweinshorthistory.com
and click "Study Questions."**

EPILOGUE

Cortéz may have used the old vocabulary of vassalage when speaking of his conquests in the Americas, but clearly the *reality* was so changed that we are right to see the years around 1500 as the turning point between the Middle Ages and a new phase of history. The Middle Ages began when the Roman provinces came into their own. They ended as those provinces—now vastly expanded, rich, and powerful, now "Europe," in fact—became in turn a new imperial power, its tentacles in the New World, Asia, and Africa. In the next centuries, as Europeans conquered most of the world, they (as the Romans had once done) exported themselves, their values, cultures, diseases, inventions, and institutions, while importing, usually without meaning to, many of the people, ideas, and institutions of the groups they conquered. In another phase, one not yet ended, former European colonies—at least some of them—have become, in turn, the center of a new-style empire involving economic, cultural, and (occasionally) military hegemony. It remains to be seen if this empire, too, will eventually be overtaken by its peripheries.

Does anything now remain of the Middle Ages? Without doubt. Bits and pieces of the past are clearly embedded in the present: universities, parliaments, ideas about God and human nature, the papacy, Gothic churches. We cling to some of these bits with ferocious passion, while repudiating others and allowing still more to float in and out of our unquestioned assumptions. Many things that originated in the Middle Ages are now so transformed that only their names are still medieval. And beyond that? Beyond that, "persistence" is the wrong question. The past need not be replayed because it is "us" but rather because it is "not us," and therefore endlessly fascinating.

GLOSSARY

aids In England, this refers to payments made by vassals to their lords on important occasions.

The Annunciation See Virgin Mary (below).

antiking A king elected illegally.

antipope A pope elected illegally.

Book of Hours A prayer book for lay devotion, meant to be read eight times a day either at home or in church. It normally contained the church calendar; a lesson from each of the gospels; prayers and other readings in honor of the Virgin Mary (see below) based on simplified versions of the Divine Office (see Office below); the penitential psalms; the Office of the Dead; and prayers to saints. Some were lavishly illustrated, and even humble ones were usually decorated.

bull An official document issued by the papacy. The word derives from *bulla*, the lead impression of the pope's seal that was affixed to the document to validate it.

canon law The laws of the church. These were at first hammered out as need arose at various regional church councils and in rules issued by great bishops, particularly the pope. Early collections of canon law were incomplete and sometimes contradictory. Beginning in the ninth century, commentators began to organize and systematize them. The most famous of these treatises was the mid-twelfth-century *Decretum* of Gratian, which, although not an official code, became the basis of canon law training in the schools.

cathedral The principal church of a bishop or archbishop.

church To the Roman Catholics of the Middle Ages, this had two related meanings. It signified in the first place the eternal institution created by Christ, composed of the whole body of Christian believers, and served on earth by Christ's ministers—priests, bishops, the pope. Related to the eternal church were individual, local churches (parish churches, cathedrals, collegiate churches, chapels) where the daily liturgy was carried out and the faithful received the sacraments.

cleric A man in church orders.

collegiate church A church for priests living in common according to a rule.

The Crucifixion The execution of Jesus by hanging on a cross (*crux* in Latin). The scene, described in some detail in the Gospels, was often depicted in art; and free-standing crucifixes (crosses with the figure of Jesus on them) were often placed upon church altars.

dogma The authoritative truth of the church.

empire Refers in the first instance to the Roman Empire. Byzantium considered itself the continuation of that empire. In the West, there were several successor empires, all ruled by men who took the title "emperor": there was the empire of Charlemagne, which included more or less what later became France, Italy, and Germany; it was followed in the tenth century (from the time of Otto I on) by the empire held (after a crowning at Rome) by the German kings. This could be complicated: a ruler like Henry IV was king of Germany in 1056 at the age of five; he took the real reins of power in 1066; but he was not crowned emperor until 1084. Nevertheless, he *acted* as an emperor long before that. That "German" empire, which lasted until the thirteenth century, included Germany and (at least in theory) northern Italy. Later "German" empires, such at that of the Habsburgs, did not include Italy. Some historians call all of these successor empires of Rome the "Holy Roman Empire," but in fact that term was not used until 1254. The Holy Roman Empire, which had nothing to do with Rome, ended in 1806. By extension, the term empire can refer to other large realms, often gained through conquest, such as the Mongol Empire or the Ottoman Empire.

episcopal As used for the Middle Ages, this is the equivalent of "bishop's." An "episcopal church" is the bishop's church; an "episcopal appointment" is the appointment of a bishop; "episcopal power" is the power wielded by a bishop.

excommunication An act or pronouncement that cuts someone off from participation in the sacraments of the church and thus from the means of salvation.

gentry By the end of the Middle Ages, English landlords consisted of two groups, lords and gentry. The gentry were below the lords; knights, squires, and gentlemen were all considered gentry. Even though the term comes from the Late Middle Ages, it is often used by historians as a rough and ready category for the lesser English nobility from the twelfth century onward.

The Flagellation The scene in the Gospels (Matt. 27:26 and Mk. 15:15) where Christ is scourged by his executioners prior to his Crucifixion (see above). The scene was frequently depicted by artists.

fresco	A form of painting using pigments on wet plaster, frequently employed on the walls of churches.
grisaille	Painting in monochrome grays highlighted with color tints.
Guelfs and Ghibellines	Guelf was the Italian for Welf (the dynasty that competed for the German throne against the Staufen), while Ghibelline referred to Waiblingen (the name of an important Staufen castle). In the various conflicts between the popes and the Staufen emperors, the "Guelfs" were the factions within the Italian city-states that supported the papacy, while the "Ghibellines" supported the emperor. More generally, however, the names became epithets for various inter- and intra-city political factions that had little or no connection to papal/imperial issues.
illumination	The term used for paintings in medieval manuscripts. These might range from simple decorations of capital letters to full-page compositions. An "illuminated" manuscript is one containing illuminations.
layman/ laywoman/laity	Men and women not in church orders, not ordained. In the early Middle Ages it was possible to be a monk and a layperson at the same time. But by the Carolingian period, most monks were priests, and, although nuns were not, they were not considered part of the laity because they had taken vows to the church.
Levant	The lands that border the eastern shore of the Mediterranean; the Holy Land.
liturgy	The formal worship of the church, which included prayers, readings, and significant gestures at fixed times appropriate to the season. While often referring to the Mass (see below), it may equally be used to describe the Offices (see below).
The Madonna	See Virgin Mary (below).
Maghreb	A region of northwest Africa embracing the Atlas Mountains and the coastline of Morocco, Algeria, and Tunisia.
Mass	The central ceremony of Christian worship; it includes prayers and readings from the Bible and culminates in the consecration of bread and wine as the body and blood of Christ, offered to believers in the sacrament of the "Eucharist," or "Holy Communion."
New Testament	This work, a compilation of the second century, contains the four Gospels (accounts of the life of Christ) by Matthew, Mark, Luke, and John; the Acts of the Apostles; various letters, mainly from Saints Paul, Peter, and John to fledgling Christian commu-

nities; and the Apocalypse. It is distinguished from the "Old Testament" (see below).

Office   In the context of monastic life, the day and night were punctuated by eight periods in which the monks gathered to recite a precise set of prayers. Each set was called an "Office," and the cycle as a whole was called the "Divine Office." Special rites and ceremonies might also be called offices, such as the "Office of the Dead."

Old Testament   The writings of the Hebrew Bible that were accepted as authentic by Christians, though reinterpreted by them as prefiguring the coming of Christ; they were thus seen as the precursor of the "New Testament" (see above), which fulfilled and perfected them.

Presentation in the Temple   An event in the life of Christ and his mother. See The Virgin below.

referendary   A high Merovingian administrative official responsible for overseeing the issuing of royal documents.

relief   This has two separate meanings. In connection with medieval English government, the "relief" refers to money paid upon inheriting a fief. In the history of sculpture, however, "relief" refers to figures or other forms that project from a flat background. "Low relief" means that the forms project rather little, while "high relief" refers to forms that may be so three-dimensional as to threaten to break away from the flat surface.

sacraments   The rites of the church that (in its view) Jesus instituted to confer sanctifying grace. With the sacraments, one achieved salvation. Cut off from the sacraments (by anathema, excommunication, or interdict), one was damned.

scriptorium   (pl. scriptoria) The room of the monastery where parchment was prepared and texts were copied, illuminated, and bound.

summa   (pl. summae) A compendium or summary. A term favored by scholastics to title their comprehensive syntheses.

The Virgin/ The Virgin Mary/ The Blessed Virgin/ The Madonna   The Gospels of Matthew (1:18-23) and Luke (1:27-35) assert that Christ was conceived by the Holy Spirit (rather than by a man) and born of Mary, a virgin. Already in the fourth century the Church Fathers stressed the virginity of Mary, which guaranteed the holiness of Christ. In the fifth century, at the Council of Chalcedon (451), Mary's perpetual (eternal) virginity was declared. Mary was understood as the exact opposite of (and antidote to) Eve. In the medieval church, Mary was celebrated with four feasts—her Nativity (birth), the Annunciation (when the Angel Gabriel announced to her that she would give birth to the Messiah), the Purification (when she presented the baby Jesus in the temple and was herself cleansed after giving birth), and her Assumption (when she rose to Heaven). (The Purification is also called the Presentation in the Temple.) These events were frequently depicted in paintings and sculpture, especially in the Later Middle Ages, when devotion to Mary's cult increased and greater emphasis was placed on her role as intercessor with her son in Heaven.

APPENDIX: LISTS

LATE ROMAN EMPERORS

(Usurpers in italics)

Maximinus Thrax (235-238)
Gordian I (238)
Gordian II (238)
Balbinus and Pupienus (238)
Gordian III (238-244)
Philip the Arab (244-249)
Decius (249-251)
Trebonianus Gallus (251-253)
Aemilian (253)
Valerian (253-260)
Gallienus (253-268)
Claudius II Gothicus (268-270)
Quintillus (270)
Aurelian (270-275)
Tacitus (275-276)
Florian (276)
Probus (276 282)
Carus (282-283)
Numerianus (283-284)
Carinus (284-285)

In the West	In the East
Maximian (Augustus) (285-305)	Diocletian (Augustus) (284-305)
Constantius (Caesar) (293-305)	Galerius (Caesar) (293-305)
Constantius (Augustus) (305-306)	Galerius (Augustus) (305-311)
Severus (Caesar) (305-306)	Maximin (Caesar) (305-309)
Severus (Augustus) (306-307)	Galerius (Augustus) (305-311)
Constantine I (Caesar) (306-308)	Maximin (Caesar and Augustus) (305-313)

Maxentius (in Italy) (306-312)

Constantine I (Augustus) (307-337)   Licinius (Augustus) (308-324)

Domitius Alexander (in Africa) (308-311)
Constantine I and Licinius (313-324)
Constantine I (324-337)

Constantine II (337-340)
Constans (340-350)   Constantius II (337-361)
Magnentius (350-353)
Julian Caesar (355-361)   Gallus Caesar (361-364)
Julian Augustus (360-363)

Julian (361-363)
Jovian (363-364)

Valentinian (364-375)   Valens (364-378)
Gratian (367-383)   Theodosius I (379-395)
Valentinian II (375-392)
Maximus (383-388)
Eugenius (392-394)

Theodosius I (394-395)

Honorius (394-423)   Arcadius (395-408)
(Stilicho regent) (395-408)
                                                                  Theodosius II (408-450)
Constantius III (421)
John (423-425)   Marcian (450-457)
Valentian III (425-455)
Petronius Maximus (455)   Leo I (457-474)
Avitus (455-456)
Majorian (457-461)
Libius Severus (461-465)
Anthemius (467-472)
Olybrius (472)
Glycerius (473)

Julius Nepos (473-475)
Romulus Augustulus (475-476)

Zeno (474-491)
Anastasius I (491-518)
Justin I (518-527)
Justinian I (527-565)
Justin II (565-578)
Tiberius II Constantine (578-582)
Maurice Tiberius (582-602)

BYZANTINE EMPERORS AND EMPRESSES

Justinian I (527-565)
Justin II (565-578)
       Tiberius, Caesar and regent (574-578)
Tiberius II Constantine (578-582)
Maurice Tiberius (582-602)
Phocas the Tyrant (602-610)
Heraclius (610-641)
Constantine III Heraclius (641)
Heraclonas (Heraclius) Constantine (641)
       Martina, regent
Constans II (Constantine) Heraclius the Bearded (641-668)
Constantine IV (668-685)
Justinian II the Slit-Nosed (685-695, 705-711)
Leontius (Leo) (695-698)
Tiberius III Apsimar (698-705)
Philippicus Bardanes (711-713)
Anastasius II Artemius (713-715)
Theodosius III (715-717)
Leo III the Isaurian (717-741)
Constantine V Name of Dung (741-775)
       Artavasdus, rival emperor at Constantinople (741-743)
Leo IV the Khazar (775-780)
Constantine VI the Blinded (780-797)
       Irene the Athenian, regent
Irene the Athenian (797-802)
Nicephorus I the General Logothete (802-811)
Stauracius (811)
Michael I Rhangabe (811-813)

Leo V the Armenian (813-820)
Michael II the Amorian (820-829)
Theophilus (829-842)
Michael III the Drunkard (842-867)
   Theodora, regent (842-856)
Basil I the Macedonian (867-886)
Leo VI the Wise (886-912)
Alexander (912-913)
Constantine VII Porphyrogenitus (913-959)
   Nicholas Mysticus, regent (913-914)
   Zoë Carbonopsina, regent (914-920)
   Romanus I Lecapenus, coemperor (920-944)
Romanus II Porphyrogenitus (959-963)
Basil II the Bulgar-Slayer (963-1025)
   Theophano, regent (963)
   Nicephorus II Phocas, coemperor (963-969)
   John I Tzimisces, coemperor (969-976)
Constantine VIII Porphyrogenitus (1025-1028)
Romanus III Argyrus (1028-1034)
Michael IV the Paphlagonian (1034-1041)
Michael V the Caulker (1041-1042)
Zoë Porphyrogenita (1042)
Constantine IX Monomachus (1042-1055)
Theodora Porphyrogenita (1055-1056)
Michael VI Bringas (1056-1057)
Isaac I Comnenus (1057-1059)
Constantine X Ducas (1059-1067)
Michael VII Ducas (1067-1078)
   Eudocia Macrembolitissa, regent (1067-1068)
   Romanus IV Diogenes, coemperor (1068-1071)
Nicephorus III Botaniates (1078-1081)
Alexius I Comnenus (1081-1118)
John II Comnenus (1118-1143)
Manuel I Comnenus (1143-1180)
Alexius II Comnenus (1180-1183)
   Andronicus Comnenus, regent (1182-1183)
Andronicus I Comnenus (1183-1185)
Isaac II Angelus (1185-1195)
Alexius III Angelus (1195-1203)
Isaac II Angelus (again) (1203-1204)

Alexius IV Angelus, coemperor
Alexius III Angelus, rival emperor
Alexius V Ducas Murtzuphlus (1204)
Alexius III Angelus, rival emperor
Alexius III Angelus (in Thrace) (1204)
Theodore I Lascaris (at Nicaea) (1205-1221)
John III Ducas Vatatzes (at Nicaea) (1221-1254)
Theodore Ducas, emperor at Thessalonica (1224-1230)
John Ducas, emperor at Thessalonica (1237-1242)
Theodore II Lascaris (at Nicaea) (1254-1258)
John IV Lascaris (at Nicaea) (1258-1261)
Michael VIII Palaeologus, coemperor at Nicaea (1259-1261)
Michael VIII Palaeologus (at Constantinople) (1261-1282)
Andronicus II Palaeologus (1282-1328)
Andronicus III Palaeologus, coemperor (1321-1328)
Andronicus III Palaeologus (1328-1341)
John V Palaeologus (1341-1376; 1379-1391)
Anna of Savoy, regent (1341-1347)
John VI Cantacuzenus, coemperor (1347-1354)
Andronicus IV Palaeologus (1376-1379)
Manuel II Palaeologus (1391-1425)
John VIII Palaeologus (1425-1448)
Constantine XI Palaeologus (1449-1453)

POPES AND ANTIPOPES TO 1500* (Antipopes in Italics)

Peter (?-c.64)	Soter (c.166-c.175)
Linus (c.67-76/79)	Eleutherius (c.175-189)
Anacletus (76-88 or 79-91)	Victor I (c.189-199)
Clement I (88-97 or 92-101)	Zephyrinus (c.199-217)
Evaristus (c.97-c.107)	Calixtus I (Callistus) (217?-222)
Alexander I (105-115 or 109-119)	*Hippolytus (217, 218-235)*
Sixtus I (c.115-c.125)	Urban I (222-230)
Telesphorus (c.125-c.136)	Pontian (230-235)
Hyginus (c.136-c.140)	Anterus (235-236)
Pius I (c.140-155)	Fabian (236-250)
Anicetus (c.155-c.166)	Cornelius (251-253)

* Only since the ninth century has the title of "pope" come to be associated exclusively with the bishop of Rome.

Novatian (251)
Lucius I (253-254)
Stephen I (254-257)
Sixtus II (257-258)
Dionysius (259-268)
Felix I (269-274)
Eutychian (275-283)
Galus (283-296)
Marcellinus (291/296-304)
Marcellus I (308-309)
Eusebius (309/310)
Miltiades (Melchiades) (311–314)
Sylvester I (314-335)
Mark (336)
Julius I (337-352)
Liberius (352-366)
Felix II (355-358)
Damasus I (366-384)
Ursinus (366-367)
Siricius (384-399)
Anastasius I (399-401)
Innocent I (401-417)
Zosimus (417-418)
Boniface I (418-422)
Eulalius (418-419)
Celestine I (422-432)
Sixtus III (432-440)
Leo I (440-461)
Hilary (461-468)
Simplicius (468-483)
Felix III (or II) (483-492)
Gelasius I (492-496)
Anastasius II (496-498)
Symmachus (498-514)
Laurentius (498, 501-c.505/507)
Hormisdas (514-523)
John I (523-526)
Felix IV (or III) (526-530)
Dioscorus (530)
Boniface II (530-532)

John II (533-535)
Agapetus I (535-536)
Silverius (536-537)
Vigilius (537-555)
Pelagius I (556-561)
John III (561-574)
Benedict I (575-579)
Pelagius II (579-590)
Gregory I (590-604)
Sabinian (604-606)
Boniface III (607)
Boniface IV (608-615)
Deusdedit (also called Adeodatus I) (615-618)
Boniface V (619-625)
Honorius I (625-638)
Severinus (640)
John IV (640-642)
Theodore I (642-649)
Martin I (649-655)
Eugenius I (654-657)
Vitalian (657-672)
Adeodatus II (672-676)
Donus (676-678)
Agatho (678-681)
Leo II (682-683)
Benedict II (684-685)
John V (685-686)
Conon (686-687)
Sergius I (687-701)
Theodore (687)
Paschal (687)
John VI (701-705)
John VII (705-707)
Sisinnius (708)
Constantine (708-715)
Gregory II (715-731)
Gregory III (731-741)
Zacharias (Zachary) (741-752)
Stephen II (752-757)

Paul I (757-767)
Constantine (II) (767-768)
Philip (768)
Stephen III (768-772)
Adrian I (772-795)
Leo III (795-816)
Stephen IV (816-817)
Paschal I (817-824)
Eugenius II (824-827)
Valentine (827)
Gregory IV (827-844)
John (844)
Sergius II (844-847)
Leo IV (847-855)
Benedict III (855-858)
Anastasius (Anastasius the Librarian) (855)
Nicholas I (858-867)
Adrian II (867-872)
John VIII (872-882)
Marinus I (882-884)
Adrian III (884-885)
Stephen V (885-891)
Formosus (891-896)
Boniface VI (896)
Stephen VI (896-897)
Romanus (897)
Theodore II (897)
John IX (898-900)
Benedict IV (900-903)
Leo V (903)
Christopher (903-904)
Sergius III (904-911)
Anastasius III (911-913)
Lando (913-914)
John X (914-928)
Leo VI (928)
Stephen VII (929-931)
John XI (931-935)
Leo VII (936-939)
Stephen VIII (939-942)

Marinus II (942-946)
Agapetus II (946-955)
John XII (955-964)
Leo VIII (963-965)
Benedict V (964-966?)
John XIII (965-972)
Benedict VI (973-974)
Boniface VII (1st time) (974)
Benedict VII (974-983)
John XIV (983-984)
Boniface VII (2nd time) (984-985)
John XV (or XVI) (985-996)
Gregory V (996-999)
John XVI (or XVII) (997-998)
Sylvester II (999-1003)
John XVII (or XVIII) (1003)
John XVIII (or XIX) (1004-1009)
Sergius IV (1009-1012)
Gregory (VI) (1012)
Benedict VIII (1012-1024)
John XIX (or XX) (1024-1032)
Benedict IX (1st time) (1032-1044)
Sylvester III (1045)
Benedict IX (2nd time) (1045)
Gregory VI (1045-1046)
Clement II (1046-1047)
Benedict IX (3rd time) (1047-1048)
Damasus II (1048)
Leo IX (1049-1054)
Victor II (1055-1057)
Stephen IX (1057-1058)
Benedict (X)(1058-1059)
Nicholas II (1059-1061)
Alexander II (1061-1073)
Honorius (II) (1061-1072)
Gregory VII (1073-1085)
Clement (III) (1080-1100)
Victor III (1086-1087)
Urban II (1088-1099)
Paschal II (1099-1118)

Theodoric *(1100-1102)*
Albert *(also called Aleric) (1102)*
Sylvester *(IV) (1105-1111)*
Gelasius II (1118-1119)
Gregory *(VIII) (1118-1121)*
Calixtus II (Callistus) (1119-1124)
Honorius II (1124-1130)
Celestine *(II) (1124)*
Innocent II (1130-1143)
Anacletus *(II) (1130-1138)*
Victor *(IV) (1138)*
Celestine II (1143-1144)
Lucius II (1144-1145)
Eugenius III (1145-1153)
Anastasius IV (1153-1154)
Adrian IV (1154-1159)
Alexander III (1159-1181)
Victor *(IV) (1159-1164)*
Paschal *(III) (1164-1168)*
Calixtus *(III) (1168-1178)*
Innocent *(III) (1179-1180)*
Lucius III (1181-1185)
Urban III (1185-1187)
Gregory VIII (1187)
Clement III (1187-1191)
Celestine III (1191-1198)
Innocent III (1198-1216)
Honorius III (1216-1227)
Gregory IX (1227-1241)
Celestine IV (1241)
Innocent IV (1243-1254)
Alexander IV (1254-1261)
Urban IV (1261-1264)
Clement IV (1265-1268)
Gregory X (1271-1276)
Innocent V (1276)
Adrian V (1276)
John XXI (1276-1277)
Nicholas III (1277-1280)

Martin IV (1281-1285)
Honorius IV (1285-1287)
Nicholas IV (1288-1292)
Celestine V (1294)
Boniface VIII (1294-1303)
Benedict IX (1303-1304)
Clement V (at Avignon, from 1309) (1305-1314)
John XXII (at Avignon) (1316-1334)
Nicholas *(V) (at Rome) (1328-1330)*
Benedict XII (at Avignon) (1334-1342)
Clement VI (at Avignon) (1342-1352)
Innocent VI (at Avignon) (1352-1362)
Urban V (at Avignon) (1362-1370)
Gregory XI (at Avignon, then Rome from 1377) (1370-1378)
Urban VI (1378-1389)
Clement *(VII) (at Avignon) (1378-1394)*
Boniface IX (1389-1404)
Benedict *(XIII) (at Avignon) (1394-1417)*
Innocent VII (1404-1406)
Gregory XII (1406-1415)
Alexander *(V) (at Bologna) (1409-1410)*
John *(XXIII) (at Bologna) (1410-1415)*
Martin V (1417-1431)
Clement *(VIII) (1423-1429)*
Eugenius IV (1431-1447)
Felix *(V) (also called Amadeus VIII of Savoy) (1439-1449)*
Nicholas V (1447-1455)
Calixtus III (Callistus) (1455-1458)
Pius II (1458-1464)
Paul II (1464-1471)
Sixtus IV (1471-1484)
Innocent VIII (1484-1492)
Alexander VI (1492-1503)

CALIPHS

Early Caliphs

Abu-Bakr (632-634)
Umar I (634-644)
Uthman (644-656)
Ali (656-661)

Umayyads

Mu'awiyah I (661-680)
Yazid I (680-683)
Mu'awiyah II (683-684)
Marwan I (684-685)
'Abd al-Malik (692-705)
al-Walid I (705-715)
Sulayman (715-717)
Umar II (717-720)
Yazid II (720-724)
Hisham (724-743)
al-Walid II (743-744)
Yazid III (744)
Ibrahim (744)
Marwan II (744-750)

Abbasids★

al-Saffah (750-754)
al-Mansur (754-775)
al-Mahdi (775-785)
al-Hadi (785-786)
Harun al-Rashid (786-809)
al-Amin (809-813)
al-Ma'mun (813-833)
al-Mu'tasim (833-842)
al-Wathiq (842-847)
al-Mutawakkil (847-861)

al-Muntasir (861-862)
al-Musta'in (862-866)
al-Mu'tazz (866-869)
al-Muhtadi (869-870)
al-Mu'tamid (870-892)
al-Mu'tadid (892-902)
al-Muqtafi (902-908)
al-Muqtadir (908-932)
al-Qahir (932-934)
al-Radi (934-940)

★ Abbasid caliphs continued at Baghdad— with, however, only nominal power—until 1258. Thereafter, a branch of the family in Cairo held the caliphate until the sixteenth century.

Fatimids

'Ubayd Allah (al-Mahdi) (909-934)
al-Ka'im (934-946)
al-Mansur (946-953)
al-Mu'izz (953-975)
al-'Aziz (975-996)
al-Hakim (996-1021)
al-Zahir (1021-1036)
al-Mustansir (1036-1094)
al-Musta'li (1094-1101)
al-Amir (1101-1130)
al-Hafiz (1130-1149)
al-Zafir (1149-1154)
al-Fa'iz (1154-1160)
al-'Adid (1160-1171)

OTTOMAN EMIRS AND SULTANS

Osman (1299–1326)
Orhan (1326–1360)
Murad I (1360–1389)
Bayezid I (1389–1402)
Ottoman Civil War (1402–1413)
Mehmed I (1413–1421)
Murad II (1421–1444, 1446–1451)
Mehmed II the Conqueror (1444–1446, 1451–1481)
Bayezid II (1481–1512)

SOURCES

MAPS

1.4 Tours, *c.*600. Copyright © Henri Galinié.

3.1 The Byzantine Empire, *c.*917. Mark Whittow, *The Making of Orthodox Byzantium 600–1025* (University of California Press, 1996), p.166, Copyright © 1996 Mark Whittow. Reprinted by permission of the University of California Press.

5.1 The Byzantine Empire and the Seljuk World, *c.*1090. Christophe Picard, *Le monde musulman du XIe au XVe siècle* © SEDES / HER, 2000. Reprinted by permission of Éditions SEDES, Paris.

6.4 The German Push to the East, Twelfth to Fourteenth Centuries. Adapted from *Atlas of Medieval Europe*, ed. Angus Mackay and David Ditchburn (Routledge, 1997), p. 98.

7.6 The Village of Toury, Fourteenth and Fifteenth Centuries. Copyright © Samuel Leturcq.

7.7 The Lands of Toury, Fourteenth and Fifteenth Centuries. Copyright © Samuel Leturcq.

8.4 The Duchy of Burgundy, 1363–1477. Adapted from *Atlas of Medieval Europe*, ed. Angus Mackay and David Ditchburn (Routledge, 1997), p 163.

PLATES

1.1 Landscape, Pompeii. Museo Archeologico Nazionale, Naples, Italy. Scala / Art Resource, NY. Reprinted by permission of Art Resource.

1.2 Theseus and the Minotaur Slayer, Pompeii. Roman fresco from the House of Gavius Rufus, Pompeii (*c.*79). Museo Archeologico Nazionale, Naples, Italy. Erich Lessing / Art Resource, NY. Reprinted by permission of Art Resource.

1.3 Meleager on a Roman Sarcophagus. Relief on façade of Casino Algardi in Villa Doria Pamphilj, Rome. Reprinted by permission of Presidenza del Consiglio dei Ministri.

1.4 Head from Palmyra. Studio Zouhabi, Palmira-Syria. Museum # Palmyra B 2253/8089. Photograph by Ingrid Stüben in *Ebla to Damascus: Art and Archaeology of Ancient Syria: An Exhibition from the Directorate-General of Antiquities and Museums, Syrian Arab Republic*, ed. Harvey Weiss (Washington DC: Smithsonian Institution Traveling Exhibition Service, 1985).

1.5 Decorated Coffer from Jerusalem. Limestone Ossuary Roman/Jewish from Jerusalem (1st Cent.?). British Museum. Dept code: AN 126392, 00032535001, © The Trustees of the British Museum. Reprinted by permission of the British Museum / Art Resource, NY.

1.6 Tombstone, near Carthage. Limestone Tombstone from near Carthage (2nd Cent.?). Collection ref 125345, Neg #: D 650, © Copyright The Trustees of the British Museum. Reprinted by permission of the British Museum.

1.7 Base of the Hippodrome Obelisk. Emperor Theodosius, seated between his two sons, receives homage from vanquished enemy. Base of the Egyptian obelisk imported by Emperor Theodosius and erected in the Hippodrome in Constantinople (c.390). Obelisk of Theodosius I, Istanbul, Turkey. SEF / Art Resource, NY. Reprinted by permission of Art Resource.

1.8 Saint Cyprian Fresco. SS Giovanni e Paolo, Rome, view of confessio (late 4th Cent.). Reprinted by permission of the Soprintendenza archeologica di Roma.

1.9 Sarcophagus of Junius Bassus. Sarcophagus of Junius Bassus, Roman prefect. Museum of the Treasury, St. Peter's Basilica, Vatican State. Scala / Art Resource, NY. Reprinted by permission of Art Resource.

1.10 Reliquary of Theuderic. Theuderic Reliquary. Merovingian. Gold-plated sliver, pearls, precious stones. Treasury, Abbey, St. Maurice, Switzerland. Erich Lessing / Art Resource, NY. Reprinted by permission of Art Resource.

1.11 Mosaic from San Vitale, Ravenna. Emperor Justinian I, Bishop Maximianus, and attendants. Mosaic from the North wall of the Apse (c.540–548). San Vitale, Ravenna, Italy. Cameraphoto Arte, Venice / Art Resource, NY. Reprinted by permission of Art Resource.

1.12 Woven Icon of the Virgin. Egypt, Byzantine period, 6th Century. Slit and dovetailed tapestry weave; wool, 178 x 110 cm. Copyright © The Cleveland Museum of Art, 203. Leonard C. Hanna, Jr., Bequest, 1967.144. Reprinted by permission of The Cleveland Museum of Art.

2.1 Silk Band. Silk Fragment from the Keir Collection, Manor House. Photograph © 2008 A.C. Cooper Ltd. Reprinted by permission of A.C. Cooper Ltd., and Manor House.

2.2 Dome of the Rock. "Detail of Dome of the Rock, interior, Jerusalem, Israel." Copyright © Sonia Halliday Photographs. Photo by Jane Taylor. Reprinted by permission of Sonia Halliday Photographs.

2.3 Belt Buckle from Sutton Hoo. "Gold Belt Buckle from the Ship-Burial at Sutton Hoo, Suffolk." Early 7th century. British Museum, London, Great Britain. Copyright © British Museum / Art Resource, NY. Reprinted by permission of Art Resource.

2.4 Saint Luke, Lindisfarne Gospels. Miniature of St. Luke, Cott.Nero.D.IV f137v. Picture No. 1000283.011. Copyright © The British Library Board, All Rights Reserved. Reprinted by permission of the British Library.

2.5 Carpet Page, Lindisfarne Gospels. Carpet page introducing St. Luke, Cott.Nero.D.IV f138v. Picture No. 1008151.011. Copyright © The British Library Board, All Rights Reserved. Reprinted by permission of the British Library.

2.6 First Text Page, Gospel of Saint Luke, Lindisfarne Gospels. Incipit page to St. Luke's Gospel, Cott.Nero.D.IV fol. 139. Picture No. 1006796.011. Copyright © The British Library Board, All Rights Reserved. Reprinted by permission of the British Library.

2.7 Franks Casket. Adoration of the Magi, when the three wise men visited the newborn Christ (ca. 700 CE). British Museum, London, Great Britain. Copyright © The Trustees of The British Museum / Art Resource, NY. Reprinted by permission of the British Museum / Art Resource, NY.

3.1 The Empress Eudocia and Her Sons, Homilies of Gregory Nazianzus. Eudocie Ingerina et ses fils (879–882). Folio B. Copyright © BnF. Reprinted by permission of Bibliothèque nationale de France.

3.2 Ezekiel in the Valley of Dry Bones, Homilies of Gregory Nazianzus. Le Prophète Ezéchiel dans la Vallée des ossements (879–882). Folio. 438v. Copyright © BnF. Reprinted by permission of Bibliothèque nationale de France.

3.3 Bowl from Iraq. Islamic, attributed to Iraq, Bowl, Abbasid period (750–1258), 9th Century, glazed and polychrome luster-painted earthenware. The Metropolitan Museum of Art, H.O. Havemeyer Collection, Gift of Horace Havemeyer, 1941 (41.165.1). Photograph copyright © 1985 The Metropolitan Museum of Art. Reprinted by permission of the Metropolitan Museum of Art.

3.4 Great Mosque, Córdoba. Interior of Mosque, Córdoba, Spain. Umayyad caliphate (Moorish). Scala / Art Resource, NY. Reprinted by permission of Art Resource.

3.5 Sacramentary of Saint-Germain-des-Prés. Sacramentaire de Saint-Germain-des-Prés (early 9th century). MS lat 2291, folio. 14v. Copyright © BnF. Reprinted by permission of Bibliothèque nationale de France.

3.6 Saint Mark, Soissons Gospels. Saint Marc écrivant. Saint Jean-Baptiste et un ange (800–810). MS lat. 8850, folio 81v. Copyright © BnF. Reprinted by permission of Bibliothèque nationale de France.

3.7 First Text Page, Gospel of Saint Mark, Soissons Gospels. Baptême du Christ. Christ servi par les anges. Trinité (800–810). MS lat. 8850, fol. 82r. Copyright © BnF. Reprinted by permission of Bibliothèque nationale de France.

3.8 Saint Mark, Coronation Gospels Evangelist Markus (c.800). Krongungsevangeliar Fol. 76v. Copyright © Kunsthistorisches Museum, Wien oder KHM, Wien. Reprinted by permission of KHM.

3.9 Utrecht Psalter. Utrecht Psalter (c.820–835), University Library Utrecht, Ms. 323, fol. 4v, Universiteitsbibliotheek Utrecht. Reprinted by permission of the University of Utrecht Library.

4.1 The Raising of Lazarus, Egbert Codex. Raising of Lazarus, Codex Egberti (977/993). Stadtbibliothek Trier MS 24, fol. 52v. Photo by Anja Runkel. Reprinted by permission of Stadtbibliothek Trier.

4.2 Christ Asleep, Hitda Gospels. Christ Asleep in the Seastorm, Hitda Gospels (*c.*1000–1020), MS 1640, fol. 117r. Hessische Landes- und Hochschulbibliothek Darmstadt. Reprinted by permission of Universitäts- und Landesbibliothek Darmstadt.

4.3 Saint Luke, Gospel Book of Otto III. Saint Luke, Gospel Book of Otto III (*c.*998–1001), Clm 4453, fol. 139v. Reprinted by permission of Bayerische Staatsbibliothek München.

Seeing the Middle Ages Otto III Enthroned, Aachen Gospels. Liuthar-Evangeliar, Thronbild Kaiser Ottos III, um 1000. Photo by Pit Siebigs. Copyright © Domkapitel Aachen. Reprinted by permission of Domschatzkammer Aachen.

5.1 San Miniato. View of the façade, Cathedral, San Miniato, Italy. Scala / Art Resource, NY. Reprinted by permission of Art Resource.

5.2 Bowl, North Africa. Pisa, Museo Nazionale di San Matteo, bacino ceramico, late 12th century. Reprinted by permission of Museo Nazionale di Pisa.

5.3 Gloria with Musical Notation, Saint-Evroult. Gloria de la notation musicale (12th cent.). Latin 10097, fol. 32v. Copyright © BnF. Reprinted by permission of Bibliothèque nationale de France.

5.4 Durham Cathedral, Interior. Nave looking east, Cathedral Durham, Great Britain. Anthony Scibilia / Art Resource, NY. Reprinted by permission of Art Resource.

5.5 Sant Tomàs de Fluvià, The Last Supper, Painted Vault. Romanic monuments: Paintings recently found and restored in San Tomàs de Fluvià (Toroella). Photograph by Heinz Hebeisen. Reprinted by permission of iberimage.

5.6 Vézelay, Anger and Lust. Capital from Vézelay with Devil, Lust and Despair. Copyright © Kathleen Cohen. Reprinted by permission of Kathleen Cohen and San José State University.

5.7 Leaning Tower (Bell Tower) of Pisa. Leaning Tower (Campanile), Pisa. Romanesque. Begun 1173. Tower of Pisa, Pisa, Italy. Scala / Art Resource, NY. Reprinted by permission of Art Resource.

5.8 Santiago de Compostela, Interior. Main altar in Churrigueresque style (1656–1703) with the effigy of St. James (Iago) (*c.*1211). Cathedral, Santiago de Compostela, Spain. Scala / Art Resource, NY. Reprinted by permission of Art Resource.

5.9 Fontenay Abbey Church, Interior. Nave looking east. Abbey, Fontenay, France. Anthony Scibilia / Art Resource, NY. Reprinted by permission of Art Resource.

6.1 Reliquary Casket for Charlemagne's Arm. Gilded copper and wood, 12th CE. Photograph by Arnaudet. Louvre, Paris, France. Réunion des Musées Nationaux / Art Resource, NY. Reprinted by permission of Art Resource.

6.2 Notre Dame of Paris, Exterior. Notre-Dame, exterior, right side, Paris, France. Scala / Art Resource, NY. Reprinted by permission of Art Resource.

6.3 Notre Dame of Paris, Interior. Notre-Dame, interior view of central nave toward altar. Notre-Dame, Paris, France Scala / Art Resource, NY. Reprinted by permission of Art Resource.

6.4 Lincoln Cathedral, Interior. Center nave of Lincoln Cathedral, looking east, 2nd quarter 13th century. Cathedral, Lincoln, Great Britain. Erich Lessing / Art Resource, NY. Reprinted by permission of Art Resource.

6.5 San Francesco at Assisi. The interior of the Upper Basilica from the east, after the earthquake of 1997. Interior, Upper Basilica of St. Francis, Assisi. Photo by Ghigo Roli, 2002. Franco Cosimo Panini Editore © Management Fratelli Alinari. Alinari / Art Resource, NY. Reprinted by permission of Art Resource.

6.6 Reims Cathedral, West Portal, Saint Joseph (c.1240). Photograph by Hürlimann, Thomas, 1967. Copyright © Swiss Foundation of Photography. SODRAC 2007.

7.1 Pietro Lorenzetti, *Birth of the Virgin*. Lorenzetti, Pietro (c.1342). Birth of the Virgin. Museo dell'Opera Metropolitana, Siena, Italy. Scala / Art Resource, NY. Reprinted by permission of Art Resource.

7.2 Virgin and Child. Madonna and Child, Ivory (1330–1350). Reprinted by permission and courtesy of Loyola University Museum of Art, Martin D'Arcy S.J. Collection, Chicago, Illinois.

7.3 Jean Pucelle, *Hours of Jeanne d'Evreux*. Heures de Jeanne d'Evreux by Jean Pucelle. Fol. 15v/16r. I. Walther, N. Wolf: Codices illustres; Köln 2005, S. 208.

7.4 Tomb and Effigy of Edward II. Gloucester Cathedral, tomb of Edward II murdered in 1327 (1330s). Photograph by Angelo Hornak. Reprinted by permission of Angelo Hornak Library.

7.5 The Motet S'Amours. The Motet S'Amours (c.1300) MS H196, fol. 170r. Reprinted by permission of Bibloiothèque Universitaire de Médecine de Montpellier (Montpellier University Library of Medicine).

7.6 Saint John, "Dominican" Bible. Bible de Saint John "Dominican" (mid 13th century). Latin 16722m, fol. 205v. Copyright © BnF. Reprinted by permission of Bibliothèque nationale de France.

7.7 Saint John, "Aurifaber" Bible. Miniature initial of St. John. Aurifaber (mid 13th) Württ. Landesbibliothek, Stuttgart, Cod. Bibl. Qt. 8, 402v. Reprinted by permission of Württembergische Landesbibliothek.

7.8 Nicola Pisano, Pulpit (1265–1268). Fratelli Alinari, Firenze.

7.9 Giotto, Arena Chapel, Padua. Giotto di Bondone, Scrovegni Chapel. View of the interior, looking toward the altar (1304–1313). Scrovegni Chapel, Padua, Italy. Scala / Art Resource, NY. Reprinted by permission of Art Resource.

7.10 Giotto, *Massacre of the Innocents*, Arena Chapel. Giotto di Bondone, Massacre of the Innocents (1304–1313). Scrovegni Chapel, Padua, Italy. Scala / Art Resource, NY. Reprinted by permission of Art Resource.

8.1 Woodcut from *Der Ackermann aus Böhmen*. *Der Ackermann aus Böhmen* woodcut (c.1462). Herzog August Bibliothek Wolfenbüttel: 1462 Ethica 20, 10 recto.

FIGURES

5.1 Saint-Germain of Auxerre. Christian Sapin (dir.), *Archéologie et architecture d'un site monastique. 10 ans de recherche à l'abbaye Saint-Germain d'Auxerre* (Auxerre: Centre d'études médiévales, Paris: CTHS, 2000) (*Mémoires de la section d'archéologie et d'hisotire de l'art, vol. X*), Fig. 3, p. 10 and Fig. 371, p. 312. Reprinted by permission of Christian Sapin.

5.2 A Model Romanesque Church: Santiago de Compostela. John Beckwith, *Early Medieval Art* (New York: Thames & Hudson, 1964), p.163, ill.155. Reprinted by permission of Thames & Hudson Ltd.

5.3 Schematic Plan of a Cistercian Monastery. *Making of the West*. Lynn Hunt et al. Bedford / St. Martin's, 2001. Adapted from Wolfgang Braunfels *Monasteries of Western Europe*. Princeton, NJ: Princeton University Press, 1972, p. 75. © Dumont Buchverlag GmbH.

7.1 Single Notes and Values of Franconian Notation. From *Anthology of Medieval Music*, edited by Richard Hoppin. Copyright © 1978. W.W. Norton & Company, Inc.

Every effort has been made to contact copyright holders; in the event of an omission or error, please notify the publisher.

INDEX

Page numbers for illustrations are in italics.

bishops, 27, 47, 119, 159, 190, 228. *See also* entries
    for individual bishops
  appointment and investiture of, 166 (*See also*
    Investiture Conflict)
  Ottonian, 166
  in Peace of God, 159
  in Truce of God, 159
Black Death, 306, 322–23
Black Sea region, 42, 146. *See also* Ukraine
  Hun invasion (376), 43
Boethius (480–524), 163
  Consolation of Philosophy, 45
  works of, in translation, 163
Bohemia, 326
Bohemond (Norman ruler in Sicily), 195
Bologna, 203, 233, 325
  Black Death in, 306
  University of, 243
Bonaventure, Saint (1217–1274), 286–87
Boniface, Saint (*c.*672–754), 89, 119
Boniface VIII, pope (1294–1303), 279–80
  Clericis Laicos (1296), 280
  Unam Sanctam (1302), 280
Boniface IX, pope (1389–1404), 325
Books of Hours, 283, 286
  definition of, 350
  of Jeanne d'Evreux, *284*, 294
Bosporous, 195
Bourges
  Pragmatic Sanction of (1438), 326
Bouvines, battle of (1214), 229
bowl, Iraq, *111*
bowl (or *bacini*), North Africa, *187*
Brethren of the Common Life. *See devotio moderna*
British Isles, 80, 87–92, 225. *See also* England; Ireland; Scotland; Wales
Bruges, 183
Brunelleschi

Foundling Hospital, 329, *330*
Bruno of Cologne, 210
bubonic plague, 64. *See also* Black Death
Bulgaria, 63, 102, 120, 143, 147, 310
Bulgars, western. *See* Bulgaria
bull
  definition of, 350
Burchard of Worms, 166
Burgundian laws, 45
Burgundian tapestries, 334, 340
Burgundians, 41, 45, 314
Burgundofara (nun), 86–87
Burgundy (early medieval kingdom), 85, 87
Burgundy (late medieval duchy), 312, 314, 317,
  331, 334, 340
burhs, 163
Buyids, 147–49, 179
Byzantine emperors, 68. *See also* names of individual emperors
Byzantine empire, 61–64, 67–68, 98, 101–5, 108,
  139–41, 143, 145, 179–81, 221
  armies, 62
  end of (1453), 310
  iconoclasm at, 62, 68, 70, 74, 98, 101–2, 105
  navy of, 62
  themes in, 63, 102–4, 143
Byzantine Orthodoxy, 147
"Byzantine Palace" at Ephesus, 66
Byzantines, artistic influence
  in Islamic world, 75
  in West, 121, 133, 166
Byzantium. *See* Byzantine Empire;
  Constantinople

caballeros villanos, 275
Caesarius, bishop of Arles (*r.*502–542), 48
Caffa, 266, 306
Cairo, 74, 150, 306. *See also geniza*

First (1096-1099), 193–95
Fourth (1202-1204), 221, 257
Northern, 257, 269
against Ottoman Turks, 331
Peasants, 194
Second (1147-1149), 197, 216, 257
Third (1189-1192), 228
Ctesiphon, 63, 74
curia, 189, 193, 205
curiales, 45, 67
currency. *See* coinage
Cyprian, Saint, bishop of Carthage, 32
Cyprus, 143, 228

da Gama, Vasco (*c.*1460-1524), 343–44
da Vinci, Leonardo. *See* Leonardo da Vinci
Dalasseni, 145. *See also dynatoi*
Anna Dalassena, 181
Theophylact Dalassenus, 145
Damascus, 63, 74, 109, 197
Great Mosque at, 75, 117
Dance of Death, 308
Danegeld, 154, 198
Danes. *See* Denmark; Scandinavia; Vikings
Dante Alighieri (1265-1321)
Commedia (*Divine Comedy*), 288
Danzig, 269
dar al-ilm, 150
David (Donatello), 329, *329*, 342
Decretum (Gratian), 193
Decretum (*c.*1020) (Burchard of Worms), 166
demesne, 126
demons, 31
Denmark, 257
Deor, 90
devotio moderna, 342
Dhuoda, 129
Diarmait Mac Murchada (Dermot Mac
Murrough), 258

Dias, Bartholomeu (*c.*1450-1500), 343
Diet of Besançon (1157), 231
Diet of Roncaglia (1158), 233
Digenis Akritas, 145
Digest (533), 54
Dijon, 314
Diocletian, emp. (*r.*284-305), 21, 25
Divine Comedy (Dante), 288
Divine Office, 48, 127
definition, 353
doge, 319
dogma
definition of, 351
Dome of the Rock (Damascus mosque), 75, *78*
Domesday Book, 198
Dominic, Saint (1170-1221), 254
Dominicans, 253–54, 265, 280, 286
Domrémy, 314
Donatello (*c.*1386-1466)
David, 329, *329*, 342
Donation of Constantine, 119
Dorestad, 125
Dorset, 306
dowries, 86
Duns Scotus, John (*c.*1266-1308), 287
Dunstable, John (*c.*1385-1453), 317, 340
Durham cathedral, 207, *208*
dynatoi, 143, 145, 172, 181, 221

Easter, 88
Ecclesiastical History of the English People (Bede), 83
Eckhart, Meister, 287
economy, 211
Abbasid, 111–12, 151
Anglo-Saxon, 80
Bedouin, 70–71
Byzantine, 66–67
Carolingian, 125
Cistercian, 214

commercial revolution, 183–85, 267, 269

of Crusader States, 196

gift, 85

of Haithabu, 161

Italian, 81, 161, 236

late medieval, 297, 299–300, 323

Umayyad, 75

Edessa, county of, 195–97, 220. *See also* Crusader
States

Edgar, king (England) (*r.c.*959-975), 163

Edict of Milan (313), 28

education. *See* intellectual culture

Edward the Confessor, king (*d.*1066), 198

Edward I, king (England) (*r.*1272-1307), 273, 278,
280

Edward II, king (England) (*r.*1307-1327)
effigy, 283, *285*

Edward III, king (England) (*r.*1327-1377), 306, 312,
317, 321

Edward IV, king (England) (*r.*1461-1483), 318

effigy (tomb)
of Edward II, 283, *285*

Egbert Codex, 166, *167*, 169

Egbert of Trier (*r.*977-993), 166, 169

Egypt, 110, 112, 149, 220–21, 265. *See also* Fatimids
conquered by Persians (619), 63
Mamluks of, 221, 265

Einhard (*d.*840), 120–21

Elbe River, 257

Eleanor of Aquitaine (*d.*1204), 225, 238, 240

Eliezer ben Nathan, 195

Embolos, 64

empire. *See also* Byzantine empire; Germany;
Holy Roman empire; Italy; Roman empire
definition of, 351

England, 253, 286, 297
Angevin, 224–25, 227–28, 260n3, 314
Anglo-Saxon, 45, 80, 82, 87–88, 161–63
baronial revolt in, 228–29, 278

Black Death in, 306

Cistercians in, 211

civil war (1135-1154) in, 224

Domesday Book at, 198

Franciscans in, 253

Hundred Years' War in, 305, 312, 314, 317

Jews in, 255–56, 273

Lollards in, 325

Norman, 185, 197

Parliament of, 278

Statute of Laborers (1351), 306

Vikings in, 152, 154

Wars of the Roses (1455-1487) in, 318

Wat Tyler's Rebellion (1381) in, 322

English church
appointments in, 163

English Peasants' Revolt (1381), 322

enquêteurs, 279

Entombment of Christ (Raphael), 329, *332*, 333

Ephesus, city of, 64, *65*, 66
Embolos, 64, 66

Ephesus, Council of (431), 29

epic poetry. *See* poetry, vernacular

epidemic diseases, 24, 64, 66, 306, 308
Black Death, 306
Plague of Justinian, 66, 101, 305

episcopal
courts, 166
definition of, 351
elections, 187

Estates General, 279, 322

Estonia, 257

Ethelbert, king (*d.*616), 88

ethnogenesis, 42

Eton, 340

Eucharist, 28, 31, 54, 252–53, 255, 281. *See also*
Corpus Christi; Mass; transubstantiation

Euclid, 112

Eudocia, empress and her sons, *106*, 108

Lyon, 254

Macedonian Renaissance, 105, 141
Madeira, 344
madrasas, 180, 331
Magdeburg, 166
    Tagino of, 166
Maghreb, 149, 180, 219, 267, 269
    definition of, 352
Magna Carta (1215), 229, 278
Magyars. *See* Hungarians
mahdi, 149
Maine, 230
Mainz, 194, 343
Majolus, abbot, 155
Majorca, 269
Malik Shah I, sultan (*r.* 1109-1116), 179–80
Mamluk Sultanate, 221, 265
al-Ma'mun, caliph (*r.* 813-833), 111, 113
Man in a Red Turban (van Eyck), 340, *341*
manors, 125–26
manse (*mansus*), 126, 238
al-Mansur, caliph (*r.* 754-775), 110
Mantes-la Jolie, 245
Mantua, 329
manuscripts, 105, 127, 210. *See also* intellectual
        culture; Renaissance
    in British Isles, 89–93
    at Byzantium, 105
    Carolingian, 126, 129, 133
    Carthusian, 210
    at Córdoba, 150
    and *devotio moderna*, 342
    thirteenth century, 291
Manzikert, battle of (1071), 179
Marcel, Étienne (*d.* 1358), 322
Marco Polo (1254-1324), 266
marriage (customs and laws), 113, 143
    at al-Andalus, 117

Byzantine, 67
clergy and, 188
clerical, 47, 70, 98, 181, 188, 193
dowries, 86
English, 228
Islamic, 72, 117
Merovingian, 86
ministerials and, 277
nicolaitism, 188
polygyny, 70–72
post-Carolingian, 158
marriage (sacrament of), 252
marriage alliances, 165, 181
Martel, Charles (mayor 714-741), 118–19
Martin, Saint, 46, 49, 183
Martin le Franc
    Le Champion des dames, 340
Martin V, pope (1417-1431), 325
martyrdom, 31, 75, 117, 228
Mary. *See* Virgin Mary
Mary of Burgundy, 317
Mary of Oignies (1177-1213), 254
Mass, 30, 127, 213, 252, 283. *See also* Divine
        Office; manuscripts; music
    definition of, 352
Massacre of the Innocents (Giotto), 296. *See also*
        Padua, Arena Chapel
Matarazzo, Francesco, 333
Matilda, daughter of Henry I of England, 225
Matilda of Tuscany, 191
Maurice de Sully, 244
Maxentius, emp. (*r.* 306-312), 28
Maximilian of Hapsburg, 317
mayor of the palace (Merovingian), 85, 118
Meath, 258
Mecca, 73–74
    Ka'ba, 71–73
Medici, 323, 329, 331
    Cosimo de' (1389-1464), 331

Odoacer (barbarian), 43
Offices. *See* Divine Office
Old Church Slavonic, 104
Old Testament
    definition of, 352
Olivi, Peter (1248-1298), 287
oratores, 156
Order of the Garter, 319
Order of the Golden Buckle, 319
Order of the Golden Fleece, 319
Order of the Sisters of Saint Francis, 254
orders (social), 156, 275, 279
Oresme, Nicole (*c.*1320-1382), 287
Orléans, 314
Osman (*r.*1281-1382), 309–10
Ostrogoths, 42–44, 56
Oswald, king (*r.*633-641), 88
Oswy, king, 89
Otto I, king and emp. (*r.*936-973), 155, 165–66
Otto II, 166, 169
Otto III, 166, 171
Otto III enthroned, Aachen Gospels, *171*
Ottoman empire, 309–10, 331
Ottonian art, 169
Ottonians, 152, 166. *See also* Germany
Oviedo, 117
Oxford, 204–5
    University of, 243–44

Padua
    Arena Chapel, 291, 294, *295–96*
Palermo, 204
Palestine, 25
Palmyra
    "Woman's Head" from, *36*, 37
Pamiers, 280
pandemics. *See* epidemic diseases
papacy. *See* popes
papal courts, 193

papal monarchy, 193, 324
papal primacy, 190, 193
papal supremacy, 190
paper, 126
papyrus, 105
parchment, 105, 126
Paris, 190, 198, 201, 203, 205, 264, 273, 279, 290, 322
    Black Death in, 306
    churches, 81
    famines, 299
    Notre Dame, 244–45, *246*, *248*
    population, 269
    representative assembly at (1302), 279
    theology at, 204
    University of, 243, 287
parish, 157
Parlement, 279, 302n10
Parliament (English), 278
Pascal III, pope (*r.*1164-1168), 232
Pastoral Care, 98, 152
pastoralism, 70, 81, 179, 263–65. *See also* agriculture
patricians, 270
Paul, Saint (*d.c.*65), 25
Paulinus, bishop of York, 83
Pavia, 97, 233. *See also* Italy
Peace of God, 159, 182
Peace of Lodi, 321
Peace of Venice (1177), 233
peasants, 221, 223
    Anglo-Saxon England, 80
    Byzantine, 67
    Carolingian, 126, 129
    in Francia, 81
    in Italy, 160
    Ottoman, 310
    Western, 157–58, 236, 238, 299–300, 306, 321
Peasants' Crusade, 194
Pechenegs, 143, 181
Pelagius (*d.*after 418), 29

art in, 32–41

Christianity in, 56

crisis of the third century, 24, 46, 56

redefined under Justinian, 56

taxation in, 25

taxes, 45

The Romance of the Rose, 288

romance poetry. *See* poetry, vernacular

Romanesque art and architecture, 207–8, 211, 213

Romanus I Lecapenus (r.920-944)

Novel (New Law), 145

Rome, 24, 119, 160, 205, 329

Sack of (410), 40, 54

Romulus Augustulus, emp. (deposed 476), 43

Roncaglia, 233

Rudolph of Habsburg, emp. (r.1273-1291), 235

Rugi, 43

Rule of Saint Benedict, 48, 123, 200, 205, 211, 213, 254

Rum, 180, 264

Runnymede, 229

ruralization, 67, 160

Roman Empire, 45–47

Rus. *See* Kievan Rus

Russian Primary Chronicle, 146

Sacramentary of Saint-Germain-des-Prés, 127, *128*

sacraments

definition of, 353

sacristy, 205

al-Saffah, caliph, 110

Safi, 267

Saint-Amand, 126–27

Saint Cyprian fresco, 40, *40*, 54

Saint-Denis, 201, 244, 297, 323

Saint-Evroult, 207

Saint-Evroult, Gloria with Musical Notation
(12th cent.), *207*

Saint-Germain of Auxerre, 205, *206*, 207

Saint-Maurice d'Agaune, 48–49, *49*

Sant Tomàs de Fluvià, 207

"The Last Supper," *209*

saints, 31. *See also* entries for individual saints

military, 145

power of, 31

Saladin (r.1171), 220–21, 228

salat, 73

Salerno, 204

Salerno, University of, 243

Salian kings and emperors

genealogy of, 189

Samanids, 147

Samarkand, 74, 310

Samarra, 110

San Francesco in Assisi, 245, *250*

San Miniato, 185, *186*

Santiago (Saint James) de Compostela, 199, 207,
210, 212–13

sarcophagus of Junius Bassus, 40, *41*

Sardica. *See* Serdica

Sasanad Persia. *See* Persia

Sasanid Empire. *See under* Persia

Saxony, 120, 257. *See also* Germany; Ottonians

Scandinavia, 145, 147, 164

scholastic

definition of, 286–87

scholasticism, 286–87, 300

scholastics, 204

schools. *See* intellectual culture

Scotland, 88, 90, 225, 278

Franciscans in, 253

Vikings in, 152

scriptorium, 126–27, 291

definition of, 353

scutage, 228

Second Bulgarian Empire, 223

Seljuks, 177–80, 193, 264

Senegal river, 343

seneschals, 279

Sutton Hoo buckle, 89, *89*

Swiss Confederation (Switzerland), 308, 319

Sword-Brothers, 257

Symeon Stylites, Saint (396-459), 31

synagogue, definition of, 194

Synod of 754, 68

Syria, 110, 149, 179, 181, 209, 220–21, 264–65. *See also* Damascus; Umayyads

Taborites, 326

Tabriz, 266

tagmata, 102–4

taifas, 149, 190, 193, 199

taille, 299

Talmud, burning of (1242), 273

Tamerlane. *See* Timur the Lame

Tana, 266

taxation, 45, 109, 142, 179

    at al-Andalus, 117

    Byzantine, 62, 209, 221

    Carolingian, 121

    Danegeld, 154, 198

    English, 198, 228, 322

    Frankish, 118

    French, 201, 299, 321–22

    Islamic, 110–12, 148

    in Italian city-states, 236, 270

    in Italy (Lombard), 98

    of Jews, 273

    late Roman, 25

    Muslim, 73

    Ottoman, 310

Tertiaries, Franciscan, 254. *See also* laity, piety of

Tertry, battle of (687), 118

Teutonic Knights, 257

themes, 63, 102–4, 143

Theodore of Sykeon, Saint, 67

Theodoric the Great, king (r.493-526), 43, 45

Theodosian Code (438), 45, 56

Theodosius I, emp. (r.379-395), 28, 123

Theodosius II, emp. (r.408-450), 54

theology (university discipline), 204–5, 243, 286–87

Theophanu, 169

Theophilus, emp. (r.829-842), 105, 108

Theseus, 32, *34*, 329

Thessalonica, 105

Theuderic

    reliquary, 49, *49*

Thietmar of Merseburg, bishop (975-1018), 166, 190

Thousand and One Nights, 111

Thrace, 310

three-field system, 125, 157, 182

Timur the Lame (1336-1405), 310

Toledo, 96, 200, 204

    Third Council of, 96

Topkapi palace, 331

Torquemada, Tomás (1420-1498), 327

Tournai, 324

Tours (France), 46, 48, 184. *See also* Gregory, bishop of Tours

    representative assembly at (1308), 279

    Saint-Martin of, 46, 49, 183

Toury, 297

towns. *See* cities

trade (long distance), 81, 125, 151, 185, 216, 265, 267, 323. *See also* economy; Hanseatic League; Mediterranean; merchants; North Sea

    Byzantine, 223

    Mediterranean, 47, 184

translations, 204

transubstantiation, 253, 281, 288, 325

Treaty of Benevento (1156), 233

Treaty of Troyes (1420), 314

Treaty of Verdun (843), 123

Trier, 24, 47, 166

Tripoli, county of, 196. *See also* Crusader States

trivium, 203

Vistula River, 257

vizier, 220

Vladimir, (Basil) Grand Prince (d. 1015), 146–47

Waldensians, 255

Waldo, 255

Wales, 88, 225, 278

Walter de Manny, 312, 319

warriors, portrayal in art, 150

Wars of the Roses (1455-1487), 318

Wat Tyler's Rebellion (1381), 322

wattle and daub, 184

wealth. *See* economy

weaponry, 120, 150, 155, 195, 310, 312, 317, 319
    Greek Fire, 62
    longbows, 312

Wearmouth, 89

Welf dynasty, 232

Welfs, 123, 231

Wessex, 154

Weyden, Rogier van der (d. 1464)
    Columba Altarpiece, 338 39, 340
    (workshop of) The *Carrying of Christ to the*
        Tomb, 333

Whitby, Synod of (664), 89

white monks, 211. *See also* Cistercians

Why God Became Man (Anselm), 216

Wijster (German settlement), 41

William of Aquitaine, 157

William IX, duke (Aquitaine) (1071-1126), 238

William of Ockham (1270?-1349), 287, 325

William of Rubruck, 265

William the Conqueror, king (1066-1087), 197–98

William the Marshal, 242

Winchester, England, 184

Winfrith. *See* Boniface, Saint

Wittenberg, 343

women, 126, 195, 240, 283, 306, 326. *See also*
    names of individual women

as booty, 70

at Byzantine imperial court, 141

in Carolingian renaissance, 129

in Córdoba, 150

courtly love and, 240

education of, 129

in guilds, 242

in Islam, 72, 112, 114

Merovingian, 86

mystics, 314

Order of the Sisters of Saint Francis, 253–54

Ottonian, 166, 169

and sumptuary legislation, 308

and troubadours, 239

and universities, 243

as vassals, 156

Worms, 166, 194
    Concordat of (1122), 191

writs, 163, 227

Wulfilas (c. 311-383), 29

Würzburg, cathedral of, 127

Wyclif, John (c. 1330-1384), 325–26

Yaroslav the Wise (r. 1019-1054), 145–46

Yazid II, caliph (r. 720-724), 68

Yeavering, Northumbria, *82, 83*

Yersinia pestis, 306

York, 255

Yorkists, 317

Zachary, Pope, 119

Zähringen, duke of, 183

zakat, 73

Zanj (slaves), 148

Zaragoza, 199

Zengi, 197, 220

Zeno, emp. (r. 474-491), 43

Zirids, 147

Zoë, 141